POETRY & MYSTICISM

Colin Wilson

City Lights Books
San Francisco

10 9 8 7

"Los with the sun," from *Jerusalem*, by William Blake

Part one was first published by City Lights Books in 1969;
part two was published by Hutchinson & Co. Ltd. in 1970.

Library of Congress Cataloging-in-Publication Data

Wilson, Colin, 1931-
  Poetry & mysticism.

  1. Poetry. 2. Mysticism. 3. Poetry, Modern—20th
century—History and criticism. I. Title.
II. Title: Poetry and mysticism.
PN1077.W56 1986   809.1   85-29140
ISBN 0-87286-182-1 (pbk.)

City Lights Books are available to bookstores through our primary distributor:
Subterranean Company, P.O. Box 168, 265 S. 5th Street, Monroe, Oregon 97456.
1-503-847-5274. Toll free orders 1-800-274-7826. Our books are also available
through library jobbers and regional distributors. For personal orders and catalogs,
please write to City Lights Books, 261 Columbus Avenue, San Francisco, CA
94133.

CITY LIGHTS BOOKS are edited by Lawrence Ferlinghetti and Nancy J. Peters
and published at the City Lights Bookstore, 261 Columbus Avenue, San Francisco,
CA 94133.

Acknowledgements

I wish to acknowledge the kindness of Messrs Faber and Faber for their permission to quote poems by T. S. Eliot, W. H. Auden, Rupert Brooke and A. L. Rowse, and Messrs Macmillan for permission to quote from the poems and autobiographical writings of W. B. Yeats. I also wish to thank Mrs Helen Kazantzakis, Kimon Friar, Prof. Athena G. Dallas, and Pandelis Prevelakis, for help in the writing of the chapter on Kazantzakis, and Messrs Secker and Warburg and Bruno Cassirer for permission to quote from English translations of his books.

C. W.

Contents

Everyone is familiar with the phenomenon of feeling more or less alive on different days. Everyone knows on any given day that there are energies slumbering in him which the incitements of the day do not call forth, but which he might display if these were greater. Most of us feel as if a sort of cloud weighed upon us, keeping us below our highest notch of clearness in discernment, sureness in reasoning, or firmness in deciding. Compared with what we ought to be, we are only half awake. Our fires are damped, our drafts are checked. We are making use of only a small part of our possible mental and physical resources. In some persons, this sense of being cut off from their rightful resources is extreme, and we then get the formidable neurasthenic and psychasthenic conditions, with life grown into one tissue of impossibilities, that so many medical books describe.

Stating the thing broadly, the human being thus lives usually far within his limits; he possesses powers of various sorts that he habitually fails to use. He energizes below his *maximum*, and he behaves below his *optimum*. In elementary faculty, in co-ordination in power of *inhibition* and control, in every conceivable way, his life is contracted like the field of vision of an hysteric subject—but with less excuse, for the poor hysteric is diseased, while in the rest of us it is only an inveterate *habit*—the habit of inferiority to our full self—that is bad.

William James: *The Energies of Man*

Part one

Introductory

In March 1968, I sat in a San Francisco bar with Lawrence Ferlinghetti, and we discussed the death of a girl who had taken an overdose of a new psychedelic drug, and failed to return from her 'trip'. Ferlinghetti admitted to having many reservations about the use of psychedelics, and I tried to explain briefly my own view that mystical experience is a normal potentiality of everyday consciousness, and not something that has to be snatched by inducing states over which we have no control. He suggested that I should write a short book about it, to be published by City Lights Press. It struck me that such a book might be a good vehicle for an 'interim report' on certain ideas I had developed since the writing of *Introduction to the New Existentialism* in 1965. Accordingly, the first part of this book was written under the title *Poetry and Zen* and duly published by City Lights. On reading the published version, it struck me that the ideas needed to be exemplified in discussions of individual poets. The chapters on Yeats, Rupert Brooke, A. L. Rowse and Kazantzakis were added in Deya, Majorca, in the autumn of 1969. The chapter on Kazantzakis had originally been written at the request of his wife, Helen Kazantzakis, as a tribute on the tenth anniversary of his death; it has been considerably altered in this version.

Because the book was written as an 'interim report', the tone is casual and personal. I have preferred to leave it like this, rather than editing it into something more formal, in the hope that it gains in spontaneity what it loses in elegance.

I must explain briefly why I consider that mysticism is no longer a subject that matters only to certain unusual individuals.

Man has achieved his present position by being the most

aggressive and enterprising creature on earth. And now he has created a comfortable civilisation, he faces an unexpected problem. Bourgeois society *reduces* man. The comfortable life lowers man's resistance, so that he sinks into an unheroic sloth. If an animal that has been used to hard food is fed on a diet of mush, it gets tooth decay. *The comfortable life causes spiritual decay just as soft sweet food causes tooth decay.*

This problem lies at the *core* of the work of every major writer of the 20th century. T. E. Hulme talked about original sin —meaning the problem I have stated above—and declared that man needs a strict discipline if anything half-decent is to be got out of him. He looked back nostalgically to the ages of dogmatic Christianity. When the 1914 war started he became an ardent militarist, and attacked Bertrand Russell's pacifism in an article called 'The Kind of Rubbish We Oppose'. It seemed to him that Russell was simply leaving out of account man's tendency to spiritual decay under conditions of prolonged peace.

Hulme was killed in the war. It is interesting to speculate what he would have done when he realised that neither the church nor militarism can solve the problem at this point in history. T. S. Eliot accepted Hulme's religious solution. The result was an increasing pessimism about modern civilisation. Christian mysticism may answer Eliot's individual needs: it leaves the general problem of spiritual tooth decay untouched.

In *The Man Without Qualities* Musil considers three solutions. His hero, Ulrich, belongs to the small percentage of people who crave purpose, discipline, adventure. The Austrian army satisfies the craving for discipline and he develops a philosophy based upon his contempt for the sloppiness of civilians. One day, he challenges a rich businessman to a duel—and soon discovers that the real power lies in the hands of these civilians. He leaves the army in disgust. His second attempt at a solution is to become an engineer. Here, surely, he feels, is the road into the future: the discipline of girders and rivets and steel cables. Then he discovers that engineers do not share his idealistic view of their profession; for them it is just a job. He drops engineering. What remains? Civilian life in a disintegrating empire that can offer him no place, except in an absurd patriotic campaign in which everyone is at cross purposes. He falls back upon seduction, and manages to sleep with every eligible woman in the novel, including his own sister. But there is no solution; only the ironic observation of spiritual tooth-rot.

Hemingway also achieved his vision of discipline during the war. In the story *Soldier's Home* he describes the return of the war hero to his mid-western home town, and the increasing feeling of suffocation, boredom, self-contempt. But if man can only achieve his full potentialities under crisis, then the answer is surely to seek out crisis—in the excitement of the bull fight, big game hunting, shark fishing, war? The decline of his work after *A Farewell to Arms* reveals that he also chose the wrong solution. The mindless violence of *For Whom the Bell Tolls* is even less satisfying than the convoluted intellectualism of *The Man Without Qualities*.

Proust perceived that the decay—which springs out of boredom and self-disgust—would be arrested if man could re-possess his own past. He was right; but how can it be done? His method—of imaginative re-creation of the past—fails to restore the insight that came as he ate a madeleine dipped in tea.

The solution suggested by Hermann Hesse in his novels is a variant on Hemingway: cease to stand apart from life; hurl yourself into it; deny yourself no experience: seduction, drugs, drink, sexual perversion, even murder (in *Steppenwolf*). He states and re-states the problem with admirable persistence; but no answer emerges.

Joyce, like Proust, turns to the re-creation of his own past. Faulkner, in the early novels, sets out to create an agony of emotional tension, that can be resolved only by self-destruction. Kafka admits that he cannot distinguish life from a nightmare. In *Doktor Faustus,* Thomas Mann meditates on how pleasant it would be if man could escape the second-rateness by selling his soul to the devil. D. H. Lawrence brooded on the idea that sex might be the gateway to the suffocated life-forces, he also toyed with a kind of fascism. Greene and Waugh reverted to Hulme's solution and subjected themselves to the discipline of the Catholic Church.

Most of these writers I have mentioned are dead, and the problem remains unsolved. And the failure to solve it enfeebles literature. In retrospect, it seems that literature has been in steady decline since the 1890s. After the Victorian giants came the generation of Shaw and Wells, then of Eliot and Joyce, then of

Hemingway and Faulkner, then of Greene and Waugh, Auden and Dylan Thomas. And the fifties generation, of Osborne, Amis, Braine and the rest, has decided to ignore the problem and stick to personal issues.

I assert that literature will continue to mark time until the problem is solved, and that each new generation will continue to be a head shorter than the preceding one.

The problem is how intelligent human beings can escape the enstiflement of bourgeois society and the sleep of triviality it brings. It is a disturbing thought that the totalitarianism of Hitler, Mussolini, Stalin, was also an attempt to solve it by introducing universal discipline, the secular equivalent of the church of the Middle Ages. Kierkegaard once suggested jokingly that one way to escape the boredom would be for Denmark to borrow vast sums of money from other governments, and spend it all on public entertainments—circuses, fiestas, games. Hitler turned the joke into earnest with his torchlight processions and Olympic games. We should not discount the possibility that if the intellectuals shirk the problem, opportunist politicians may seek cruder solutions.

The aim of this book is to show that there *is* a solution on the psychological level, and to suggest how it might be applied.

A final point. It may seem that I am using the word mysticism in altogether too broad a sense. Its traditional meaning, after all, is 'direct experience of God', or of the 'absolute'. I would argue that there is no fundamental difference between the aesthetic experience and the mystical experience. The case of Ramakrishna, cited in Chapter Two, makes this clear. No one would deny that the vision of the Divine Mother that came when he was about to commit suicide was a mystical experience in the strictest meaning of the word. But what of his earlier experience—when the sight of a flock of white cranes flying past a black storm cloud induced such ecstacy that he lost consciousness? Equally clearly, this is not a mystical, but an aesthetic experience. It is what T. E. Hulme meant when he spoke of 'beauty that is her own eunuch'. Where is the dividing line? It makes equal sense to say that the experience with the cranes was a mild mystical experience, or that the vision of the divine mother was an overwhelming aesthetic experience.

I have tried to demonstrate that the psychological mechanisms are identical in each case. This does not mean that I am attempting to reduce mysticism to a matter of psychological mechanisms, any more than understanding the anatomy of the eye explains our perception of colour. Where the mechanisms end, the mystery begins.

1

Absurd Good News

Ever since I was thirteen, I have been obsessed by the question of the nature of mystical experience. This 'quest of the mystical' began as a devotion to poetry, developed into an interest in comparative religion—with the emphasis on the east—and in recent years has become the scientific pursuit of the psychological mechanisms of the 'intensity experience'. I am convinced that at some point in his evolution, man will achieve complete control over those floodgates of inner-energy that create the mystical experience. I also believe that he will do this by a *learning process,* exactly as he might learn to play Beethoven sonatas or drive a helicopter. I do not believe there is any useful short-cut to mystical experience—either psychedelic drugs or so-called yogic disciplines. I am not denying that these are both means of achieving states of 'intensity consciousness', any more than I would deny that you can 'play' a Beethoven sonata by putting on a gramophone record or working the pedals of a player-piano. But if you wanted to learn to play the Beethoven sonata in the real sense of the word, you would have to start at the beginning, doing scales and learning to sight-read music. Where mystical experience is concerned, we have the equivalent of 'scales'—i.e. practical exercises—in yogic disciplines. But what we most emphatically do *not* have is the equivalent of a musical score—the detailed objective knowledge of what goes on in states of 'intensity consciousness'. In my own investigations, I have preferred the careful, plodding attempt to create a kind of mental 'musical notation' to the mystical vagaries of some writers on 'cosmic consciousness'.

In this chapter, I shall start in a typically western manner by talking about the nature of poetry.

Luckily, there is no need for lengthy deliberations on the nature of poetry; it can be defined fairly simply. There are certain experiences in which we get a sense of what G. K. Chesterton called 'absurd good news', the sudden feeling that everything is good, and that the human inability to see this is sheer stupidity, a kind of colour-blindness. It happens most notably in the sexual orgasm. It often happens when one first smells spring in the air. It can happen when you are setting out on a holiday, or relaxing in a pub with your first drink of the evening. It can happen to people convalescing from illness—observe the opening paragraphs of Poe's story *The Man of the Crowd*. It happened to W. B. Yeats for no particular reason, when he happened to be sitting in a London teashop:

> My fiftieth year had come and gone
> I sat, a solitary man,
> In a crowded London shop,
> An open book and empty cup
> On the marble table-top.
> While on the shop and street I gazed
> My body of a sudden blazed;
> And twenty minutes more or less
> It seemed, so great my happiness,
> That I was blessed and could bless.

Yeats is full of these sudden insights, particularly in his later years, when he had got over his romantic self-pity about the 'wrong of unshapely things'. In a poem called *The Gyres,* which begins by repeating some of the ominous prophecies of *The Second Coming,* he has the lines:

> What matter? Out of cavern comes a voice,
> And all it knows is that one word 'Rejoice!'

Dylan Thomas was particularly fond of the poem called *Lapis Lazuli,* that mocks at the poets of the thirties with their social consciousness and cries of doom, and ends by describing three Chinamen carved on lapis lazuli; they look down on the 'tragic scene' of contemporary Europe, and

> Their eyes mid many wrinkles, their eyes,
> Their ancient, glittering eyes, are gay.

Auden, who was one of the socially conscious poets, was so impressed by the lines from *The Gyres*—which obviously expressed a conviction of his own—that he paraphrased them in his poem *In Sickness and in Health*:

> Yet through their tohu-bohu comes a voice
> Which utters an absurd command—Rejoice.

Most of Auden's poetry fails to rise above the romantic neurosis, obsession about the decay of beauty and the swift flow of time:

> In headaches and in worry
> Vaguely life leaks away,
> And Time will have his fancy
> Tomorrow or today.

This is a poetic expression of the Graham Greene mood; an unsympathetic reader might feel that it sounds more like dyspepsia than despair. But in this same poem (*As I Walked Out One Evening*), he has the lines:

> O look, look in the mirror,
> O look in your distress;
> Life remains a blessing
> Although you cannot bless.

What comes across from these examples, very clearly, is the feeling that when we see things as they really are, we immediately experience the imperative: Rejoice.

As I go about my everyday business, I am trapped in a net of my own making. I know roughly what I can expect to achieve today, what I can hope for if things go smoothly. If things go unexpectedly smoothly, or a present arrives in the post, I shall say 'How delightful', like a child that has been coaxed into laughing. If things go badly, I shall allow myself to experience an increasing apathy or annoyance, and when I get home in the evening I shall say: 'God, it's been one of *those* days'. I am *in control,* passing my own judgements on what is good or bad, what shall make me smile or frown. But in the sudden moments of intensity, this control vanishes; I am suddenly hit by the objective world, by the reality of things I had been discounting. When Auden writes:

> As I walked out one evening,
> Walking down Bristol street,
> The crowds upon the pavement
> Were fields of harvest wheat.

he is not really *seeing* the crowds; he remains in control, discounting them, imposing his own concepts on them. Both a crowd *and* a field of harvest wheat are far more important than Auden will allow in this rather mannered image. When Yeats or Poe look out of their tea-shop window at the crowd, their 'imposing' mechanism has gone off duty; the mind lies wide open, and the crowd is observed as open mindedly as if it were a crowd of Martians who have just emerged from a space ship in Piccadilly Circus.

There is a story told about the Hitler régime. A German comedian used to make fun of the Nazis in his act; he would snap to attention and shout 'Heil . . .'; then a puzzled expression would cross his face and he would mutter: 'What the hell's his name?' This was reported to Hitler, who sent for the comedian, and made him do his act in front of the Nazi top-brass; then they all sat there with frozen faces; not one of them cracked a smile during the comedian's act. Apparently the lesson served its purpose; the man stopped joking about the Nazis.

This image expresses the adult attitude to experience. *We* decide what is funny and what isn't; what is good and what is bad. But supposing the comedian is so funny that it becomes impossible not to smile, and then to abandon oneself to laughter? This is what happens in all 'intensity experiences'; we cease to act as judges and critics, and become innocent and passive.

But it will be pointed out that even when I am laughing helplessly at a comedian, my judgement has not gone to sleep; on the contrary, I am laughing because it is awake. The judge and censor who has gone to sleep is only my top level, the 'me' I wish to impose on the world, the 'me' I wish to be accepted at his face value. It is a deeper 'me'—equally capable of judgement and criticism—who laughs.

It should now be clear what I mean when I speak about the 'psychological mechanisms' that interest me. When I am engaged in some simple activity, such as typing this page, I seem to myself to be a fairly simple, unified being. In the same way, if my car is running well, it seems to be a simple, unified mechanism. I *know* my car is not a simple mechanism because I have looked under the bonnet. But it requires a great deal of training in self-observation to become aware how many wheels and levers have to move when I do something as straightforward as laughing. The study of the wheels and levers is the key to mystical experience. For one thing ought to be plain from the above discussion: that mystical—or poetic—experience is somehow very simple, like drawing aside a curtain, or turning on a light switch. But if you blunder into a completely dark room, you may feel the walls for hours before you find the switch. Turning on the light is simple only when you know where the switch is.

Now the peculiarity of poetry—as also of great music and painting—is that it has the same power as the sexual orgasm—of twitching aside the curtain, of pressing the switch. But how does it work? Consider what happens when you set out on a holiday— that strange bubbling of vitality from the core of the being. This is a holiday: its purpose is for you to *open up* and *absorb*. When you are working at everyday tasks, you aren't supposed to open up; you have to be in control, 'giving' rather than 'absorbing'. Before you set out on a holiday, you have already passed on a message to your subconscious mind: the personality will be off duty for the next week or so. It is like taking off a uniform and putting on civilian clothes. You have quite consciously *told* your mind that it can relax, open up. The actual words 'Relax, open up', would not have the desired effect, because it would be your personality that hears them, and to be effective, they must be heard by a deeper level. Good poetry has this power of getting straight through to the deeper level, of issuing the order 'Relax' and being obeyed. There is a release of tension, a sigh of relief. And whenever this happens, you confront the basic fact about mystical experience: that somehow, *you do it yourself*. It is exactly like knowing where to find the 'Stop' button on a dynamo. Every time it happens, you become aware of the same splendid truth: that headache and the worry and the 'thousand natural shocks that the flesh is heir to' are *not* an inescapable part of human existence. The dynamo of 'concern' can be turned off, and living ceases to be a process of giving-out, of *output*, and suddenly becomes a process of taking-in, of input. It seems a very obvious discovery, yet we forget it every day. It is completely absurd, just as if I should keep forgetting the existence of food and drink, so that every time I get depressed and hungry, I should assume that my condition is inevitable, due to the 'thousand natural shocks that flesh is heir to', and fail to realise that all I have to do is to relax and eat a hot meal.

This is a point of vital importance, and I must underline it. When tragic poets talk about 'the human condition' they are completely overlooking it. Where my physical metabolism is concerned, I know how to balance input and output. Even on a holiday, I spend a day water-skiing or swimming or clambering up mountains; then, in the evening, I eat good food, drink a bottle of wine, and perhaps listen to music, knowing that this is all that is needed to counteract the fatigue of the day and to prepare me for another strenuous day tomorrow. But psychologically speaking, man is still a long way from this insight. And this is because the psychological process of intake is far more complicated than the physical, and *at this point in evolution,* is not nearly so instinctive. It will become so, and this is man's main hope for the future. But at the moment, he cannot stop the dynamo from grinding on and on. This applies more to intelligent than to stupid people, because their intelligence makes them aim at more self-control. Eliot says:

> I pray that I may forget
> Those matters that with myself I too much discuss
> Too much explain.

Yeats speaks of:

> The old mill of the mind
> Consuming its rag and bone. . . .

T. E. Lawrence says: 'I . . . lamented myself most when I saw a soldier with a girl, or a man fondling a dog, because my wish was to be as superficial and as perfected, and my jailer held me back.' His jailer . . . those upper levels of the personality that refused to be switched off, that are like an over-tired person who cannot get to sleep.

All great art has this odd power of reaching past the jailer,

and pressing the 'Off' button. That is what poetry is about. It is a
formula for inducing 'holiday consciousness' without the need for
a holiday.

Consider for a moment the mechanism of how poetry does this.
Let us think in terms of the romantic poetry that actually treats
this problem of the jailer, the 'thought-riddled nature' (to borrow
another phrase of Lawrence's). This is from the end of *The Waste
Land* and refers specifically to the jailer:

> . . . I have heard the key
> Turn in the door once and turn once only
> We think of the key, each in his prison
> Thinking of the key, each confirms a prison
> Only at nightfall, aetherial rumours
> Revive for a moment a broken Coriolanus

Read in its context—and even, to some extent, out of it—this
passage has the effect of causing the relaxation of tension that is
the essence of poetry. Note the lack of full stops where there should
be full stops, giving it an air of exhaustion, as if the poet is too
weary to bother with such things. Speaking of the prison has the
effect of leading one, so to speak, to *face and accept* this tragic
aspect of the human predicament; it is like a sick man being told
the worst by his doctor; at least, there can now be no further
shock. If I am 'weary and overwatched', my 'jailer' sits on guard,
vigilant, looking outward, prepared for fresh emergency, and the
waste of my vital energies continues like a leak. The moment I
accept the notion of man's tragic destiny (or my own). the
watcher can go off duty; he knows the worst. The leak stops.
Thus pessimistic art serves the purpose of stopping the leak, the
first step towards recovery. In the above example, the talk of
'nightfall' and 'aetherial rumours' increase this soothing effect,
brings visions of blue dusk and murmurs of

> old unhappy far-off things
> And battles long ago.

The reference to Coriolanus is slightly more complicated.
Coriolanus, the proud Roman who regards the common people
as scum and cannot bring himself to beg for their support, is
obviously a symbolic figure for the author of *The Waste Land*.

In reading Shakespeare's play, one may feel that his 'noble pride' is actually a shallow, Evelyn Waugh-ish snobbery: but one can also understand why, for Eliot, he is an archetypal symbol. If Eliot had stated in black and white exactly why he found Coriolanus so important, he would have been accused of fascism or élitism; there was an emotional commitment to the idea of aristocracy and authority and distaste for 'the mob'. (The uncomplimentary references to Jews in his poems *have* led to accusations of anti-semitism.) Coriolanus becomes the symbol of the poet, the intellectual aristocrat in an age of the dictatorship of the proletariat, of 'the mob'. (Yeats and Rowse have felt much the same and said it more openly.) The reference to 'a broken Coriolanus' suddenly raises the poetry from its minor key of exhaustion to the thunderous crash of real tragedy. The inner tensions are suddenly released; the energies that were 'saved' by the acceptance of exhaustion and despair respond to the climax, and overflow.

The effect I have described is the chief emotional device in all Eliot's poetry, from *Prufrock* to the *Four Quartets*. Weariness and depression are transformed into beauty, always by the same device: full acknowledgement of the tragedy and futility of human existence, and then a cautious ascent into a major key by contemplating some favoured symbol of past grandeur. In *The Hollow Men* there is acknowledgement of the total futility and worthlessness of all human values, modulated to sadness, then to resignation:

> Sunlight on a broken column
> There, is a tree swinging
> And voices are
> In the wind's singing
> More distant and more solemn
> Than a fading star.
>
> Let me be no nearer
> In death's dream kingdom
> Let me also wear
> Such deliberate disguises
> Rat's coat, crowskin, crossed staves
> In a field*

* This is a reference to a tarot card showing men squabbling.

> Behaving as the wind behaves
> No nearer—
>
> Not that final meeting
> In the twilight kingdom

Here, the last two lines, with their sudden ominous suggestion of an end to all the futility and lies, are like a clash of cymbals.

Eliot's method is the basic romantic method, raised to a new level of sophistication. In Verlaine, Dowson, Swinburne, the poetry stays on a level of exhaustion and sadness:

> I am tired of tears and laughter
> And of men who laugh and weep . . .

It is interesting to recall that one of Eliot's earliest enthusiasms was John Davidson's *Thirty Bob a Week,* a Kiplingesque lament of a half-starved clerk with a family:

> For like a mole I journey in the dark
> A-travelling along the underground
> From my Pillar'd Halls and broad Suburban Park,
> To come the daily dull official round;
> And home again at night with my pipe all alight,
> A-scheming how to count ten bob a pound.
>
> And it's often very cold and very wet
> And my missus stitches towels for the hunks;
> And the Pillar'd Halls is half of it to let—
> Three rooms about the size of travelling trunks.
> And we cough, my wife and I, to dislocate a sigh,
> When the noisy little kids are in their bunks.

The rather grim self-pity of Davidson remains in the minor key; there is no catharsis. But it achieves a power beyond most of that of Davidson's poetry because it strikes the minor key so savagely. This is even more true of James Thomson's *City of Dreadful Night,* whose influence Eliot also acknowledged. Thomson was an alcoholic who drank and starved in gloomy London lodging houses; he turned out bad love poetry to an imaginary girl and made a little money from hack journalism. There is a kind of pathetic cheerfulness in his *Sunday at Hampstead—An Idle Idyll by a Very Humble Member of the Great and Noble London Mob.* One day, he decided to bare his teeth:

Because a cold rage seizes one at whiles
To show the bitter old and wrinkled truth
Stripped naked of all vesture that beguiles,
False dreams, false hopes, false masks and modes of youth;
Because it gives some sense of power and passion
In helpless impotence to try to fashion
Our woe in living words howe'er uncouth.

The poem is Thomson's masterpiece because this savage
pessimism never lets up, and it raises despair *to a form of strength*.
The age of Shelley and Keats, with their soothing melancholy,
was definitely over.

With *The City of Dreadful Night*, Thomson becomes almost a
great poet. But not quite. The main trouble with poetry is that it
knows itself to be dealing in illusion. One might say that it
achieves catharsis by telling lies. Auden defines its function in his
poem *In Memory of W. B. Yeats*:

Sing of human unsuccess
In a rapture of distress;

In the deserts of the heart
Let the healing fountain start,
In the prison of his days,
Teach the free man how to praise.

It brings emotional relief through the imagination; it teaches
man how to praise, not by pointing to the wonders of the universe, like science, but by creating wish-fulfilment fantasies. This
phrase should be understood in its broadest sense. Wagner liked
to use the word 'wahn', which means literally 'illusion', but which
Wagner uses in the sense of a kind of legal fiction, 'play acting'.
He tells his patron, King Ludwig of Bavaria, that the king must
stand above the illusions of Church and patriotism that comfort
the common people, sustained only by the power of art, the
'kindly life-saviour who does not really lead us *beyond* this life,
but lifts us up *above* it and shows it as a game'. This, then, is
poetry, a kind of ointment that soothes the wounds made by life,
but cannot cure them. In old age, Yeats believed he was being

ruthlessly honest when he expressed the same view of art as a kind of ladder that allows you to clamber above the mud of life, but that has no power to transport you out of it permanently.

> . . . Now that my ladder's gone
> I must lie down where all the ladders start,
> In the foul rag-and-bone shop of the heart.

The ladder is 'wahn'.

But in the opening words of his great monologue in the third act of *The Mastersingers,* Hans Sachs uses 'wahn' in an altogether harsher sense when he cries: 'Wahn, wahn, Uberall! Wahn!', and goes on to speak of human spite and conflict. Here it means something closer to 'Mad, mad!', or 'deluded fools!' Here Wagner uses the word in the sense in which it might have been used by Schopenhauer or Buddha. Here there is an entirely different attitude to human existence; for what distinguishes Buddhism or Schopenhauer's philosophy from 'poetry' is that it is definitely not 'wahn'. Its attitude to existence is grimly clinical. The Buddha surveys the world and says: 'Suffering! Stupidity! Cowardice! These are the basic realities of human existence.' What he actually *says* is practically identical with what Thomson says in *The City of Dreadful Night.* What makes it different is that Gautama's words are not intended to soothe or 'teach the free man how to praise'. They are intended as the analysis which precedes a course of action. He sees human life as the pursuit of happiness, and he believes firmly that this is as destructive as the moth's interest in candle flames, or the fly's in fly-paper. Although Buddha professes to believe neither in God nor the devil, his outlook really presupposes some great demonic force that has created life as a sadistic joke. And the solution is simple. 'Don't touch. *All* berries are poisonous.' Schopenhauer said much the same thing twenty-three centuries later: the world is an illusion the only reality is the Will—the will to live, to procreate, to achieve happiness. And just as sexual desire leads you into frenzied pursuit, and ends by leaving you high and dry, wondering what it was all about, so all willing leaves you with empty hands. The world is fairy gold.

I have to admit that there was a time in my mid-teens when I found these doctrines deeply satisfying. In your teens, you

are always making a fool of yourself. You are always chasing
objects of desire, and falling flat on your face. You are always
plunging into impassioned monologues, and then discovering
that you have communicated nothing at all. The Buddha said:
Don't make any effort. Don't even bother to desire that girl;
you're merely wasting vital energy.

I will admit that if this was *all* Gautama said, Buddhism would
have been forgotten in the year he died. It was the next part of his
doctrine that aroused the enthusiasm. What do I do instead of
pursuing sex or fame? *I attempt to widen my perception until I contemplate the whole world.* For all intelligent human beings have had
some brief experience of moments of contemplation, when consciousness seems to widen and become aware of the sheer
interest and complexity of the world. And when you are in this state,
you cease to feel the same intense desire for individuals or objects,
because you are aware of so many. The beam of your desire is
spread-thin, as it were. And it's a delightful state: to think about
a girl who has been causing you sleepless nights, and to feel only a
kind of patronising interest in her, complete lack of involvement.
You can breathe deeply again; the thorn has gone out of your
foot. You had been subject to the delusion that happiness involves
getting what you want. Now you suddenly know that happiness
is *wanting nothing*. It is by no means a matter of being exhausted or
indifferent. On the contrary. This sense of being a bird, of looking
down on the world from a great height, produces a keener satisfaction than you ever experienced in the satisfaction of desires.

According to Gautama, this feeling of delight and freedom is
only the beginning. In such a state, your mind can focus on wider
horizons, broaden its beam of *perception* from its usual narrow
compass to a sense of the richness and complexity of the world.
But there is no reason why a man who has made this discovery
should not continue to broaden his beam of perception until it
embraces the whole universe, until it contemplates the notion of
infinite space and time, and recognises the total unimportance of
human existence against this vast canvas. Man ceases to be man:
that is, a creature who pursues his own aims and desire, and becomes an enormous mirror that reflects reality. And if ordinary
'contemplation' brings a sense of delight and relief, then this
universal contemplation would bring a detached ecstacy beyond
anything we can imagine, the ultimate peace and delight of Nirvana.

I have never read any western exponent of Buddhism who understood this; that Buddhism is an extremely positive religion. Its world rejection is quite unlike the Christian 'renunciation'. You wouldn't call it renunciation if you rejected cold tea for champagne. This also explains why exponents of Buddhism feel only a patronising contempt for Christianity—as well as for Judaism, Mahommedanism and the more traditional forms of Hinduism. The basic Buddhistic vision is identical with the basic vision of science; it has no use for 'belief' or dogma; it aims at pure contemplation, as detached and unprejudiced as a scientist examining an unknown virus under the microscope.

But anyone who has ever fallen under the spell of Buddhism— or other eastern religion, for that matter—will have discovered the drawback. You can determinedly withdraw your mind from the objects of sense, assure yourself that you are free of all desire—and nothing whatever happens. You just sit there. You cannot 'contemplate' merely by wanting to contemplate. In fact, you soon realise that contemplation is closely bound up with desire. When you first perform that mental act of rejecting your desires and obsessions, the feeling of freedom is magnificent, and the mind is launched like a rocket, powered, by the desire you are rejecting. This is why religious conversions are such emotionally violent experiences. When there is nothing more to reject, the mind becomes static. And there is a world of difference between serenity and mere lack of motion.

I would not go so far as to reject the whole Buddhist concept of contemplative objectivity; it can be achieved in flashes. But I *am* inclined to believe that when the aspirant sits cross-legged and concentrates the gaze at the end of his nose, his immediate aim should not be a state of contemplation. It is too negative. The mind requires a more positive aim.

Zen Buddhism is only Buddhism by name; in content, it is more closely related to Hinduism or Taoism. Both these religions recognise that there are other ecstacies besides that of purely objective contemplation. The Buddhist mistrusts the delight he feels on a spring morning; the Hindu accepts it as another aspect of God, a glimpse of something bigger. The Taoist would not call it God, but his attitude towards it would amount to the same thing.

With Hinduism, we are closer to the position I outlined at the beginning of this chapter: the belief that there is a sort of curtain between man and 'reality', and that when some chance twitches the curtain aside, the effect is of 'absurd good news', sheer delight. Its attitude to these moments of insight is altogether more *active* than that of the Buddhist. There is always a reason for the moments of insight. Yeats has not bothered to describe his process of thought or feeling when his 'body of a sudden blazed' in the teashop; but from his description, I would be inclined to believe that it is an example of what I call 'the rainbow effect': that is, the delight that comes after a storm, when the air is still full of raindrops, and the sun emerges, creating a rainbow. The delight here is a matter of the contrast with the storm, a feeling of convalescence, of rebirth. This is obviously what Poe experienced in *The Man of the Crowd*. Pascal's mystical revelation—which he wrote out on a sheet of paper and kept sewed in the lining of his coat for the rest of his life—occurred when he was recovering from illness. He headed it with the word FIRE.

It may seem that I am overemphasising the difference between the Buddhist Nirvana and the Hindu vision of Brahman, the 'all'. Surely, in the last analysis they are the same thing? I do not deny this. All the same, the difference between the Hindu and the Buddhist approach to this reality is about as basic as it could be. The Buddha's feeling was that once you have glimpsed this ultimate reality, you are quite clear about one point: that our human life and human preoccupations are *irrelevant* to it, as irrelevant as if you happened to be an octopus who was interested in astronomy. If his aim is to grasp this reality, man would be better off as a pure, abstract spirit.

The Hindu approach is the reverse of this. In the *Bhagavad Gita*, Krishna explains to the warrior Arjuna that the world as perceived by men is an illusion that hides the reality of God. But the soul of man is also God. In some paradoxical sense, you can reach God either by turning completely inwards or completely outwards. 'Eternity opens from the centre of an atom' said William Blake, expressing the same notion. But at the climax of the *Gita*, after the instruction is over, Krishna allows Arjuna a glimpse of the totality of God:

> Universal form, I see you without limit,
> Infinite of arms, eyes, mouths and bellies

See, and find no end, midst or beginning.
Crowned with diadems, you wield the mace and discus,
Shining every way—the eyes shrink from your splendour
Brilliant like the sun; like fire, blazing boundless.*

This vision—the ultimate 'bird's eye view'—or rather, god's-
eye-view—reveals meanings that are ungraspable from the worm's
eye of everyday human consciousness. From this moment, all is
seen to be justified. All is good. There is no more shrinking, no
more doubts and hesitations. At the beginning of the *Gita* (which
is a part of the *Mahabarata,* a Hindu epic poem), Arjuna has
refused to go into battle because he recognises faces in the oppos-
ing army and is torn by pity. Krishna assures him that his scruples
are absurd: 'Go out and fight... by me these men are slain already.'
Observe that the vision of God does not lead Arjuna to sit
cross-legged and contemplate. It fills him with courage and purpose, the desire to begin living at a hundred miles an hour.

Clearly, this is why Yeats's Chinamen are so gay. It is the
secret of the visionaries. Human beings are playing for enormous
stakes, stakes so big that they cannot even begin to grasp them.
And like the Indians who sold Long Island for a few dollars,
they are grotesquely, comically unaware of the value of the life
they possess.

Nietzsche begins his essay on Schopenhauer by asking what
are the universal characteristics of human beings, and replies:
Laziness and timidity. This is not true. Some people are not lazy.
Some are not timid. But *all* human beings are narrow, blind, petty,
stuck in the present. Our problem is narrowness of vision. The
poet is a man whose vision sometimes expands beyond the usual
human limit, and is startled by how enormous and beautiful the
universe is. It is the one thing that all poets have in common,
even the pessimistic ones like Thomson, Leopardi, Eliot.

The sky is blue, the air soft, each leaf lies,
Each blade of grass, all motionless; the sun
Pitilessly dazzles my tear-swollen eyes.†

* Isherwood translation.
† S'apre il ciel, cade il soffio, in ogni canto,
  Posan l'erbe e le frondi, e m'abbarbaglia
  Le luci il crudo Sol pregne di pianto.
                                      Leopardi, Fragment 38

O City city, I can sometimes hear
Beside a public bar in Lower Thames Street,
The pleasant whining of a mandoline
And a clatter and a chatter from within
Where the fishermen lounge at noon: where the walls
Of Magnus Martyr hold
Inexplicable splendour of Ionian white and gold.

But few poets are as concerned as Yeats with the contrast between this vision of total goodness and our human pettiness:

What were all the world's alarms
To mighty Paris when he found
Sleep upon a golden bed
That first dawn in Helen's arms?

Nabokov's Humbert had described a sexual orgasm: 'a glowing tingle which *now* had reached that state of absolute security, confidence and reliance not found elsewhere in conscious life'. Paris has stolen Helen; he is in trouble; so is Troy; but surging upwards on that enormous wave of 'security, confidence and reliance' he knows that all these considerations are absurd; he falls asleep with the trust of a baby.

The characteristic of the really great writer is the ability of his mind to suddenly *leap beyond* his ordinary human values, into sudden perception of universal values. Jane Austen, Dickens, Thackeray, Trollope, never get outside their own value-systems —although these systems, in themselves, are broader than those of their contemporaries. Other major writers of the 19th century had definite moments in which they became aware of the 'universal value system'—Balzac, Hugo, Tolstoy—but such awareness is an accident in the general pattern of their work; it has nothing to do with the over-all weltanschauung of *Les Misérables*, the *Comédie Humaine*, *War and Peace*. Only two major figures place the values glimpsed in moments of intensity at the centre of their work: Nietzsche and Dostoevsky. Nietzsche only refers to them obliquely; but the volcanic life-affirmation of Zarathustra and the vision of a 'transvaluation of all values' can be traced back to certain moments of pure affirmation in his earlier years; an experience on a hill called Leutch when a thunderstorm released the 'power-orgasm', and another on the road near Strasbourg. In both cases, Nietzsche was depressed and tired, and in both cases,

c

something occurred that would normally have depressed him still further: on Leutch, the sight of a shepherd killing a goat, on the Strasbourg road, the sight of his old regiment riding into battle. The crash of the storm, the thunder of the cavalry, released the power orgasm, and led to the 'transvaluation of values'—in the latter case, to the sudden conviction that 'the strongest and highest will to life lies in the Will to war, the Will to Power'. Like Pascal, Nietzsche was almost permanently ill, so these moments of affirmation-consciousness were probably connected with periods of recovery or convalescence.

The case of Dostoevsky is even more interesting. His 'glimpses' stemmed from a single experience: when he was about to be shot for treason in the Semyonovsky Square, and was pardoned at the last minute. The prospect of immediate death brought sudden awareness of the absolute value of life; it acted in the same way at Arjuna's vision of God. From then on, Dostoevsky was a man of widely separated halves. He remained a typical Russian—emotional, impulsive, self-pitying, generous—but a part of him looked down ironically on the 'human' Dostoevsky, recognising the complete triviality of most of his values. Dostoevsky was epileptic, and, according to his description of a seizure in *The Idiot,* the fits were preceded by moments of pure 'affirmation-consciousness'. All his novels are studies of 'human' sufferings, sufferings due to pride, to poverty, to the gambler's obsession, to sexual infatuation. He wallows in humiliation; perhaps the most typical scene in all his work is the one in *The Idiot* where the characters at a party propose to relate their meanest action. His neurotic self-contempt leads him to lay a most un-Nietzschean emphasis on the Christian virtues of pity, kindness, humility; and to a large extent, his novels are about the clash between violent, wilful human beings and naturally saintly ones. And then come the moments of total affirmation-consciousness when the opposition ceases to matter. Alyosha Karamazov is miserable because Father Zossima's body begins to rot almost immediately after his death and the other monks believe this is a sign of inner-corruption; as he looks at the stars, the floodgates burst; he wants to embrace the whole universe. The petty human values have been completely transcended; not by 'Christian' values, but by a vision similar to Arjuna's.

It is in the novel called *The Demons* (or *The Possessed*) that Dostoevsky sees most clearly that the Christian-non-Christian conflict is less important than the conflict between life-negation and life-affirmation. Stavrogin is perhaps the most important character created by Dostoevsky. He is rich, spoilt, good-looking, gifted—and bored. The boredom arises from his basically passive attitude to his own existence. He expects far more out of it than life normally gives, like a romantic schoolgirl going to her first ball. When it fails to give him the experiences he demands, he loses interest, becomes detached and indifferent. He tries vice and crime to see if they set his vital compass working again, but they don't. He ends by killing himself, although he concedes that this is a pointless thing to do, since he has no more motive for dying than for going on living. He is a man who has become devoid of all motive.

His counterweight in this novel is Kirilov, who also commits suicide, but for the opposite reason, Kirilov has had a mystical experience. He does not describe it, but its nature becomes clear from his comment that 'everything's good'. When seen in the perspective of this vision, even the suffering of children ceases to be bad. What has happened is that he has had the experience of pure affirmation, and seen that *it is objectively true,* that it corresponds to objective reality. This means that he now discounts all his human 'values', the worm's eye view. He wishes to test this certainty that 'all is well' by an irreversible experiment—suicide. The logic of this may not be clear—but then, Dostoevsky was more intent on finding powerful dramatic symbols to express his ideas than in logic. Stavrogin's suicide is equally illogical.

But what is important here is this contrast between the man who is trapped in his own boredom, and feels that life is meaningless and pointless—i.e. *that he has exhausted the world of interest*—and the man who is aware that life is infinitely interesting, infinitely good. We all contain a Stavrogin and a Kirilov. Dostoevsky is right to show Stavrogin turning to crime as the expression of his sense of futility. Crime represents a choice based upon a certain lack of optimism, the absence of the feeling of infinite potentiality.* There are moments when everyone experiences Kirilov's insight: that the world is infinitely interesting—*self-evidently* so. Yet to everyday consciousness, it is equally self-evident that the

* See my *Casebook of Murder* (1969).

world is not infinitely interesting. Not that only, but that it is we who endow it with interest. Look at that child playing with her doll. Is the doll really 'interesting'? And the answer seems to be: No; she only finds it interesting because she is innocent and ignorant. She is endowing it with interest, and we could not do the same because we know more than she does. And once you begin to see the world in this way, it becomes horribly plain that *all* human activity is the outcome of a kind of immaturity. You look around at this world, full of people with 'convictions'—patriots, Jehovah's Witnesses, left-wingers and right-wingers, men who sail yachts single-handed round the world or cross the Atlantic in a rowing boat—and you shudder. Isn't it obvious that all human activity springs out of unintelligence? Or at least, out of a kind of enthusiastic innocence that more fastidious souls cannot share? Surely Koheleth was right when he said that 'all is vanity'?

And then, quite abruptly, your 'input motor' starts working again, perhaps for some quite trivial reason, like the madeleine dipped in tea that reminded Proust of his childhood at Combray. The springs of the 'secret life' begin to flow, and like Yeats, you are suddenly 'blessed, and could bless'. Obviously, Koheleth had left something important out of his calculations.

The poet is the man in whom the Kirilov element is, for some reason, naturally stronger than the Stavrogin. Why can we not imagine Wordsworth or Shelley becoming criminals? They were poor enough. They also experienced moments of depression and exhaustion, as can be seen from the *Lines Written in Dejection near Naples,* or the *Ode on Intimations of Immortality*. But no matter how tired they got, they could remember the 'other' moments so clearly that their one desire was to recover them. Shelley asks the 'spirit of beauty':

> Why dost thou pass away and leave our state,
> This dim vast vale of tears, vacant and desolate?

Obviously, the man who has experienced the 'spirit of beauty' with the intensity described in the *Hymn to Intellectual Beauty* can never sink to the level of life-devaluation necessary for crime.

Another important point arises from this. Not only is Shelley himself incapable of crime; but his poetry is capable of arousing the same consciousness of 'intellectual beauty' in others, and combatting *their* tendency to life-devaluation. Shaw provides an example. He started writing at the age of twenty, but he was nearly fifty before he achieved real success. The first ten years of his writing life were devoid of any kind of success; in the next decade, he became known as a journalist, and began to write plays that never achieved performance. This kind of long-term act of faith is also the opposite of criminality. To imagine Shaw becoming a criminal, we have to imagine two distinct steps: first, total discouragement that leads him to abandon literature; second, an increasingly defensive and resentful attitude towards the society that denies him success, until he forgets his 'long range' policy, and decides to grab what he can get.

It will be seen now why I say that Kirilov's suicide is basically unbelievable. The Kirilov vision of meaning is associated with long-range purpose, purpose that is capable of dispensing with returns for a very long time. Although it would not be true to say that human beings without purpose become criminals, it would be true to say that criminality cannot exist in association with long-term purpose.

Be it noted that when one feels possessed by 'long term purpose', one's *sense of oneself* also alters in quality. When I feel angry, miserable, anxious, bored, the self I am aware of might be called my 'short-term self': that is, I have no sense of duration. I feel somehow inferior to the material objects around me. In moments of intensity, or moments when I plan some project in the future, I become aware of my strength and durability, of my *long-term self*. I shall not explore this concept here, but its presence will be sensed throughout the book.

2

The Robot

The basic assertion of this book is that 'mystical vision' occurs when we get a sudden 'bird's eye' view of life; when, for a moment, we 'pull back' from it and see more of it, instead of being confined to the narrow focus of our usual worm's eye view. This seeing-more-of-it always brings a feeling of exaltation, delight. Now the interesting question is: what actually *happens* when I suddenly swing from the worm's eye view to the bird's eye view? What takes place, physically and psychologically speaking?

I have invented a useful concept for dealing with this basic psychological problem; I call it the 'robot'. When a human being learns anything difficult—to talk, to write, to calculate, to drive a car, to type, to speak a foreign language—he has to begin by concentrating upon the details of what he wishes to learn. Even when he has learned a basic French vocabulary, he finds it difficult to read French, because he is still thinking in English, and he has to translate each word into English. But gradually, the 'remembering' process is passed on to a deeper level of his being, a kind of robot in his subconscious mind, and the robot can read French without having to translate it back into English. It is in every way more efficient than his conscious personality.

This robot is a labour-saving device. He is a kind of electronic brain who stores information. When an activity has been performed often enough, he takes it over, and what is more, he does it a great deal more efficiently than I could do it consciously. I drive my car automatically; if I think about it, I do it less well. This is illustrated by the anecdote of the centipede, to whom a spider said: 'How on earth do you move a hundred legs at the same time? I have trouble enough with eight.' 'Oh, it's perfectly easy,' said the centipede, 'I simply do this . . .' at which point he tripped and fell on his nose.

It should be noted that it is not mere repetition of an action that leads the robot to learn it efficiently; it is *how much effort you put into learning it*. A boy learning French at school may study it for several hundred hours in a year, and still learn very little. The following year, he goes for a holiday in France, and suddenly *wants* to express himself; the consequence is that he learns more in two weeks than he learned in a year at school.

All animals possess a robot to some extent—otherwise they would not be able to learn. But man has the most efficient robot of all. The cleverer he is, the more efficient the robot. But the very efficiency of his robot is one of his greatest problems. A man living alone in his country cottage, tending his roses, feels far more the master of his house than a millionaire with servants and gardeners. The sheer size of the millionaire's house alienates him from it. Compared to most animals, man is psychologically a millionaire. Of course, it is possible that a millionaire is so full of vitality that he knows everything that goes on in his house. But if he ever gets ill or tired, the servants will take over. It is easy for man to lose all sense of vitality and free-will, and to live an almost robot existence. Because you will observe that the sense of freedom, of being vitally alive, tends to occur when you are doing something for the first time. The amateur actor gets more excitement out of it than the professional. The most blasé person becomes a schoolboy again if you get him to do something at which he is totally inexperienced: riding a horse, skiing, appearing on television. The more intelligent a man is—the quicker he learns things—the more quickly the activity is passed on to his robot, to be performed automatically. This is the great disadvantage of the robot: that it not only drives your car and talks French, but also takes the excitement out of skiing or listening to a symphony. The robot has taken over too many of our functions. The consequence is that when life is peaceful, we find it difficult to feel really alive. As Nietzsche points out, happiness is the feeling of the will. But we have passed on 99 per cent of our 'willing' to the robot.

It is important to understand that this enormous structure of the robot restricts our capacity to feel. We keep learning things and packing them into the realm of the robot until we are like some ancient archaeological site, with layer upon layer of ruined cities. Whenever I acquire some new skill, it gives me pleasure, but the moment the robot takes over, the pleasure vanishes.

I should point out that this pleasure is, in theory, recoverable. I may become acquainted with the symphonies of Beethoven through the radio, and finally become so familiar with them that they cease to be a source of pleasure. Years later, I buy a good record player and the latest version of the symphonies in stereo, and I find my plesaure in them just as intense as when I first discovered them. And surely everyone has had the experience of lending someone a book, and re-reading it when it is returned, just from the sheer pleasure of seeing it again?

It should now be possible to understand exactly why Stavrogin finds life so strangely boring. Challenge keeps the will healthy as exercise keeps the body healthy. If the will remains unexercised for too long, it runs to fat, becomes short-winded. When it is in this state, nothing seems worth doing; life becomes flat and pointless.

I have coined the term 'acceptation' to describe this state of forgetfulness—its relation to 'acceptance' should be obvious. I think acceptation as being like the shadow of an eclipse spreading across the moon. And I have elsewhere coined the term 'St Neot margin' for the area covered by the shadow, and explained how I happened to be travelling through St Neots in Huntingdonshire when I was suddenly struck by the notion that there is an area of the mind that can be stimulated by pain or inconvenience but not by pleasure. Camus wrote a novel about a man who lives all the time in such a state, *L'Etranger*. The hero goes to the cinema, goes to his mother's funeral, sleeps with his mistress, all in a mood of indifference, which is only broken at the end when he loses his temper with a priest on the eve of his execution. He then makes the curious comment: 'I had been happy and I was happy still'. He had been happy, even when bored? How can the paradox be explained? By the concept of the robot. We have many layers, and since each achievement passed on to the realm of the robot represents a satisfaction, one might say that the robot contains layer upon layer of compacted happiness, that can be shaken up only by the effort of will aroused by crisis. It is significant that Camus was so fascinated by Stavrogin that he did a stage version of *The Possessed*.

Once understood, this notion of the layers of compacted 'intentions' (which derives from Husserl), will be seen to be as vital to the understanding of human psychology as the Copernican hypothesis about the sun to astronomy. All the tragedy and failure of the 19th century are due directly to the failure to grasp it. But before I speak of it more fully, there are some other matters that require mention.

The older—and more complex—we become, the more we become slaves of the robot—slaves of the machine that was intended to give us greater control over our environment, 'for that is the end of all slavery', as Shaw says. 'Shades of the prison house begin to close', and the less spontaneously arise those moments in which we experience 'the glory and the freshness of a dream'. But this is not an absolute matter; it is a matter of vital economy. A businessman may tie up most of his capital in various enterprises, so that he has none immediately available; but if a real emergency arises, he can realise it quickly enough. In more primitive societies, constant challenges and dangers kept the older adults 'on their toes' and prevented life-devaluation from setting in. (Even today, in the remote part of Cornwall I live in, it is still possible to meet clay-workers of eighty or ninety who have the alertness of a man forty years younger.) But as life becomes more civilised and automatised man is thrown back increasingly upon his own resources, his inner-richness, for his sense of values. And nothing can destroy a man so quickly as 'freedom'—freedom from these external demands. We have all come across cases of a man who has worked for fifty years and dreams of retirement to a country cottage with a rose garden— and who dies within a year of retiring. Freedom is a corrosive.

I have elsewhere cited the example of Sri Ramakrishna to illustrate this matter of the 'shades of the prison house'.* Ramakrishna was born in 1836, and Swami Nikhilananda has described how he had his first experience of spiritual ecstasy at the age of six. He was eating puffed rice from a basket as he crossed a paddy field when a storm cloud blew up. When it covered most of the sky, a flock of white cranes flew across it. The beauty of the contrast of black cloud and white birds so over- whelmed him that he collapsed and became unconscious.

(It is no derogation of the mystical content of the experience to

* *The Outsider,* Chapter 9.

suggest that Ramakrishna may have suffered from some from of epilepsy—the experience sounds very like Dostoevsky's.)

As he grew older, these experiences stopped happening. In his late teens, he became a priest at the temple of Kali at Dakshineswar, and spent his days meditating and singing hymns. But the moments of intensity were infrequent. And since affirmation-consciousness so often tends to be a by-product, and attempts to seize it directly are so seldom successful, he found them becoming steadily less frequent. Until one day, in a state of total misery, he seized a sword and was about to plunge it into himself. 'Suddenly the blessed Mother revealed Herself. The buildings with their different parts, the temple, and everything else vanished from my sight, leaving no trace whatsoever, and in their stead I saw a limitless, infinite, effulgent Ocean of Consciousness. As far as the eye could see, the shining billows were madly rushing at me from all sides . . .' And once again, Ramakrishna lost consciousness.

What happened is clear enough; it is the experience of Camus's Meursault on the eve of his execution, but intensified by this physical peculiarity of Ramakrishna—epilepsy or whatever—to the point of unconsciousness. Restiffe de la Breton has described (in *M. Nicholas*) how, when he was in his early teens, an older girl began to kiss him, and then to masturbate him; at the crucial moment, he collapsed in a faint. He ascribes this to his youth and physical frailty.

Obviously, crisis can change the balance of power in the robot; it can, so to speak, shake up these layers of compacted happiness as if they were gravel in a sieve, releasing the happiness into consciousness.

Students of Zen will grasp immediately that what I have said above is the essence of Zen. Suzuki writes: 'This body of ours is something like an electric battery in which a mysterious power latently lies. When this power is not properly brought into operation, it either grows mouldy and withers away, or is warped and expresses itself abnormally.' 'Zen, in its essence, is the art of seeing into the nature of one's own being.' But, as everyone knows, the peculiarity of Zen Buddhism is its method of 'shock'. Ramakrishna knew all about the Divine Mother, but he needed the self-administered shock of the sword to release this knowledge as conscious *insight*. Zen is a system of such shocks—always bearing in mind that it must be built upon a foundation of study. In extreme cases, the master may suddenly kick the pupil, or simply offer him a flower as the answer to some question about the Ultimate. But there is also a continual attempt to jar the mind into sudden recognition by epigrammatic lessons. A master called the disciple, who said 'Yes?' The master called him several times more, and each time the disciple answered 'Yes?' The master then said 'I apologise for calling you by your name, but it should be you who apologises to me.' It takes a moment for the meaning to dawn: that the state of affirmation-consciousness involves a total loss of ego-feeling; the disciple should apologise for feeling that his name is his identity.

In another case, a famous samurai asked the master whether there was a heaven and hell. The master deliberately provoked him by saying 'You don't look like a soldier of the emperor—you look more like a beggar,' and various other derogatory remarks, until the enraged soldier drew his sword. 'Now you have opened the gates of hell,' said the master. The soldier sheathed his sword and bowed. 'Now you have opened the gates of heaven,' said the master.

It can be seen from these examples that Zen tries to teach by 'action parables'. But *what* it is teaching is in no way different from what might be taught by a Hindu, a Christian or a Sufi. I have chosen these two examples because, in the context of the above analysis, they strike me as dubious. It is true that the upper-levels of the personality vanish in moments of affirmation-consciousness—as with Yeats in his tea-shop. It is also true that it may be salutary for conceited people to mortify the ego. But to suppose that one can achieve affirmation-consciousness by trying to consciously suppress the ego is naïve. It *may* work sometimes, for *any* part of the will may achieve the right result; but it is basically irrelevant. The story of the soldier has more in common with Christianity than Buddhism. Losing one's temper leads one to identify with the upper levels of the personality and leads away from affirmation-consciousness in exactly the same way as being conceited; conversely, controlling it is a step in the right direction. These are useful reminders to the aspirant, but neither are relevant to the question of the affirmation-insight.

Eugen Herrigel's *Zen in the Art of Archery* might also be mentioned in this connection. The aim of Herrigel's teacher was

to persuade him to shoot the arrow 'subconsciously', to stop
trying: i.e. to let the robot take over completely. He had to stop
making conscious efforts to direct it. But there is no profound
spiritual message to be drawn from all this. My robot is now
typing for me, and if I try observing how my fingers work as I
type, I shall start doing it badly. Herrigel's slowly increasing skill
proves nothing about Zen; only about the way we acquire habits;
Pavlov would have been as competent to discuss it as a Zen
master. The actual value of this type of exercise is in making the
aspirant fully aware that he *has* deeper levels. I become aware of
the same thing if I start to type the word 'outhouse' and find my
fingers automatically typing 'outsider' because I have done it so
often, or if I type 'apeg' instead of 'page'. Just as in shorthand,
there are single signs—even a dot—that stand for words, and
just as a compositor may keep certain words permanently in print
because he uses them so often, so my robot apparently has his
own methods of achieving efficiency, which 'I' only discover by
accident. (I put 'I' in inverted commas because I want to emphasise
that, in a sense, the robot is more 'me' than 'I' am.)

If these remarks on Zen sound disparaging, this is not because
I do not recognise its importance, but because I wish to emphasise
that it has nothing to tell us that we cannot say just as precisely in
western terminology. In recent years there has been a revival of
the fashion to exalt eastern modes of thought and disparage the
western. There are even converts who speak of the spiritual meaning of the Japanese tea ceremony and flower arrangement—whose
significance is basically in no way different from the ceremonial of
the Catholic Church. (The function of rituals—like that of birth-
days or Christmas—is to 'remind'.) This kind of thing does more
harm than good, just as patriotism and racialism does more harm
than good; it separates rather than joins, emphasises differences
rather than similarities.

The point I wish to underline here is that poetry and Zen are
fundamentally similar; they have the same aim. I have pointed
out that the affirmation experience is usually a by-product of other
experiences, and tends to arise from *contrast*. The first day of
spring produces such a pleasant shock because we have got into
the habit of thinking of winter as permanent. But this is not to
say that the best way to capture the affirmation experience is not
to try. All art is humanity's attempt to capture the affirmation

experience so it can be re-created. The simplest form of art is romantic art—the poetry of Wordsworth or Shelley, the music of Beethoven or Sibelius, the painting of the expressionists, the sculpture of Rodin. Classical art—the music of Monteverdi or Bach, for example—seeks to direct the mind beyond the human, to a kind of Buddhistic remoteness. Its roots are in religious ritual, as are those of Greek tragedy. But a symphony of Sibelius tries to *mould* the emotions of the hearer as directly as a sculptor moulds clay. And it is interesting that a large percentage of records of Sibelius's music carry pictures of pine forests on the cover. In his best music, Sibelius aims to paint nature, to produce the sense of great forests, the northern lakes, trees laden with snow. It is the attempt to by-pass the upper levels of the personality, to appeal to the impersonal in man.

Let us consider the phenomenology of the poetic experience more closely. On the morning of July 31st, 1802, William Wordsworth and his sister Dorothy crossed Westminster Bridge on top of the Dover coach, en route to France. Dorothy wrote: 'The city, St Pauls, with the river and a multitude of little boats made a most beautiful sight. . . . The houses were not overhung by their cloud of smoke, and they were spread out endlessly, yet the sun shone so brightly. . . .' The impression was brief but intense—it cannot have taken the coach more than half a minute to cross the bridge, even going slowly—and Wordsworth wrote, a month later, the famous sonnet beginning: 'Earth has not anything to show more fair'. As one reads it, one assumes that Wordsworth stood on Westminster Bridge early in the morning—I had always assumed he was standing on the Big Ben side, since otherwise the sun would be in his eyes—and sank into a state of deep serenity, a kind of Buddhistic stillness, in which he had no trouble in finding exactly the right word to express his sense of awe: 'a sight so *touching* in its majesty'—how often do we think of majesty as being 'touching'? In fact, the coach whirled them across the bridge with much clattering—it would be cobbled—and they emerged for a moment from the unbeautiful buildings of Victoria Street—which had another name in those days—on to the great bridge. It was July, and within a couple of hours the sun would be unbearably hot; but at this time, the air was still cool and fresh—again, the sense of contrast. They were setting off for

France, a country Wordsworth loved; and in those days, the journey from London to Calais would be as strenuous and adventurous as a train journey across outer Mongolia nowadays. Wordsworth is already in high spirits, and the glimpse of the city in the early morning sunlight intensifies the mood. But how can he get all this into a sonnet—the knowledge that it was going to be a hot day, that in a few minutes the coach will be back among the gloomy houses of the Westminster Bridge Road, a slum area; above all, the holiday feeling of setting out on a journey? He might get it into a novel; but to capture it in a poem, he has to take a snapshot of a moving object, so to speak. And so the poet stands on Westminster Bridge and meditates:

> The city now doth like a garment wear
> The beauty of the morning, silent, bare . . .,

When, in fact, the coach was clattering noisily.

As we read the poem, we create the idea of a majestic river (at this stage of the poem, we have nothing more to go on); then we add ships, domes, towers, theatres and temples, and the line 'all bright and glittering in the smokeless air' adds a radiance to the mental creation. And now comes the contrast:

> Never did sun more beautifully steep
> In his first splendour, valley, rock or hill.

The negative nature of the phrase does not matter ('never did sun . . .'); what it has done is to remind us of valleys, of mountains. And with the next line, we are back on Westminster Bridge, deepening the feeling of peace still further:

> Ne'er saw I, never felt a calm so deep.
> The river glideth at his own sweet will.
> Dear God, the very houses seem asleep . . .

The river, of course, has no will; but after inducing the deep calm, Wordsworth turns the attention back to the river; 'at his own sweet will' suggests irresponsibility, freedom from worry, a schoolboy on holiday. The exclamation 'Dear God' would have been a mistake earlier in the poem; but at this stage, he has convinced us, and it expresses the reader's emotion too; the calm and peace is allowed to burst its banks for a moment, although only

for a moment, since the next words again refer to the peace of
the houses. The last line:

And all that mighty heart is lying still

is not a good line compared to the rest of the poem; considered on
its own, it is a little too gushing, has a little too much brassy
uplift, the 'land of hope and glory' feeling. But here, it again
brings in the element of contrast; the notion of London as it will
be later in the day; the noise and bustle.

What Wordsworth has done in fourteen lines is to induce
Yeats's tea-shop mood, when 'I was blessed and could bless'. It is
fundamentally the Zen experience. We might observe that the
poem means more to us when it has been read several times. The
effect is definitely hypnotic; one knows what line is coming next,
and savours it like a mouthful of wine. Joyce uses an identical
technique in one of the best known passages of *A Portrait of the
Artist as a Young Man,* the one in which Stephen wades in the sea
on a still day. The tone is set in the sentence about seaweed:
'Emerald and black and russet and olive, it moved beneath the
current, swaying and turning. The water of the rivulet was dark
with endless drift and mirrored the highdrifting clouds. The
clouds were drifting above him silently and silently the seatangle
was drifting below him; and the grey warm air was still . . .'
Here, the effect is deliberately hypnotic, like swinging a bright
object back and forth before one's eyes. The passage—too long to
quote—goes on to evoke sights and sounds of the beach—'a
waste of wild air and brackish waters and the sea-harvest of
shells and tangle and veiled grey sunlight and gayclad lightclad
figures of children and girls and voices childish and girlish in the
air'. The mention of girls here introduces another element into the
evocation, the sexual. (After all, children can be girls as well as
boys.) Earlier in the novel we are shown the sexual agonies of
Stephen's adolescence, so the mention of girls here carries overtones. Then, in the next paragraph, Stephen looks at a young girl
—presumably twelve or thirteen—standing looking out to sea.
'She seemed like one whom magic had changed into the likeness
of a strange and beautiful sea bird.' But the sexual element is
present here, deliberately muted: 'Her long slender bare legs were
delicate as a crane's and pure save where an emerald trail of seaweed had fashioned itself as a sign upon the flesh. Her thighs,

fuller and softhued as ivory, were bared almost to the hips where
the white fringes of her drawers were like feathering of soft white
down. Her slate blue skirts were kilted boldly about the waist
and dovetailed behind her. Her bosom was as a bird's soft and
slight. . . .' Joyce had a fetichistic interest in drawers, and a girl
with her dressed tucked into the waist would normally have
aroused a perfectly simple desire in him. What happens here is
that the desire is aroused, but it is allowed to blend with the other
elements of the scene: the sense of peace and delight in nature;
like gunpowder allowed to burn in the open, it has lost its explosive power. The end of the passage utilises the device we have
already noted in Wordsworth:

'The first faint noise of gently moving water broke the silence,
low and faint and whispering, faint as the bells of sleep; hither and
thither, hither and thither: and a faint flame trembled on her cheek.

—Heavenly God! cried Stephen's soul, in an outburst of pro-
fane joy.—'

It is worth noting that the passage could not be described as
perfectly written. At times, the writing is not far from the sort of
thing turned out by sentimental female novelists: 'He was alone
and young and wilful and wildhearted . . .'. This does not matter
greatly; it may detract from the mood of the passage, but the total
hypnotic effect makes this unimportant. We do not stop in the
middle of the Westminster Bridge sonnet to reflect that 'bright
and glittering' mean the same thing, or point out that 'I listened
motionless and still' in the *Solitary Reaper* poem is another case of
tautology.

I have quoted the passage from Joyce because one can study the
workings of poetry more clearly there than in most poems.
Like music (Joyce was a musician) it aims at making the emotions
sway like a snake to the snakecharmer's flute, and it mixes its
emotions as skilfully as a good cook mixes his ingredients. A
great deal of the world's poetry aims at evoking emotions of peace,
of rest in nature: Keats's *Ode to the Nightingale* and the *Bright Star*
sonnet, and much of the poetry of Coleridge, Cowper, Swinburne,
Tennyson, Verlaine, Baudelaire. But the hypnotic technique can
evoke other moods. Whitman's catalogues of names and places
produce a feeling of zest, of love of life; Hart Crane's *The Bridge*
captures something of the vast complexity of America; some of
the poetry of Brecht and Mayakovsky aims at producing a jazzy

sensation akin to drunkenness. The point to observe, though, is that poetry tends to turn outwards, to the larger-than-human, whether it is Brooklyn Bridge or the west wind.

But one of the most important things to note is that the central device of poetry is contrast, the change of mood. It aims at creating a kind of shadow-play in the mind, in which forms change shape as easily as in a dream. If you rub your eyelids with your fingers, then stare towards a light with your eyes closed, great splotches of colour will change shape, and if you let your imagination work on them, they will turn into almost anything you want. Poetry aims at the same sort of effect; so does music. The final section of *The Waste Land*—'What the Thunder Said'—is a particularly clear example, because it uses so many images and moods in quick succession:

> After the torchlight red on sweaty faces
> After the frosty silence in the gardens . . .

And after the long, remarkable passage evoking a waterless desert, 'Dead mountain mouth of carious teeth that cannot spit', the poem becomes a phantasmagoria:

> Who are those hooded hordes swarming
> Over endless plains, stumbling in cracked earth
> Ringed by the flat horizon only . . .
> which rises to a surrealistic climax:
> A woman drew her long black hair out tight
> And fiddled whisper music on those strings
> And bats with baby faces in the violet light
> Whistled and beat their wings
> And crawled head downward down a blackened wall
> And upside down in the air were towers
> Tolling reminiscent bells that kept the hours
> And voices singing out of empty cisterns and exhausted wells.

After all this evocation of dryness and exhaustion, the breaking of the storm has the same emotional effect as a thunderstorm after weeks of drought:

> Only a cock stood on the rooftree
> Co co rico co co rico
> In a flash of lightning. Then a damp gust
> Bringing rain.

D

This passage raises another question. The cock here is the cock that crowed when Peter denied Jesus—Christian images in the earlier part of the poem make this clear. The rain here is associated with the coming of the Messiah. In his early poems, Eliot is uncompromisingly hostile to Christianity. Yet plainly, *The Waste Land* does not represent an *intellectual* conversion. Leslie Stephen said of Gibbon's conversion that 'he believed in Catholicism as he might have believed in the authenticity of a disputed document'; this could certainly not be said of Eliot. What he has discovered is that in this chef's mixture of ideas and emotions that constitutes poetry, Christianity is a valuable ingredient, with its notion of a man dying on the cross for the sins of men. This very phrase in itself is a poetic image; it points *outwards* at 'le condition humaine'. In *Sweeney Among the Nightingales,* Agamemnon is used as a symbol of human suffering and death and the trick of contrast is used with superb power. A gangster is apparently about to kill a female informer:

> The host with someone indistinct
> Converses at the door apart,
> The nightingales are singing near
> The convent of the Sacred Heart,
>
> And sang within the bloody wood
> When Agamemnon cried aloud,
> And let their liquid siftings fall
> To stain the stiff dishonoured shroud.

Agamemnon or Jesus; it does not matter. A poet is concerned with symbols that can evoke certain feelings, as the mere name of the Divine Mother could plunge Ramakrishna into samadhi. The word itself becomes the kick of the Zen master, releasing the mind from its narrowness, producing affirmation-consciousness.

Observe another point about the examples given—it is particularly obvious with regard to the *Westminster Bridge* sonnet and Joyce's passage about the water. Poetry makes us *slow down*. It is as if I was in a hurry, panting and rushing, and someone said: 'Stop it. Slow down. Relax for a moment.' The basic difference between poetry and prose is not so much a matter of the form as of the content. Prose is always in a hurry to get somewhere;

it is either telling a story or pursuing an argument. When you read a poem—even if it is in a *vers libre* that is indistinguishable from prose—you automatically slow your mind down to a walk knowing that it can only produce its effect if the mind is relaxed. This underlines another vital point about mystical experience. *It has a close-up effect, as if reality were being seen through a microscope.* (Psychedelic drugs produce this effect, while marihuana causes time to stand still.)

This is related to the observations I have already made about 'holiday consciousness'. Man is a purposive animal; he is always hurrying forward. The more you are in a hurry, the more you tend to ignore your surroundings, just as if you read a book in a hurry, you tend to skip every other word. But even 'normal' perception works like this. Most people will read

PARIS

IN THE

THE

SPRING

as 'Paris in the spring', because the eyes skip over the words. This faculty of grasping reality at a speed has cost the human race a great deal of effort to acquire; it is not something we can afford to lose. But it is equally important to train the senses to slow down when there is no need for hurry, to arrest the impatient forward flow. Why does a beautiful view often fail to move us, while a painting of the same view immediately touches the aesthetic sense? Because we automatically slow down the senses to look at a painting. If we could learn the same trick when looking at scenery—or indeed at anything—it would be a major step in the direction of controlling the 'mystical faculty'.

This is an important recognition in trying to define the 'mental act' that produces mystical experience. Look at the second hand of your watch. You can see it moving without any difficulty. But now look at the minute hand. You know it is moving, yet it doesn't appear to be. Try staring at the minute hand of the largest clock you have in the house. With a little effort, it becomes possible to actually *see* its movement. But you have to concentrate hard. If you are distracted, or thinking of something else, you won't notice the movement.

This teaches something important about consciousness. It

skips. It seldom focusses on anything for more than a second or two together.

This is obviously a serious defect. If you had a record player that changed speeds every few seconds, and even stopped periodically, you would agree that it would give you a very distorted impression of a Beethoven symphony. But this is exactly what your senses do with regard to the world.

For a Wordsworth, contemplating Thirlmere from the slopes of Helvellyn, or taking a moonlight row on Windermere, the senses suddenly begin to work properly. Instead of skipping and jumping, switching from one thing to another, then turning-off altogether in a flash of introspection, they faithfully and continuously record every sound, every sight, every breath of wind. Consciousness is slowed down and focussed.

But if you can train your senses to perceive the movement of the minute hand of a clock, what is to stop you from training them to 'slow down' when you look at a tree or a puddle?

3

The Relationality of Consciousness

The basic psychological problem of human beings is the tendency of consciousness to 'congeal'. When Wordsworth looked at the Thames from Westminster Bridge or the daffodils besides Grasmere, his consciousness was somehow free and fluid, like running water in the sunlight. When we are in the same situation for any length of time, consciousness thickens, becomes a jelly, then eventually turns into a kind of sticky mud.

But in this state of congealed consciousness, a single word or a smell or a fragment of a tune can suddenly produce a state of delight—like Proust's madeleine dipped in tea. Why? And if I am sitting in a room, rather dull and bored, and rain starts to patter on the window, does it often produce a flash of pleasure? In this latter case, the reason is fairly easy to grasp. My consciousness has shrunk within the bounds of the room; I know that a whole world exists 'out there', but it is not real to me; just an idea. As the rain patters on the windows, it becomes a reality. I am in here, warm and dry, and out there, rain is falling on roofs, on the leaves of trees, on the grass in fields. In a sense, the rain is a negative stimulus, falling on the St Neot margin.

When I was sitting in the room, I was aware of nothing but the room; there was a kind of 'singleness' about my consciousness. When the rain began to fall on the window, it was as if I was in two places at once: in the room, and out there in the rain. My consciousness had achieved a *double* nature. We might say that when I sat in the room, I was in a state of mono-consciousness, and that when the rain began to fall, it suddenly became a state of *duo-consciousness*.

The concept of duo-consciousness explains a great deal about poetry. Why do children enjoy sitting around the fire on

Christmas night, listening to ghost stories? They wouldn't enjoy the stories if they were sitting in a lonely barn, listening to the sound of the wind. It is because they are warm and secure. But warmth and security are easily taken for granted. They are in mono-consciousness. The ghost story, and the thought of the wind and snow outside, produce duo-consciousness.

Again, why is the beginning of a holiday always so delightful? Because I am, so to speak, in two places at once. I can very clearly remember my home, which I have left, and my everyday life, and I am now amid new scenery. There is a startled recognition that the world is huge and very beautiful, and that this fact had become *totally concealed* from my consciousness by habit. Later on in the holiday, I shall be enjoying myself, but I shall have forgotten my home; so no matter how pleasant the seaside, I am back in mono-consciousness.

The interesting thing is that duo-consciousness often just *happens*, either for no definable reason (as in Yeats's London tea-shop) or for some quite unpredictable reason (like Proust recalling his childhood because of the taste of the madeleine). Whenever duo-consciousness happens, one experiences intense happiness affirmation. If it happened when you were looking at a grain of sand, you would see a world in it. If it happened when you were looking at a rotting corpse, you would feel overwhelmingly happy, and the corpse would seem somehow good and positive. This explains that strange bit of dialogue between Kirolov and Stavrogin:

'Ever seen a leaf—a leaf from a tree?'

'Yes'

'I saw one recently—a yellow one, a little green, wilted at the edges. Blown by the wind. When I was a little boy, I used to shut my eyes in winter and imagine a green leaf, with veins on it, and the sun shining. . . .'

'What's this—an allegory?'

'No; why? Not an allegory—a leaf, just a leaf. A leaf is good. Everything's good.'

'Everything?'

'Everything. Man's unhappy because he doesn't know he's happy . . . he who finds out will be happy at once, instantly. . . .'

'And what about the man who dies of hunger, and the man who insults and rapes a little girl. Is that good too?'

'Yes, it is. And the man who blows his brains out for the child, that's good too. Everything's good.'

'When did you find out you were so happy?'

'I was walking about the room. I stopped the clock . . . It was twenty minutes to three.'

Dostoevsky knew that duo-consciousness is only experienced in flashes, but for the sake of the novel, he has made it a more-or-less constant state for Kirilov.

Let me add, by way of a parenthesis, that I can see no *a priori* reason why consciousness should not expand beyond the duo-stage. Multiple-consciousness should be possible. But anyone who has experienced duo-consciousness with any frequency will recall the strain it entails, the desire to return—with re-charged batteries—to intellectual mono-consciousness. Multiple-consciousness would probably 'blow our fuses', as the divine vision blew Ramakrishna's. (It is a disturbing thought that Rama-krishna died of a cancer at the age of fifty.) All our human work is done in a state of mono-consciousness; and this is as it should be. It is true that I can chop wood, dig the garden, and change the spark plugs in my car in a state of duo-consciousness. But it would be a waste. Duo-consciousness is like a visit to a mountain top; it shows me my direction. But in order to move forward, I have to descend into the valley. The view from the mountain top serves a very important purpose—particularly if I do not happen to possess a compass. But if I stayed up there all the time, nothing would get done.

This notion of duo-consciousness can be used as a springboard for expounding one of the most difficult but important and rewarding concepts of the 'phenomenological mysticism' we are surveying, that of the *relationality of consciousness*. In everyday affairs, the word 'real' is almost synonymous with 'close'. 'Out of sight, out of mind', we say. When Shaw's Cleopatra wants to convince Caesar that she is real, she jabs him with a pin. As I sit in this room, the objects surrounding me are obviously real; so are my children, because I can hear them quarrelling upstairs. If I look out of the window, I can see the garden; that is also quite real to me, but not as real as it will be in summer, when I alternate writing with mowing the lawn. Across the sea which is also visible from my window, there are other lands, for example, New

York is about three thousand miles away. I was in New York a few months ago, and I talked to my agent there on the telephone only yesterday. And yet I cannot claim that New York is a reality to me. But the other day on the beach, I caught an ozoney sort of smell that reminded me of the New York subway, and for a few seconds, I might actually have been in Grand Central Station.

It seems clear that we have two sorts of memory. It I want to recall a telephone number, or the name of a character in a book, it may take me a moment or so, but the answer will finally come popping up from the robot. The robot's business is to store 'facts' for me, just as a librarian's business is to store and arrange books. I don't want too many facts in my mind at any time. If I am overtired, or slightly feverish, the facts of the past few hours keep swimming around in my mind and prevent me from sleeping or from thinking clearly. Facts are like books; it is best to keep them on a shelf until you need them; otherwise, the place gets untidy.

My other memory has a function that is almost equally important. It can recall *the reality* of things. Everyone sees a great many places and people in a lifetime, and if they all stayed in the memory, equally real, the result would be even greater chaos than when 'facts' keep swimming around in my mind. This is obviously true where people are concerned. While I am actually talking to someone, they have a fairly full claim on my attention, but unless their interests are related to mine, I do not allow this claim to persist for long after they have gone. If I did, my life would soon become so full of people and their affairs that I would have no time for my own. William James described this tendency to ignore the reality of other people's lives in his classic essay *On a Certain Blindness in Human Beings*. But the blindness is more of an advantage than otherwise. It may mean, admittedly, that I am capable of unconscious cruelty or neglect; but without it, none of the world's work would get done, and we would still be living in caves—for a Plato or a Newton would have been impossible. In our society, a person who was too aware of the reality of other people would soon be a mental wreck. If I have a violent disagreement with someone who has parked his car across my garage doors, I cannot get any real thinking done until I have pushed it 'to the back of my mind'. It is important that I stop going over the argument in my mind and thinking of all the things

I ought to have said. And the more grown-up and self-controlled I am, the easier it is for me to 'un-realise' the man with whom I have quarrelled. In fact, even without an effort on my part, my robot will do the 'un-realising' for me.

But the reverse process is more difficult. I cannot 'real-ise' things as easily as I can un-realise them. A madeleine dipped in tea may do the trick; or it may not. And it seems that no matter how hard I try to conjure up Grand Central Station, all I get is a kind of dim carbon copy, a piece of paste jewellery that is very obviously *not* the real thing.

In *Rasselas,* Dr Johnson makes his prince complain about the perfectly happy valley in which they all live. 'I can discover within me no power of perception which is not glutted with its proper pleasure, yet I do not feel myself delighted. Man has surely some latent sense for which this place affords no gratification, or he has some desires distinct from sense which must be satisfied before he can be happy.' We have all experienced this feeling: a situation in which we ought to be ecstatically happy, and yet feel nothing. I labelled Johnson's 'latent sense' or 'faculty apart from sense' 'faculty X'. But faculty X is, of course, this power of inducing duo-consciousness. What is preventing Prince Rasselas from enjoying his happy valley is mono-consciousness.

Now it can be seen that the human mind possesses a latent power of 'real-ising' other places so they become as real as the place we are actually in at the moment. This means that the common-sense view—that only what is here, now, can be real—is false.

Let me try to make this very clear. If you think of consciousness as a sort of lake, then the here-now is like a stone tossed into it, causing ripples to spread outward. In the ordinary common-sense view of consciousness, there can only be one stone and one set of ripples. But when Proust tasted the madeleine, there were suddenly two stones, two sets of ripples. It is almost as if your mind possessed the weird power of being in two places at once. It seems to violate all the rules of common-sense—we know the body can only be in one place at once—but we have evidence that it *can* occur. The historian Arnold Toynbee, for example, has described moments in which certain events in history suddenly became as *real* for him as if he was actually there, watching them. Chesterton said: 'We say thank you when someone passes us the salt, but we don't mean it. We say the earth is round, but we don't mean it.' But an astronaut out in space can say the earth is round and *mean* it. And in very rare moments, a historian can contemplate some distant event and realise it really happened—i.e. believe in it, mean it.

If you think of consciousness as a lake, it becomes plain that if the lake freezes—or becomes thick and muddy—a stone thrown into it will have far less effect than when the water is clear. When you are tired, events hardly cause a ripple in your consciousness. You hear a piece of music that normally moves you, but nothing happens. The stone has plopped into an almost solid jelly, and it merely vibrates slightly. On the other hand, if I am wide awake and full of vitality, the same piece of music may cause something like a tidal wave in my lake, an overwhelming emotional experience. *My sense of reality extends as far as the ripples.* In fact, ripples are so important that we might almost say they *are* consciousness. When I say that a poem or a Zen exercise causes my consciousness to expand, I mean that it causes ripples.

And this brings me to what I am inclined to believe is my most important insight: the relationality of consciousness.

A few years ago, I had spent two weeks driving around in the north of Scotland, accumulating background material for a novel. I am not fond of holidays that go on too long; I miss being surrounded by books and records. So when we stopped overnight at Biggar, on our way back home, I was feeling a certain delight at the prospect of getting back into England. My assumption was that we had a hundred miles or so to reach the border.

It had been raining in the night, but when we set out in the morning, the sun was out, and everything looked green and wet. I began to experience the cheerfulness that often comes on journeys, the sense of expansion and optimism. We passed a signpost, and I saw that it was only about fifty miles to the border. My wife checked the map and we realised it was so; we had overestimated the distance, and could, in fact, easily reach Blackpool, where we could spend the night with friends.

Nothing is pleasanter than this realisation that something is going to cost less effort than you expected. The sense of expansion increased; I found myself in one of those moods of the 'glory and the freshness of a dream', of feeling far more *awake* than usual. All negative elements—doubts, fears, the sense of contingency— vanished from consciousness. It was the kind of mood I had often experienced as a child, particularly at Christmas, as if the mind itself is a Christmas tree covered with coloured lights.

It was so intense and constant that I had a chance to observe it closely. Driving down through the Lake District—which I know well—I had a sense of being able to somehow feel the presence of lakes and hills behind the hills at either side of the road. It was as if I was a spider, and my web stretched in all directions.

Thinking about it later, I began to understand the consequences of this sense of 'web-like consciousness'. Husserl pointed out that consciousness is intentional, not a passive mirror of things. I have to fire my attention at objects in order to be conscious of them. But even more important: consciousness is by nature *relational*; it has a web-like structure. Things have meaning, significance, in so far as they are related to other things. If I am reading, and my attention wanders, I stop 'taking it in'. This is not simply because I have ceased to fire my attention at the page, but because I have ceased to actively grasp the meaning of earlier pages, and to keep adding the meaning of each new sentence to what I have already grasped. In the case of a difficult book, or a problem in mathematics, this tendency to 'lose the thread' is very obvious. If you do not make the effort to 'connect up' the latest stage of the argument with all that has gone before, the latest stage will become meaningless. If I am sitting in a train, looking at the world that goes past, I am not aware of having to 'connect up' the things I now see with my past experience. But this is because I do it unconsciously. The fact remains that 'seeing' things, understanding them, responding to them, is a matter of making connections with dormant areas of my mind.

Husserl was aware of the role of 'relationality' in ordinary perception. He knew that when I look at a cube, I see it *as* a cube, even though I see only two or three sides of it. I have had previous experiences of cubes, chairs, books, birds, telephones, and a mere glimpse of any of these objects is enough to make me supply the rest of its reality from my memory, to give it significance. If I glimpse something too quickly to supply the rest of its 'reality' from memory, I fail to endow it with significance; I say 'I glimpsed something but I'm not sure what it was'.

Apply this insight to the way we grasp 'meanings' in our everyday life, and the whole problem of mysticism suddenly becomes clear. In order to understand anything, we have to make the

mental act of 'connecting up' with other things. But the more
things I can 'connect it up' with, the more meaningful it becomes.
Each object I look at has invisible threads running from it to
other things. I glance at that square object opposite. The man
who is sitting beside me says 'Good god, what's that?' I reply:
'Just a book.' 'Just a book! Good heavens, man, unless I'm
mistaken, that is the almost legendary edition of Byron's *Corsair*
pirated in Milan in 1820. . . .' My friend is a lifelong student of
Byron. What for me is 'just a book'—which I 'identify' simply by
relating it to other books on the shelf—is for him a piece of
history that makes him tremble with excitement. For him, the book
is the centre of a vast 'web' of significances; it has exploded like
a flare, revealing the web stretching into the distance in all
directions. . . .

The mind works off energy, like an electric bulb. If I am dull,
my energies are low; I am aware of only a small area of the web.
And while the things I look at *are* significant, they are not *very*
significant. Now some challenge, some crisis, some cause for
happiness, causes a gush of power from the mains. A larger area of
the 'web' is illuminated, and whatever I am looking at becomes
more significant.

Philosophy has been saddled with a narrow and passive idea of
the word 'meaning'. The meaning of a sentence or a mathematical
formula is quite precisely definable, because both are abstractions
to which we have assigned the meaning in the first place. But the
'meaning' of all other things, a book, a phrase of music, a patch of
green grass, can never be pinned down like this. Every object in
the universe is like a fragment of bone upon which an archaeolo-
gist could construct a whole prehistoric mammal, perhaps a
whole epoch.

What is at issue here is the 'reality' of things. As I type this
page, this room is real for me. I can see the garden through the
window, but this is not very real; I hardly pay it any attention.
But then, it is now December, and this room is rather stuffy. If it
happened to be April, and I was working with the doors and
windows open, I could smell the garden and hear the birds; it
would be more real to me than now. Why? Because the spring
morning has made me more wide-awake, and the relational web of
consciousness is bigger.

Hesse's Steppenwolf describes how the taste of a glass of wine suddenly makes him aware of 'Mozart and the stars'. He means that the web has suddenly become bigger, and Mozart and the stars have become realities.

The consequences of all this should be clear. So-called mystical consciousness, the moments when one has that sense of immense significances, when consciousness seems full of vibrations of meaning, is not different *in kind* from everyday consciousness; only, so to speak, in *pressure*. The web is already there, stretching in all directions, but for the most part, it is in darkness; only a tiny area around 'me' is illumined. My sense of 'significances' is entirely dependent upon the size of the illuminated area.

And here we confront the most significant twist to the argument, the key to the whole business. Consider my experience driving back from Biggar. The web had expanded; my sense of realities had deepened. What started it? The delight of a pleasant morning and the smell of rain, the pleasure of anticipating a return to familiar things, and then, as a final cause for optimism, the realisation that I was closer to home than I expected. These factors caused an expansion of the 'web', a sense of wider significances. *And from this point on, a chain reaction built up.* The wider sense of meaning created more energy, more optimism; the additional energy, flowing along the strands of the web, created a wider sense of meaning. The wider sense of meaning created more energy. . . . And so on.

More important, the converse is also true. Oblomov sits yawning on his stove. The illuminated area of his 'web' is small; most of his values are dormant. He picks up a book, but it is 'merely a book'; he reads a page but cannot get into it. But supposing the book touches some chord in his 'dormant' regions. His interest is whetted; he reads on; soon he is 'into the story', and the chain reaction has started—wider significances producing interest and concentration. The will-machine begins to work. On the other hand, if he is in a mood of resentful boredom, he will not feel it is worthwhile even to open the book. His boredom increases; that is to say, the pressure of his consciousness drops; his web narrows. With life so meaningless, it is a burden to stay awake, for everything he looks at is 'merely itself'. He thinks he has seen the truth of life. Nothing is 'interesting', everything is boring. Men only endow things with 'interest' when they have spare energy to burn. . . .

We know this to be untrue. Meaning is not 'added' by the mind. It is 'out there', in things themselves, and the larger the illuminated area of the 'web', the more it is seen as an inescapable external fact, a reality that calls the tune, no matter how much we would like to change it by wishful thinking.

The next step in the argument is the most exciting so far. When we recognise that consciousness is relational as well as intentional, we push Husserl's recognition a stage further. I perceive a cube by mentally 'adding' its remaining sides. But what about when I hear a Mozart symphony or look at a piece of magnificent scenery? If I am very dull, very tired, it is meaningless for me. In order to grasp its meaning, my consciousness needs to expand beyond its normal narrow limits of relationality. I must *supply* the additional aspects of the symphony or the scenery. And what does this mean? Well, suppose I am in a state of 'expanded web-like consciousness' when I hear the symphony. I am supplementing it with all the things I know about Mozart—and about the 18th century, and about music in general—just as I supplement the cube. Again, if I am in love, and I have just kissed the girl for the first time, the surge of energy from my mains expands the web of consciousness, and I supplement her with all kinds of intuitive vibrations of meaning; for a moment I see her as Paris saw Helen, as Dante saw Beatrice, as Faust saw Marguerite; I am aware of her simultaneously as the source of all idealism—the eternal feminine—and as a biological will to motherhood and security of the family. I myself am momentarily transformed from an ordinary, plodding sort of person to an embodiment of the eternal masculine: Faust, Casanova, Caesar, Merlin. All this is not illusion or daydreaming; on the contrary, it has a quality of reality that places it above my everyday reality.

If all this is true, then the course of human evolution is obvious enough. The chain-reaction can be started either by a flood of insight, or by a sudden 'bonus' of energy. But whenever I succeed in getting it started, I realise that the next step is connected with the 'mains' themselves, the source of energy. If I could somehow train or condition my 'generator' to produce the sudden surge of energy, I would have taken the first great step. The power of concentration of the average person is small. Why? Because he has never come to understand the nature of his consciousness and its relation to the world. His greatest act of concentration is watching a television quiz or reading a detective story. Since he lives in the devalued world of cheap mass-culture, he sees no reason to develop further powers of concentration, for there is nothing worth concentrating on; and if he accidentally sees a play by Sartre or Beckett on television he learns that man is a useless passion and that human life is a long-drawn-out defeat, which confirms the result of his own occasional moments of reflection on his destiny. When the world strikes him as boring and devalued, he assumes that this is because it *is* boring and devalued, and accepts this as a further reason for his passivity.

Human beings tend to wait until fate gives them a reason for generating excitement, optimism, intensity of will; and since most of life is a plodding business, moments of unambiguously positive consciousness are rare. Our values are dormant most of the time. There are a thousand things in my life that I would regret if I lost them; but when I am feeling bored and tired, they are forgotten; I am not aware of them as something to be grateful for. My values are dormant, 'eclipsed', because they lie in areas of the 'web' that are still in darkness. This vicious circle is of the most stupid kind, for it all depends on a simple fallacy: my belief when I am feeling dull that there is nothing *worth* making an effort for. As soon as I proceed to make a determined effort, reaching beyond my boredom to a sense of objective values, I become aware of the fallacy; for the effort of will causes a surge in the dynamo, that in turn 'lights up' more strands of the web. This recognition of the relational nature of consciousness brings mysticism within the range of ordinary psychology. More important, it solves the basic dilemma of all intelligent and sensitive human beings: the contradiction between the times when the world seems meaningful and the time when it seems meaningless; between the times when an object or a person or an experience seem valuable and important, and the times when they leave us cold. The sense of meaning is true because it involves wider relationality; just as statistics based upon a million people will be more accurate than statistics based upon a hundred people.

I would agree that one of the obstacles to achieving an *intuitive* grasp of the relationality of consciousness is our feeling that there is a qualitative difference between states of 'intensity consciousness' and states of everyday narrowness, as basic as the difference between being in the open air and being in a stuffy room. This is obviously true. In states of everyday consciousness we are conditioned to passivity, to a hypnotic state of mental inactivity; this passivity vanishes in states of wider relational consciousness; we snap out of the hypnotic trance.

Some years ago, before I had developed this recognition of the relationality of consciousness, I spoke of these two states as 'vertical' and 'horizontal consciousness'. Horizontal consciousness is flat and perceptual; it is the kind of consciousness I experience if I am idly watching a fly on the window. It is characterised by *lack of feeling*. Horizontal consciousness is devoid of values, if by values I mean something to which I respond by feeling. Vertical consciousness involves a strong sense of values.

It is easy to become trapped in horizontal consciousness—like the hero of Camus's *L'Etranger*, to be so bored that you cease to make any effort. If I do a job that bores me, I cease to make efforts of will, and my consciousness tends to become 'horizontal' for longer periods. When I am enjoying a holiday or some interesting effort, my consciousness becomes 'vertical' for long periods; it is always being charged with subtleties of feeling and response.

When I have experienced some intense feeling of satisfaction, the result is to *charge my will*. Imagine a teenager born in a slum who saves enough money to spend a day at the seaside. He finds it all so magical that he begins to plot and plan how to save enough money for a week at the seaside. Vertical consciousness is directly connected to the will; it produces a sense of worthwhileness that leads to effort. The effort is directed towards inducing more vertical consciousness. The result is a kind of cycle. Someone who has been impressed by a fragment of Wagner may take the trouble to get to know all the operas, and the operas in turn induce still more 'vertical consciousness'.

Since horizontal consciousness is purely perceptive, a grasping of symbols rather than a response to values, it has no direct connection with the will. This means that no 'cycle' can be engendered. Worse still, it means that my will-muscle falls into a state of disuse that reduces my enjoyment in being alive. Unless some external stimulus—like Faust's Easter bells—propels me back into vertical consciousness, where efforts of will are again seen to be worthwhile, I shall tend to sink deeper and deeper into a state of passivity, until even the intentionality of perception is affected, and I begin to experience a sense of the absurdity of existence—Sartre's 'nausea'.

The problem for man, at this point in evolution, is to discover the intention that converts horizontal to vertical consciousness. Vertical consciousness tends towards an expanding relationality, with values feeding the will, and the will feeding the ability to perceive values. Neurasthenic breakdown, when every molehill becomes a mountain, is connected with horizontal consciousness and the resulting sickness of the will.

How, then, can the 'relationality of consciousness' be increased? How can horizontal consciousness be converted to vertical consciousness?

It is true that there are exercises that can strengthen the 'muscle' that enables us to push back the bounds of acceptation. But these are relatively unimportant. The real problem is that we are trapped in misconceptions that always deceive us, as the matador's cape deceives the bull; that continue to deceive us a million times over the course of a lifetime. Wittgenstein once said that traditional philosophy causes a form of mental cramp, and that the aim of his philosophy was to remove this mental cramp, or to 'show the fly the way out of the bottle'. Our misconceptions involve the passive fallacy and the notion that consciousness is a plane mirror that cannot lie about the world it reflects. To really grasp the relational nature of consciousness is to cease to be suffocated and bullied by 'horizontal consciousness' and to awaken the will out of its state of hypnosis. This hypnosis is the result of our complexity; we have *forgotten* too much. Heidegger said penetratingly that the crisis of modern civilisation is due to 'forgetfulness of existence'. What he meant by this should be clear from the above discussion. When consciousness has congealed, so that there are almost no ripples going outward, *the present becomes unreal*. Why? Because, as I have explained, you cannot perceive one thing, in isolation. A thing becomes 'realler' as you see it in a wider and wider 'web' of relations to other things. When my mind is dull, I say that New York exists, but I don't 'mean' it; I have 'forgotten' the *real* existence of New York. Not only is it a kind of abstraction for me, a piece of paste jewellery, but I suffer from the delusion that this is as it should be, that is quite inevitable, since I am not actually in New York at the present moment. So here I am, completely stuck in my dull little present, half-suffocated, and the worst of it is that I don't put up a struggle because I don't see any way out. I don't believe there is a way out. This state is the opposite of mental health, and can, in fact, lead to total mental breakdown.

Clearly, to understand that there is a way out is of enormous importance. The next step follows automatically: the attempt to break through to one's deeper energy levels. If the 19th century had understood about the robot and duo-consciousness, many artistic tragedies could have been avoided. The list of men of genius who committed suicide, or died insane, or died of consumption induced by mental strain and a sense of defeat, is depressing. The interesting thing is that the more intelligent romantics understood something about the problem. In *Dejection, An Ode,* Coleridge writes about the state of 'frozen' consciousness. He describes how he looks at the stars and says: 'I see, not feel, how beautiful they are.' But he adds penetratingly:

> I may not hope from outward forms to win
> The passion and the life whose fountains are within,

He recognises, in a dim, instinctive way, that the 'passions and the life' have somehow got frozen in the realm of the robot.

The most penetrating statement of the whole problem is one of the earliest manifestations of the romantic genius, *Faust.* The poem opens with Faust in his chamber, in a state of profound depression; too much study, too much effort, has frozen his energies. 'The old mill of the mind, consuming its rag and bone' goes on grinding whether he likes it or not, and he has a sense of futility. Yet he still has insight enough to state:

> The spirit world shuts not its gates,
> Your heart is dead, your sense is shut

This is the clear recognition that when man thinks he has exhausted the world, he has really only exhausted his own mind. 'Other realities' lie out there; it is simply the 'doors of perception' that are dirty. Faust knows this, but he has no idea of how to reach the 'other realities'. He decides to kill himself, and picks up a phial of poison. What then happens is what happened when Ramakrishna seized the sword: the sudden revelation. Goethe makes the Easter bells ring, suddenly reminding him clearly of his childhood; the floodgates open; he bursts into tears, and says:

'The earth takes back her child.' He now *sees* what he only knew theoretically before: that it was his own mind that was 'weary, stale, flat and unprofitable', not the earth. But more important: that his exhaustion and despair were *superficial*; the immense springs of power are still there, in the realm of the robot, ready to be released by the necessary act of will. Faust luckily discovers this before he kills himself; Stavrogin didn't. Stavrogin took his exhaustion and lack of interest in life very seriously, believing that it was a recognition of the meaninglessness of human existence. He not only ended by taking his own life, but he did a great deal of damage along the way; he has actually raped and insulted a little girl. In fact, his various activities—including various masochistic as well as sadistic actions—are a wildly disproportionate response to his problem of being emotionally constipated like a man frenziedly battering at a door which is not actually locked, or clinging all night to the edge of a ravine that turns out to be only a few feet deep. In that sense, his suicide is almost comic.

In *Modes of Thought*, Whitehead defines life as 'a certain absoluteness of self-enjoyment'. This is certainly true of animal life, for animals can accept simple pleasures simply. Who cannot recall that feeling during childhood when you got into a bed that had been warmed by a hot-water bottle, and curled up in a tight bundle with a sigh of pleasure? Or lying in a warm bed on a winter morning, listening to the noises that indicate that your parents are already up, and knowing you can spend another ten minutes in the warmth? Animals have this immediacy of sensation beause their robot is so much less complex than ours. It may control a few very simple skills—building nests, catching game—and, of course, the sexual impulse; apart from these, the animal may add a few skills of its own—one of our dogs learned to open doors by getting its paw on the handle. If you think about a human child in any civilised country—reading and writing by the age of seven, science and foreign languages at eleven, and perhaps B.Sc. physics and mathematics by the age of seventeen—it will be apparent that the capacity of our robot must exceed a dog's by as much as a large dustbin exceeds an egg cup. And we all know what happens when things become increasingly complex. If I have a library of a dozen books, I can keep them in any order, and find the one I want immediately. If I have a thousand books, I need to classify them by subject and author, and keep them in some sort of order; this costs me a certain amount of energy and time, but it saves me a great deal more. Human beings who live in a complex modern civilisation need a huge amount of energy just to get through everyday existence. And in a large library, you cannot just reach out and lay your hand on any book you want; you may even have to climb a ladder to some shelf next to the ceiling. And the library of the British Museum is so enormous that they cannot even allow visitors access to the bookshelves. If you want a book, you have to write out a ticket for it, and the book will be brought to your desk during the next hour. Any other method would be impracticable for a library of such size; for the larger the library, the more important it is that no book should get into the wrong place. Human beings are in this position. By the age of twenty-five, most of us have learned so much that we have lost touch with most of our knowledge. A child imagines that a very clever man could sit in a room alone and simply recall one of the thousands of books he has read; in fact, the very clever man is much more likely to sit there completely bored, or glancing at the headlines of a week-old newspaper. His knowledge is too tightly packed inside him to be accessible for browsing.

It is worth bearing in mind that animals possess certain powers that human beings have lost. The homing instinct, for example, shows that animals operate on some kind of 'psychic radar' which only works occasionally for human beings. The tiger hunter Jim Corbett developed some of this 'radar' in the jungles of India, and could tell when a tiger was lying in wait for him. But then, he was living close to nature. A few human beings possess powers of second sight, prevision, thaumaturgy, etc. But they are usually very simple people. If human beings needed to recover these primitive powers for their survival, they would do so. We do not need them.

We might think of an animal as a small cottage, with one room up and one down—simple and comfortable. And a human being, by comparison, is like a skyscraper that houses a giant corporation, with everything from garages and workshops to a digital computer containing details of personnel. This seems a depressing picture, for we all have a hankering after simplicity—particularly if we happen to be poets. But it is not so depressing as it sounds, because there is something we have failed to take into account.

The whole operation is computerised, which means that there are all kinds of 'short cuts' for saving trouble. You don't have to walk from the basement to the sixtieth floor; a fast lift takes you there in seconds. In the library, you don't have to spend an hour searching for the book you want; you press a button and it falls on to your desk.

For this labour-saving mechanisation, we use the wholly inadequate word 'instinct'. A bird does not have to learn to build its nest; it leaves it to the robot, which has picked up the information via the genes. Baby eels are born in the Sargasso sea, and then find their way back across the Atlantic without the help of the parents; their ancestors have done the trip so many times that it has been programmed into the genes. (This, of course, makes nonsense of the Darwinian assertion that there is no inheritance of acquired characteristics.)

And it is this programming that is the chief reason for human beings to be optimistic about their future. Because any habit can become an instinct if we want it badly enough. Consider the sexual impulse. It is a mystery to my conscious intellect. I can understand why I need water when I get thirsty, for I can explain it precisely in chemical terms; the same with my need for food. A pregnant woman can understand why she gets a sudden craving for grapes or oranges or ice-cream, or why she cannot bear cigarettes. But although I have been living with my sexual impulse for more than a quarter of a century now, it is almost as puzzling to me as when I was thirteen. What is the 'chemical' nature of this basic hunger of the male for the female? How does it work? I am aware now of something I did not even suspect in my teens: that there is a definite need for children, even in the male impulse. Shaw asks: 'Is there a father's heart as well as a mother's?', and the answer is definitely yes. My response to my children makes me aware that they are somehow involved in the genetic programming of my sexual impulse; I think I have also solved certain other aspects of the 'sex code'. But as a whole, it eludes me. All I know is that certain of my tastes are conscious and acquired —for music, for wine, for certain kinds of exotic food. Enjoying these things, I bring to bear levels of my conscious personality, my experience, my imagination; and a person who positively dislikes music or wine may declare that my enjoyment is *all* imagination. But where sex is concerned, there can be no

doubt that it operates on a level well below imagination.
What does this mean? The point about music and poetry is
that it causes a 'movement' in my depths. When I am enjoying
music, there is a sense of relief, a flow of energy, which is analogous to the relief I may feel in a bowel-movement. You may
experience the same kind of sensation when you lie on a beach in
the sunlight, and your body seems to soak up the sunlight as if it
is thirsty. But when the sexual impulse stirs volcanically, the
seismic disturbance obviously comes from a much greater depth.
It by-passes my personality and conscious will, and turns me into
a much simpler creature.

In fact, the sexual impulse is another 'short cut', like the fast
lift or the digital computer. It is of such importance to my vital
economy that it does not come within the jurisdiction of my
conscious will.

In psychology, it is still fashionable to talk about 'instincts' as if
they were of a completely different nature from acquired tastes.
The above considerations should have indicated that this is not so.
An instinct is a *mechanical* device designed to remove some of the
burden from consciousness. It is nothing, more or less, than an
alarm clock. Some people do not need alarm clocks because they
can wake up at any hour they please simply by telling themselves
before they fall asleep 'I must be awake by six'. But if I try to do
that, I find I simply keep on waking up every half hour to glance at
the clock. And so I set the alarm, which saves me the trouble of
worrying consciously about waking up. A few miles from our
home, there is a hill with a steep drop on one side; I suppose I
have driven up and down it some hundreds of times. One day,
I drove up it with the sun blazing in my eyes, and dazzling off a
wet road; near the top of the hill, I came to a bend, and twisted
the wheel. To my amazement, my hands simply declined to twist
the wheel. My robot had driven the hill so often that it knew
the bend came further on, and that if I started to turn at that point,
I would drive off the road. In this case, it can be clearly seen that
'instinct' is an automatic device intended to supplement consciousness.

The same is true of the sexual mechanism, and in this case, it is
exceptionally easy to observe. Sex is, to some extent, a conscious
activity; I can turn my thoughts towards it, choose to be stimulated or not. But once I have 'started the ball rolling', so to speak,

I can be amazed at the strength of the forces I have set in motion. I am labouring this point because it is the answer to the problem of Faust and Stavrogin. Faust sits in his study and complains: 'I am exhausted. Life is meaningless. The life forces in me have dried up. . . .' He is quite sincere about it; he is not indulging in self-pity. BUT, he is under a misapprehension when he uses the word 'I'. The 'I' of which he is conscious through introspection is a small corner of his total being. His sexual part, for example, contains immense forces that will be released by Gretchen.

Now the point about the instincts—of which the sexual impulse can be taken as typical—is that they can supplement the energies available to consciousness with energy drawn from a deeper source. Plainly, this is what happened to Ramakrishna when he had his vision of the Divine Mother. The 'waves' that overwhelmed him were *inside* himself, a flood from the source of power, meaning and purpose, that is concealed in the depths of the robot's domain.

Consider Boehme's description of his first mystical vision. He was staring at a pewter dish with the sunlight shining on it. Through some mental process analogous to Ramakrishna's ecstasy, he was swept into a state of pure affirmation-consciousness. He went walking in the fields, afterwards, and had the illusion that he could see to the centre of the trees and blades of grass, and see their 'essence' (or 'signature', as he called it). In a state of intense duo-consciousness, things were no longer seen in isolation; the whole web of consciousness was vibrating as if a thousand flies were all stuck on it at once, so that each individual object looked at would be seen as a part of a larger plan, so to speak. This, I have no doubt, is what Boehme tried to express by saying that he could see the 'signature' of all things—that is to say, their essence, their 'purpose'.

Normally, I look at a tree, and it is simply there; I say 'It is just a tree'. On the other hand, if a pretty girl begins to take off her clothes in my presence, I do not say: 'That is just a girl'. Those great reserve energy tanks in my subconscious mind promptly flood my consciousness with intense interest. I may hardly have paid any attention to her before. I glanced at her and thought: 'That is just a girl'. But the act of removing her clothes triggers the 'alarm' mechanism; she is flooded with the significance of the eternal feminine.

This happened to Boehme when he looked at a tree. The mechanism was *exactly* the same. Instead of it being 'just a tree' it was suddenly the 'eternal tree', the essence of tree. So what is there to prevent me from experiencing the same intense, excited interest in a tree as in a girl? A naïve biologist would reply: Because the tree doesn't excite your sexual instinct as a girl does. But we have already dismissed this crude notion that instinct is something quite different from a habit or an acquired taste. It is simply deeper ingrained. There is, in fact, no *a priori* reason why human beings should not develop the same attitude towards nature as towards sex. We have developed all our instincts by wanting to. There is no reason why we should not develop a 'mystical' instinct that would counterbalance the excessive self-consciousness of our civilisation. All that is necessary is to understand the mechanisms that control the robot.

It is important to grasp that Faust and Stavrogin—and their modern derivatives in the work of Beckett, Ionesco, William Burroughs, etc.—are trapped in a vicious circle which is basically absurd—like sitting on the lid of a box and protesting that you can't get it open. An instinct begins as a conscious impulse. If you want anything badly and continuously enough—by conscious choice—that desire will become a habit, and eventually, an instinct. Having become an instinct, it will survive even after consciousness has lost its drive. When this happens, instinct now supplies the conscious mind with its meanings—so that my sexual response to a girl is thrust upon me, as it were, and may brush aside my conscious judgements. However, my subconscious is only giving me back what I have already put there—or, in the case of sex, what my ancestors put there. The 'instinct' does not come from the depths of nature or from God or some other mysterious source; it comes from my robot, and I put it there.

Nature's method of 'instinctive feedback' has one great disadvantage. Most wild creatures are under the protection of their parents for a very brief period; then they are on their own. By comparison, human beings spend a long period being fed, clothed and educated—that is, being more or less passive. The period during which a small bird opens its beak and has worms dropped into it lasts only a month or so; the period during which human beings open their mouths and expect food may last for twenty years or more. This encourages a habit of passivity, and the habit becomes deeply ingrained. Moments of intense happiness are accepted as a 'gift' from nature. And this habit of passivity leads to the total loss of motivation we find in Stavrogin and Faust. I have pointed out in *The Strength to Dream* how significant it is that most of the pessimistic modern authors were the children of rich—or well-to-do—parents—Proust, Andreyev, Beckett; the optimists—Wells and Shaw, for example—had to fight their way up from the bottom. Beethoven was playing the role of father to his brothers and sisters at the age of thirteen. The great creators threw off the passivity at an early age, so that the vital instincts were fed by the conscious will, and vice versa. Proust was spoilt —as he freely admits in his novel—with the consequence that he spent his life like a bird with its mouth open, and came to believe that life was hostile because it refused to supply him with worms.

One can see the 'passive fallacy' very clearly in a writer like Graham Greene. He is describing, let us say, an autumn evening in a London suburb. We get the bitter wind, which blows the fine grit into the faces of the exhausted men who emerge from the tube station, the trees like grey ghosts on Clapham Common, the white-faced urchins begging a penny for the guy, which lies like an exhumed corpse in the battered pram. . . . What Greene is implying is that he is merely a camera, an honest observer, striving to convey to the reader what an evening near Clapham Common is *really* like. It does not strike him that what he is describing is not Clapham Common but his own inner-world. All the adjectives imply exhaustion and *lack of will,* passivity. Consciousness is high and dry, empty, it is not fed by hidden streams from the subconscious.

But I have elsewhere quoted the passage from Greene's essay 'The Revolver in the Corner Cupboard' in which he describes how he could dissipate this sense of life-failure by playing Russian roulette with his brother's revolver; he would insert a bullet into the pistol, twirl the chambers, point it at his head, and pull the trigger. When there was just a click, he would experience a surge of delight and the sense that life is full of infinite potentialities. Plainly, the sudden 'crisis' had induced a convulsive clenching of the will, and when the crisis passed, a flow of relief and delight.

Similarly, Wordsworth told De Quincey that his moments of poetic delight came when he had been concentrating on something other than poetry, and suddenly allowed his mind to relax. This happened when he had been kneeling with his ear to the ground, to listen for the rumbling of the mail cart from Keswick. As he straightened up and relaxed, he saw a star overhead that suddenly struck him as extremely beautiful. Wordsworth's moments of affirmation-consciousness arose from the healthy activity of the will. The 'orgasm' of sudden delight arises from a convulsive *clenching and unclenching* of the will.

What is so difficult for us to grasp is that what seems to be perfectly factual and unprejudiced 'observation' of reality ('I am a camera') is actually highly prejudiced *assessment*, like a pawn-broker examining an article to decide what it is worth. The mind allows all kinds of other considerations to colour its assessments. This morning I happened to be looking at a coloured photograph of a Scottish loch, which struck me as rather disagreeable. I analysed this impression, and realised that the patches of purple heather and jutting granite boulders in the foreground struck me as rather messy, like a junk yard. So instead of looking at it and feeling 'Ah, chaotic grandeur', I experienced a negative reaction, which was actually due to a string of associations: untidiness, dirt, cold, discomfort.

Our lives are a series of such assessments, and they are mostly narrow and superficial. The relational theory of consciousness states that in order to see a thing 'truly', we must see it in the widest possible net of relations. I may feel, for example, that I know Tolstoy's *War and Peace* extremely well because I have read it ten times. Then I take a course on European history in the 19th century, and the book is transformed: against this broader background, it becomes in every way more meaningful. Greene's 'observation' of the Clapham Tube Station may be 'honest' enough in its way, but since it has almost no broader background of relations, it is bound to be 'untrue'.

Note that our feeling of 'relationality' is not often a conscious thing. In the case of *War and Peace*, my study of European history may provide it with a new background and alter my conscious assessment of the book. But if I am intensely enjoying a piece of music, this probably has nothing to do with my knowledge of the composer's life. No, what happens is that as I listen to the music, my mind begins to 'warm up', my emotions respond, my subconscious mind becomes more active, tossing up memories and impressions. The 'web of relations' is not visible to consciousness, but it is there all the same, and I can *feel* it. Our moments of happiness—and of creativity—arise from this active relation between the conscious and the subconscious. Our task, at the present point in evolution, is to learn how to promote this relation.

In all animals and most human beings the will is dependent upon the immediate challenges of the environment. Sartre says of the café proprietor in *La Nausée*: 'When his café empties his head empties too.' On the other hand Dostoevsky's Raskolnikov when he thinks about dying has the thought that he would prefer to stand on a narrow ledge for all eternity rather than die at once. Similarly the 'whisky priest' in Greene's *The Power and the Glory* has the sudden insight when he is about to be executed by a firing squad that it would have been so easy to be a saint. In both cases, crisis has made the person aware of the immense potentialities of the will, which are normally wasted because of the mind's absorption in the boring limitations of everyday existence. If we could learn to disengage the will from our minute-to-minute assessment of life-situations, and focus it upon the equivalent of the challenge of sudden death, this *waste of consciousness* would cease, and man would have entered into the next stage of his evolution. For his problem at the moment is that he does not possess the subconscious powers to back up the development of his intellect and power of conscious choice.

This will be easier to grasp if we trace the course of human evolution. We begin with the simplicity of animals, possessing their highly developed sense of self-preservation, and a strong telepathic 'sixth sense'. In the great droughts of the Pliocene, man almost disappeared, for he was a weird hybrid between a tree-ape and a ground predator like the tiger and bear, and could not rival either of them in their own domain. As conditions worsened, man should have vanished, a victim of the tree-apes and sabre-toothed tigers. No one knows quite why he did not vanish, but I think it is a fair guess that he was forced to use his only slight advantage —his intelligence. Robert Ardrey believes that he learned to use chunks of bone or tree-branches as weapons, and that this developed a coordination of brain and nerve that gradually made him the most *calculating* animal that had yet existed. This may be so; or the droughts of the Pliocene may have led him to apply more of his intelligence to stalking and trapping, to out-thinking his rivals rather than out-fighting them. At all events, it seems clear that during the Pliocene, man made his most important discovery, a discovery that has been made by no other animal—that thinking pays off to an unbelievable extent. It is natural for living creatures to live from moment to moment, by rule-of-thumb, dealing with problems as they arise, and not worrying about them in advance. It also seems to be defensible on the grounds of common sense, because surely it can do no good to anticipate trouble? You can fight a bear as easily at ten minutes' notice as at ten days'. But the Pliocene forced man to extend his powers of anticipation and his cunning as a hunter. And quite abruptly, he found himself at the top of the class, with the danger of extinction—at least by other animals—behind him. The tiger had its claws, the elephant its tusks, the crocodile its teeth; and man had his brain and his weapons.

Slowly—over more than a million years—man learned to trust his brain. It must have been a painful process, confined to a small number of unusual specimens: for among men, strength and courage were still the characteristics that led to dominance, and intelligence was not favoured by social evolution. Bertrand Russell once remarked that the greatest intellectual stride ever taken by the human race was when someone noticed that three trees and three lions and three mountains have something in common, and that a calculation involving buffalo still works if you use fingers or pebbles to represent the buffalo.

Somehow, over a very long period, man learned that abstract thought can be trusted, and his evolutionary will went into developing the brain rather than some other defence mechanism. But the activity of thinking involves a separation from physical immediacy, as anyone who tries calculating in the middle of the night discovers. And since man works for rewards—the more immediate the better—and most of his rewards are physical or emotional, the activity of thinking never became popular. It showed its first results—inevitably—in human dwellings, in making the home secure against wild animals and winter storms. Man looked further and deeper than any other animal, and his embryonic ability to reason led to the creation of religions—or rather, superstitions. A caste of priests meant that intellectual distinction became a way of achieving dominance within the tribe. Thinking brought its rewards, by way of admiration and influence. And at some fairly recent point in evolution—within the past twenty or thirty thousand years—a small number of men discovered that thinking can be a pleasurable activity in itself, that calculation need not be connected to any specific purpose to give pleasure. Perhaps the rise of mathematics and science was a consequence of the accidental discovery of wine, for wine makes a man contemplative and detached. In the warm, comfortable civilisations of the Mediterranean, thinking finally came to be regarded as just as important as war.

This new type of man was more thoroughly compartmentalised than ever before. Thinking about mathematics or ideas has this tendency to create a separate, uninvolved personality that often has difficulty coming to terms with the ordinary human world. And as civilisation has slowly grown more complex, more and more human beings have developed this 'bifurcation'—the split between natural man and reasoning man, that I discussed in the first chapter—Lawrence envying the soldier patting a dog. I say 'natural man and reasoning man'—but I might just as well say 'natural man and social man'. There was a time when the natural man was very close to the social man, and Aristotle could describe man as a political *animal*. In the more highly developed of modern civilisations, social man has had to become reasoning man. For example, the Englishman who travels to America is immediately struck by the rather abstract sounding jargon that will be used by ordinary housewives or working men. This is largely derived from psychology and technology; but quite apart from the special jargon, it seems to be true that the American tends to use longer words than his counterpart in Europe. And this seems natural to a country whose biggest cities seem so much more impersonal than any in Europe. The mind has to become more abstract just to cope with everyday living. Life in a mechanised civilisation is closer to mathematics than life in the ancient world. And man is more easily overwhelmed with trivialities.

But this summary of man's spiritual evolution has missed the most crucial point. I have said that animals are on a kind of universal radar; this means that an animal's consciousness of the world is vaguer but more unified than man's. It is an over-all vision, like looking at a landscape through a pair of binoculars. Man is not satisfied with binoculars; he wants far more clarity and definition, the kind of thing that is given by a microscope or a very powerful telescope. His intellect gives him this ability to examine things with a precision and concentration that no animal can achieve. But the disadvantage of a microscope or an astronomical telescope is that it focusses the eye upon a very small area. A dragonfly becomes a dragon; a molehill becomes a mountain. *His power of close-up vision condemns man to the trivial.*

At least, it would. Except that while man has been developing the 'microscope', he has also been developing a power to focus on distant horizons, on far objectives. He developed art and music and poetry to capture these affirmative visions of purpose. He was trying to *replace* the animal's universal radar with another mode of unified perception, which involved what is inadequately called 'imagination'. (It is an unfortunate word, because we have come to associate it with fantasy, with invention, when it is basically an *instrument of perception,* a pair of binoculars.)

There is another reason for the crisis situation that has developed —man's tendency to get bogged-down in triviality. Religion used to provide him with an arbitrary sense of purpose, of distant goals, to contrast with the triviality of everyday living. He has become intelligent enough to reject the paraphernalia of old religions without having achieved the sense of evolutionary purpose—which is implicit in music and poetry—to rescue him from the triviality. And since the immense effort of the 19th century, art has ceased to be a vehicle of heroic idealism, and is temporarily in a doldrums where it can only reflect the triviality, and take up an attitude of disgust and rejection towards it.

It would be useful at this point to introduce another concept I have found valuable in my attempts to create a phenomenology of the poetic experience: that of 'promotion'.

In the R.A.F. I had observed a rather interesting phenomenon. When an ordinary private was promoted to corporal's rank, he was often embarrassed by the promotion; giving orders made him feel a fraud. But after a week or so, he would get used to giving orders, and apparently make the interesting discovery that his new identity fitted him better than his old one. *He had been a corporal all the time,* but had not known it. And once this happened, the promotion became a reality, instead of being a kind of play acting.

If a man is placed in circumstances of boredom or misery, the opposite happens; he is 'de-moted', so to speak; his sense of his identity—of his importance—declines steadily.

Faust's 'promotion' experience on hearing the Easter bells is the fundamental poetic experience, the widening of horizons, the release from constriction, the sense of the mountain ranges of one's inner-being. The sensation is akin to blood flowing back into an arm that has 'gone to sleep' because you have been lying on it; but in ordinary consciousness, vast tracts of one's being have gone to sleep.

The really interesting question now arises. What is it that cuts us off from these wider horizons of identity, that reduces us from the sense of being human to the sense of being an insect. The answer seems to be that we stumble into a vicious circle. Excitement and challenges cause my strings to vibrate, and make me aware of my powers and potentialities. As I become aware of the wider range of notes of which my strings are capable, my desires and appetites also awaken. For after all, the strings are nothing more than *capabilities of sensation.* In order to want something, I must be capable of conceiving it; that is, of imagining the pleasure it will give me. So the more I feel the sense of expanded identity, the more I become aware of the world's potentialities for delight. Conversely, if I am in a situation without much to stimulate me, the strings do not vibrate; my sense of identity narrows; my sense of 'what is worth doing' also narrows, and I become passive. The less effort I make, the lower the water sinks in my well. Everyone is familiar with what happens on a train journey that has gone on too long; the tendency to sink into apathy. You pick up a newspaper and drop it; read a few lines of a book and close it; wonder whether it is worth going to the dining car for a cup of tea, but decide it isn't worth the effort. . . . One's apathy —the abnegation of will—means that things that would normally stimulate lose their power to arouse interest. Like an invalid's stomach, the mind becomes more and more delicate, until even the prospect of arriving at one's destination ceases to give pleasure. Because you have ceased making any effort at 'output', all 'input'

ceases. But 'input'—as in the case of the Easter bells—is precisely
what awakens will-power and vitality. And so the vicious circle
is complete. But observe that the key to the situation is the way
that *forgetfulness* steps in, cutting one off from a backward glance
at the mountains one has left behind. Without forgetfulness, one
would make further efforts, in spite of the fatigue. One would
remember that the world is not really as dull and limited as one's
senses seem to assert, and that therefore the fault lies on oneself, in
one's failure to will.

To continue with the example of the train journey: observe what
happens when you finally reach your destination. Perhaps you
are being met by someone you haven't seen for years. But if you
have allowed yourself to sink too far into a state of apathy, this
makes no difference. You reach inside you, so to speak, for a
reaction of gladness, and there is nothing there—like lowering a
bucket into a well and finding it empty. You have *allowed yourself*
to sink into this condition of life-failure, for that is what it amounts
to. It is the Koheleth state in which everything seems vain and
pointless. Auden writes:

> Put the car away; when life fails
> What's the good of going to Wales?

But now we are close to the hub of the matter. Focus upon
this notion of 'gladness'. The gladness I feel on arriving at my
destination is of quite a different nature from the kind I might
feel as I drink a mouthful of hot tea when I am tired and thirsty.
And to understand the nature of the difference is to understand
something very important indeed. In a word, the difference is
this, that 'emotional' gladness is *intentional*. It is my *chosen* response
to something that I feel is worth doing or worth having.

An example will make this clearer. In America a few years ago,
I accumulated many gramophone records. However, some of these
lacked the polythene sleeve that keeps records free of dust. I
ordered a large number of these sleeves—two hundred or so—and
on the morning they arrived, I sat on the floor with a pile of
records, and went through the lengthy procedure of putting
records into polythene bags—lengthy because it involved taking
each record out of its cardboard cover, then out of the paper
inner-sleeve, wiping the record with a sponge to clean it, then

putting it into a polythene bag and back into its cardboard cover. I was thoroughly enjoying myself when the absurd aspect of my activity struck me. If someone who had never possessed a gramophone had seen me, they might have wondered exactly where the satisfaction came in, for the job was certainly repetitive enough, and lacking any element of excitement. Why, then, was I so enjoying it? Because every time I played a record and had to return it to a paper sleeve, I felt a certain irritation, for, as every record collector knows, dust somehow manages to sneak into a paper sleeve even though it is carefully folded and sealed. Why keep the records free of dust? Because a dusty record develops crackling noises that spoil the music. And if I go one step further and ask myself why I enjoy music so much, the answer is again more complex than at first appears. I may enjoy a piece of music simply for itself, because I like the melody or the harmonies. But that is not all. Any piece of music *reminds me* of the whole realm of music, that enormous country that stretches from the pleasant lowlands of Schubert lieder and Chopin barcarolles to the mountain scenery of Beethoven and Wagner, from the cold beauty of mediaeval plainchant to the rich melancholy of Brahms and Elgar. I do not enjoy any music in isolation, and if I begin an evening by playing myself a Bruckner symphony, I may end it by playing Gilbert and Sullivan or the latest piece of Stockhausen; musical pleasure is *associative* and expansive.

All this would have to be explained to someone who saw me wiping records and putting them into polythene envelopes. But the central point would be that I had *decided* to be glad, for reasons associated with long-range motives. It is my choice, for there is nothing in the actual nature of polythene envelopes to provoke gladness.

The point I am trying to make here concerns the exact nature of the 'mistake' we make in moods of apathy or life-failure. A man who has sunk into the mood of life-fatigue described in Coleridge's *Dejection: An Ode* feels that his apathy is an objective response to the boringness of life, and that the characters of Samuel Beckett see deeper into life than the rest of us. But then, it is also objectively true that polythene bags are not in themselves objects of delight. It is my capacity for vision, for long-range purpose, that makes them so. If I do not feel gladness as I look at the stars, this is not because the stars are failing in their duty of evoking gladness, as cold tea would fail to evoke the gratitude of my stomach. I am making an elementary mistake. If I put a coin into a slot machine but fail to pull out the drawer that contains the bar of chocolate, this is not the fault of the machine, but an omission on my part.

4

The Automatic Gearbox

It is easy to explain the next development in man. He will possess the power of switching from the binoculars to the high-powered telescope at will. His sense of purpose will no longer be a direct product of the trivial ups and downs of everyday living. He will be capable of inducing duo-consciousness at will, and so cease to be a victim of his moods and emotions, or the stubbornness of his own will. I must emphasise that this new power will not depend upon some evolutionary *creed* or belief, but upon a mastery of duo-consciousness.

But here is the most important assertion in this book. The mastery of duo-consciousness is already well within our reach. Evolution has already provided us with its basic mechanisms. The central assertion of Zen—and of mysticism generally—is that in a sense, 'affirmation consciousness' is extremely easy to reach. *The Cloud of Unknowing* compares it to a spark flying upwards. Kirilov experiences it simply walking up and down the room.

What happens in such moments? We change focus, from the worm's eye to the bird's eye view. Close-upness deprives us of meaning, but we already possess the capacity to grasp the meaning. It depends on a mental act of 'pulling back'.

I can be more precise about this. Anyone who understands the principle of the automatic gearbox in cars will be able to grasp it. If you take two electric fans, and place them an inch apart, and then switch one of them on, what happens? The other fan begins to revolve in sympathy, because the air between them revolves and turns the other blades. In the automatic gearbox of a car, the two 'fans' are separated by oil instead of air, so sympathy is even stronger. In an ordinary gearbox, the two fans themselves engage their blades. But oil between them is just as efficient, and gives a much gentler start, with no sudden clash of engaging blades.

Our minds also 'revolve' in sympathy to the environment. If I speak to someone I like very much, the two fans are very close together; if it is someone I hardly know, the two fans are much further apart. But this principle of fans revolving in sympathy does not merely apply to my relations with people, but to *all* my relations—with things, with places, with knowledge. For example, when I first learn French, I talk it very slowly and deliberately. Eventually, it ceases to be a stranger; I 'sympathise' with it, and speak it easily and naturally.

Obviously, 'sympathy' is another name for the robot, and it is essential for making my life smooth and straightforward. But it can have unfortunate consequences. When a place begins to bore me, it is because I am now *too much* in sympathy with it, too close. If some place has been associated with humiliation and defeat, I may feel waves of defeat surging over me every time I go near it. This kind of 'sympathy' is a damned nuisance. The reason that few men of genius remain in their native town is that they know it too well; it induces certain personality-patterns in them, and they cannot break the grip of the robot. Freedom is experienced when you meet new challenges. and the robot has no time to come into operation. Anyone who has read the plays of Chekhov knows all about the way that people can sink into a condition of stagnation that finally becomes so associated with the environment that they are stuck in their sense of futility like wasps in treacle, and have nothing else to do but sting one another. Such people have become slaves of the robot. Blake called the robot 'the spectre' and wrote:

> Each man is in his Spectre's power
> Until the arrival of that hour
> When his humanity awakes
> And casts his Spectre into the lake.

But to return to my image of the two fans. You can imagine that if I took a sheet of metal, and inserted it between the two fans, they would instantly cease to revolve in sympathy. It is not necessary to place the fans several yards from one another; the act of 'detachment'—when the 'humanity awakes'—can be instantaneous.

Because note this: all my moments of poetry, of intensity, are moments when things strike me very *freshly*, i.e. without 'sympathy'. Habit reduces the impact of experience; the 'Zen moment' is when all vestige of 'taking for granted' has vanished. Observe what happens to Alyosha Karamazov when he experiences a 'Zen moment' looking at the stars. He has been in a condition of misery and tension because Father Zossima's body is decaying, and he suddenly wonders whether the whole idea of sanctity is a delusion, since men have to die, and they rot whether they have been saints or sinners. This is a crisis situation, and in crises, 'the humanity awakes'; the robot is firmly suppressed, because this is a time for vigilance and quick decisions. Alyosha has a dream about Cana of Galilee—the subconscious powers can work easier through dreams—with the result that the tension is suddenly relaxed. It is then that he goes out into the night and sees the stars. The tension has only just relaxed, so the robot has not had time to get back on duty. And simply looking at the stars—which he can see any time—he experiences 'Zen consciousness'.

The lesson is clear. The Zen moment comes swiftly and easily because it only depends upon the robot being turned off for a moment, or upon a sheet of metal being placed between the two fans so that habit is circumvented. Alyosha turns it off by the usual process of contraction and expansion, with which we have now become familiar.

The very simplicity of the mental act involved in the act of 'detachment', pulling back, makes it difficult to describe, although it is certainly easy enough to grasp. Perhaps the easiest approach to the problem would be to speak personally.

In my teens, I was exceptionally subject to boredom and 'life devaluation', and I was impressed by the phrase 'the great mystery of human boredom' that I came across in a book about Job. As I saw it, the mystery was this. When you are in a state of affirmation-consciousness, you look back on your boredom with a shrug, and say: 'It is easy enough to throw off.' The universe is self-evidently fascinating; it seems that all you have to do is open your eyes and look. Your whole inner-being whirrs like a dynamo, and the switch is there for anyone to see.

Then you sink into boredom; you press the switch. Nothing

happens. The dynamo sits there looking as if it has never worked in its life. It is completely lifeless—it is like pressing the starter button on a car when the battery is flat.

It seemed to me that boredom had never been recognised for the enormous and menacing problem it is; at least, not in England. In Russian novels, characters blow out their brains out of boredom. There is a speech in Chekhov's *Wood Demon*.

'You've never tasted real boredom, my dear fellow. When I was a volunteer in Serbia, there I experienced the real thing! Hot, stuffy, dirty, head simply splitting after a drinking bout. Once I remember sitting in a dirty little shed. Captain Kashkinazi was there too. Every subject of conversation long exhausted, no place to go, nothing to do, no desire to drink—just sickening, you see, sickening to the point of putting one's head in a noose. We sat, in a frenzy, just glaring at one another—he gazes at me, I at him; he at me, I at him. We gaze and don't know why we're doing it. An hour passes, you know, then another hour, and still we keep on gazing. Suddenly he jumps up for no reason, draws his sabre and goes for me. Hey presto! I, of course, instantly draw my sabre—for he'll kill me—and it started: chic-chac, chic-chac, chic-chac . . . with the greatest difficulty we were at last separated. I got off all right, but to this very day, Captain Kashkinazi walks about with a scar on his face. See how desperately bored one may get?'

And when one thinks of *this* kind of boredom, and then of the intensity of the affirmation experience, of the feeling that the whole earth is made of jewels, the endless potentialities of life, it is impossible not to feel that boredom is as strange a mystery as cancer or the Black Death: one of the most mysterious ailments of the human spirit. This is what drives Stavrogin to rape a child, and finally to kill himself—boredom has become a kind of constipation that threatens to poison the whole system, to turn one into a fungus.

The 19th century knew about this—Byron and Lermontov and Pushkin fighting duels, Shelley sailing into a storm, Lenau and Hölderlin dying insane, Kleist killing his mistress and then himself, Stifter cutting his throat, Beddoes poisoning himself with curare, Van Gogh hacking off an ear and shooting himself in the stomach. And all this mental strain and suicide was related to what I like to call 'the Bombard problem'. Alain Bombard was the Frenchman who set out to prove that one could cross the Atlantic in a rubber dinghy, living off plankton and the juices from fish. Halfway across, he made the mistake of accepting an invitation to go on board a passing ship and eating a good meal. It almost killed him, for when he went back to his plankton and squashed fish the next day, he couldn't stomach it; he vomited for days before his stomach became accustomed to his old diet. Everyday human existence is a matter of plankton and squashed fish, and the romantics have experienced the greater intensity of the affirmation experience; after this, they cannot stomach everyday life.

But the desperation of those romantics demonstrated that they were aware that part of the problem was lack of self-discipline, boredom. They sought out crisis as Ramakrishna seized the sword in the temple of Kali. Captain Shotover tells Ellie in *Heartbreak House*: 'You are looking for a rich husband. At your age I looked for hardship, danger, horror and death, that I might feel the life in me more intensely.' This is why the romantics sought out violence. Van Gogh pursued it with remarkable single-mindedness. In 1965, I saw an exhibition of his pictures at the museum in Amsterdam, and it was amazing to see the way in which the mind struggled to throw off the Spectre. There is the dullness and darkness of the early pictures; then the visionary intensity of the pictures painted in the Borinage, when he lived as a pastor among the Belgian miners and gave away his food and clothes; the light and air of the Montmartre period, the desperation and struggle of the Arles period—when he tried to cut off his ear and kill Gauguin—and finally, visionary intensity alternating with terrible depression during the last period in the mental home. But what was obvious is that he had finally achieved a certain ability to induce the 'affirmation experience' by mental effort; this is very clear from the 'Road With Cypresses', the 'Starry Night', the 'Field of Green Corn'. His main trouble was that years of failure and anxiety had turned his mind into a swamp of pessimism, so that these self-induced ecstasies were only breathing spaces. What he needed was the kind of *understanding* of the phenomenology of his 'affirmation experiences' that I have been trying to outline. As it was, he was pursuing a kind of stop-go policy, like driving a powerful car at top speed, and then slamming on the brakes every time it reaches a hundred miles an hour. In the last analysis, it was sheer *ignorance* that destroyed him.

My discovery of Van Gogh—at about the age of seventeen—was a kind of turning point. What I began to understand was not so much the phenomenology of the moments of intensity, but—far more important—the phenomenology of the moments of boredom. We know that we can summon up energies in an emergency; but we also know that we can summon energies from the subconscious under quite ordinary circumstances. If I know that I have to drive three hundred miles tomorrow, I make a mental act of concentrating my forces, in much the same way that I would go to the bank to draw out money for a holiday. If life is fairly quiet and not very interesting, and then some really tiresome problem arises, my tendency is to turn away from it, to say 'Oh no', and refuse to summon up the necessary energy to deal with it. I am like a miser who claims to be poor; I protest that I have no energy to deal with this crisis, that I am exhausted and overworked already. . . . What I am saying, in fact, is 'This is not *worth doing*'. We *judge* whether something is worth doing or not; we make an assessment. There is an act of conscious choice about it. And if I am in a dull state, my consciousness is narrow; the 'web' is small. We lay-out energy on the same principle that a businessman lays out capital: that is, upon our expectation of a return. Let us suppose that I am sitting in a chair, dull and bored. I have just put down a book that I find tiresome. The room is stuffy, but it is cold outside, so that if I open a window, it will get too cold. Note that I *assess* the situation on possible 'returns'. The fire is low and I sit up to look at the coal scuttle. It is empty. That means I have to go outside. I was willing to make the effort to pick up the scuttle and toss coal on to the fire. But to go outside and get more coal . . . that is too tiresome. *It really doesn't seem worth it.*

I am trying to emphasise the way in which situations involve continual 'assessments' of *what is worth doing*.

But now, suppose that the reason I have not refilled the coal scuttle is that I know the coal-shed to be almost empty, so that if I make a fire now, I shall not be able to have one this evening. This is yet another negative factor to take into account, and it increases my feeling that making up the fire really isn't worth the trouble. But at this moment, I hear a lorry outside; the coal man has arrived. And ten minutes later, I go out to the coal shed with a certain enthusiasm. Why? What is the difference between the

two situations I have outlined? In the first, the coal shed might
have been full of coal, but because I am bored, I still don't feel
that it is worth the effort of fetching more. In the second situation,
there was a negative stimulus present—the worry about lack of
coal—and therefore there was a certain tension in my mind.
When the coal man arrives, the tension vanishes; the resulting
mild 'affirmation experience' is enough to add purpose to the act
of fetching coal.

The point to observe here is that in the previous situation—
when I am simply paralysed with bordeom—my judgement on
the situation seems wholly fair and accurate. I say: 'Yes, I know
there is plenty of coal, but the room is stuffy, I don't want to go
on reading, I feel tired and dull, and when I look inside myself
for any positive impulse, I just can't find any. . . .' It *looks* an
accurate and just assessment, *within* the situation I have outlined.
Just as the lassitude of Beckett's characters looks reasonable
enough within the situation he creates. The fallacy here, of course,
is that one is accepting a very small web of relational consciousness as if it were a permanent criterion, a sort of absolute. When I
scrutinise the situation in order to assess it, the one thing I do
not bother to scrutinise is the degree of 'relationality' of my
consciousness. I take if for granted, for after all, consciousness is
consciousness, and surely a candle shows you a room just as
accurately as an electric bulb or brilliant sunlight . . . ? *This* is the
fallacy. It simply isn't so. What I am failing to grasp is that I
possess a 'muscle' for extending the size of the web of consciousness.

Consider this mental act of 'becoming interested' for a moment.
Dr Watson is sitting in his armchair at Baker Street, on a dull
winter afternoon; he has finished reading *The Times*, and he is
feeling rather bored. He says dully—without really being very
interested: 'I see Lord Ashton is dead, Holmes. Did you ever
meet him?' Holmes looks up and says: 'Indeed I did, Watson. It
was in connection with one of the most curious and macabre
cases of my whole career. Would you like to hear about it? It was
in 1881, the year I came down from Oxford, and I had just taken
rooms behind the British Museum. . . .' And suddenly, Watson is
all attention. He is leaning forward, wearing that little smile of
delight that children get when you say 'Once upon a time. . . '

What has Watson *done*? We say he has 'become interested', and the inadequacy of the phrase is at once apparent. It makes it sound passive; something has 'seized' his interest. But this isn't quite true. Watson's interest has pounced like a hawk on a rabbit; its talons sink into every word Holmes speaks. There is suddenly an act of concentration, of reaching out.

What would have happened if Watson had tried to make this act of concentration *without* an objective, just staring into the fire? That really depends upon how bored he was. If he was only slightly bored, it might have produced a flicker of pleasure and intensity; if he was very bored nothing would have happened. That seems plain enough. The talons have to grip something. The act of 'interest' requires an object.

But then, the 'Zen moment' reveals the universe as being full of infinite potentialities—infinite occasions for interest. When the hammer of Greene's revolver clicks on an empty chamber, when Faust's suicide attempt is interrupted by the Easter bells, there arises an absurd and incredible recognition. When the relationality of consciousness is increased, the world itself is seen to be full of potentiality In other words, the potentiality is *already there*; it is the act of concentration, of increasing the relationality, that reveals it. Our habit of passivity means that we tend to do things back to front —and to *think* back to front. We are bored; we ask for a stimulus to focus the interest: 'Would you like to hear about it, Watson?' And this way of thinking is fatal if I am trying to develop Van Gogh's power of 'affirmative vision'. This is dependent upon the recognition that if you open the sense wide enough, the vision follows.

To return to my own researches into the subject. My mid-teens were crippled by boredom and a sense of total futility. A succession of dull office jobs increased this, so that my attempts to 'shake the mind awake' were always being undone by the dreary, familiar scene that set the record running in its old groove. A short period of national service was dull enough, but there was enough movement and change of scenery to make me aware that *this* was clearly the trouble: the robot, the two fans turning in sympathy. If the continual mental effort was not to be undone, then I had to seek out situations where habit could not develop— exactly as Van Gogh had done. With this in mind, I became a kind of tramp for about a year, moving around, returning home periodically, and working for brief periods at all kinds of labouring jobs—on farms, building sites, even a fairground. This had the effect that I had anticipated: that is to say, the lack of routine, the perpetual inconvenience that kept the will from relaxing, made it easier to focus the 'distant horizons' far more constantly. The mild element of 'crisis' in such an existence kept the mind in a state of tension, so that temporary breathing-spaces were no longer taken for granted, and would produce affirmation experiences. It was important not to sink into a tramp's frame of mind: that is, of drifting fatalism, with the will focussed upon the contingencies of the present moment. But there was never much danger of this, because the pleasure of the affirmation experience was so intense that my mind was constantly trying to vault the gap between the 'worm's eye view' and the 'bird's eye view'.

I noticed something that will seem clear enough to anyone who has read the mystics, but which seems to puzzle many otherwise intelligent people. The 'affirmation experience' was always the same; it never changed in nature. It was like climbing to the top of a tower, and always looking out on the same scenery. It might vary from day to day, depending whether it happened to be sunny or rainy, so to speak; but it was visibly *the same* scenery. These experiences were not 'mystical' in the sense of being a vision of God. What was 'perceived' was something I already knew theoretically; but it was *perceived*, not simply 'known'. There was an increased knowledge of the workings of consciousness, of the assumptions and habits that condemn most human beings to a lifetime of the 'worm's eye view'; there was also a fairly certain knowledge that I would never again accept the worm's-eye-view as 'reality'. The plays and novels of Beckett, for example, seemed to me slightly silly, as if all based upon a schoolboy-howler of a mistake. Most metaphysical problems remained opaque: the problem of death, of time and space, of existence and non-existence. But it was impossible to doubt that this insight was 'truer' than the worm's eye view. There was no possibility of relativism.

What was also obvious to me was that in these moments of insight, I had taken the *logical* next step in human evolution. I think that my *precise* meaning should now be clear. Our basic problem lies in this habit of minute-to-minute 'assessment' of situations, to judge 'what is worth doing'. This does no harm for brief periods, particularly if serious realities keep intruding and forcing the mind to revise its narrow judgements, to call the bluff of its laziness posing as exhaustion. But if continued for too long—and most people do it for a lifetime—it leads to an increasing mental slovenliness and untidiness. To return to an earlier simile: it would not matter greatly if the librarian left a few dozen books lying around on tables: a hour's work can always get them back in their correct places. But if miscellaneous books are allowed to go on piling up for years, the library will be too messy to be tidied by any one person. (This is the point at which people fall back on psychiatrists.) What is worse, the messier the place becomes, the more one experiences the sense of 'nothing is worth doing'. It is a vicious circle—or spiral—where mess leads to the exhaustion of the will, and exhaustion of the will leads to more mess.

It was during the four or five years of moving around restlessly, concentrating on the 'distant horizon', that I developed the mental trick of brushing aside the worm's eye view. Van Gogh's affirmation-experiences were never subjected to logical analysis, so that he could never be sure, looking back on them later, whether they were not simply bursts of *emotional* euphoria, with no objective significance. Once I had got used to the idea that the insight had nothing to do with emotion—that it was always a vision of the same landscape—this kind of doubt ceased to be an important factor.

This 'vision' of my 'wanderjahre' period was not a consummation, like an orgasm; it always produced a strong sense that I was only at the beginning. The next problem was to map the landscape, to explain the mechanisms of consciousness and the way they can lead to affirmation-experiences or to morbid paranoia. This proved to be harder than I had anticipated, because ordinary psychology, of the kind created by Freud and Jung, proved to be quite useless. Existentialism provided a better starting point, but that was equally frustrating because the major figures—Kierkegaard, Heidegger, Sartre, Camus—were as riddled with pessimism and the 'passive fallacy' as Beckett. Sartre's world-negation seemed to me as unperceptive as Graham Greene's, merely a sign of an inability to think clearly. He keeps confusing consciousness as a general concept with personality-consciousness. So that Simone de Beauvoir can write (in *Pyrrhus and Cinéas*):

'I look at myself in vain in a mirror, tell myself my own story,
I can never grasp myself as an entire object, I experience in myself
the emptiness that is myself, I feel that I am not', and imagine
that she is describing a general characteristic of *all* consciousness,
instead of ordinary superficial mono-consciousness. As soon as
one reads Mlle de Beauvoir's volumes of autobiography, or
Sartre's *Words*, one can see exactly why they made this basic
error; neither of them possess that capacity for poetic experience
—affirmation-consciousness—that came so naturally to Wordsworth.

And the chief characteristic of the opposite of affirmation
consciousness—I suppose one might call it depression-
consciousness—is that when you are in it, it seems *totally convincing*;
like a very brilliant liar, it can account for everything in its own
terms. Aldous Huxley invented the rather useful term 'minimum
working hypothesis' about religion—i.e. what can we state definitely about it without going off into 'faith' or speculation. Well,
the minimum-working-hypothesis for depression-consciousness
is that the world is real and permanent, and *we* are not very
real and not very permanent. (One of the most convincing
expressions of it in literature is Wells's *Mind at the End of its
Tether*, that final work in which he thought the universe was
falling to pieces.)

At this point, it might seem relevant to ask the question: What
about death? Does this fundamentally optimistic philosophy
have anything to say about the final problem? If not, then surely
it has no right to condemn Sartre, Greene, Beckett and the rest
for being short-sighted?

This is not quite so. Although I do not believe the question
of death to be ultimately beyond human solution, it is *not* particularly relevant at this point anyway. Suppose I were a building
contractor, and I say: 'I think it would take me about two years
to erect a thirty storey building,' and someone replies: 'Oh no,
because you might die at any moment', this would quite clearly
be a logical *non sequitur*. What I am stating here is that the
greatest human mistake is the belief that 'the natural wakeful life
of the ego is a perceiving'—in Husserl's phrase. It isn't. At least,
the normal understanding of this idea involves a fallacy; that
perceiving is a passive occupation, like sleeping. I have tried to

show that this mistake arises from the efficiency of our human robot. This robot might be compared to a super tax-accountant, who is so efficient that he gets his hands on all your money before you receive it yourself, and deducts tax for you, so that you never have any tax bills. And when people mention tax, you say with sincerity: 'I've never paid any in my life.' The flat truth is that you are too stupid to understand your own business affairs. *However*, your invisible tax-accountant is completely dependent on you. If you stop earning money, he won't be able to support you. The same is true of the robot. The energy that sustains your everyday perception comes from *you*. So do those bonuses of duo-consciousness, that startle you as pleasantly as a tax rebate. What human beings will slowly develop, as we advance up the evolutionary scale, is a deepening consciousness of these transactions of the robot, so that the chance element disappears from the ups and downs of consciousness. And eventually the problem of death itself will come within the range of our self-knowledge—for any doctor will confirm that the body's health depends, in some strange way, upon the mind. And, at the present stage, this is all it is possible to say.

To summarise. All great changes involve a doldrums period, a time of fallowness. When a backward country changes over from agriculture to industry, the immediate result is misery and starvation for farm workers. The human race has been going into a new phase of evolution at a steadily accelerating pace, and the end is now in sight. Man deliberately abandoned the warm richness of animal consciousness for something altogether bleaker and harder. He has not done it deliberately and determinedly, but in brief spurts, with many backslidings. His attempt to conquer nature and improve his position have made life so complicated that the old phrase about the 'gift of life' begins to take on ironic overtones. Laziness and timidity are no longer qualities that can be tolerated by the force behind evolution. Human beings of the 21st century will be born into a forbidding world: a civilisation that is immense, aloof, heartless and highly mechanised. Men of genius will find it a frightening world, for it will look so impersonal and vast that there will seem to be no room for individuality. Roads to the top will be well marked, but they will involve a discouraging amount of specialisation, of adjustment to the demands of mass-organisation. And since men of genius naturally hate to conform, it seems likely that the present tendency to negative revolt will increase, as they fire off blasts of loathing at the clockwork octopus that holds them fast. This will only make things worse, for nothing destroys the will quicker than the conviction that there is no point in willing. It looks like a vicious circle; there seems every reason to assume that human beings have chosen a self-destructive route to dominance, and that things are bound to get worse, until the whole miserable chaos explodes and we plunge back into a relaxing barbarism.

This is why it has become so important that we grasp what is happening. Human consciousness has been on half-rations for a long time now; but in an important sense, this is by our own choice as a man might fast to lose weight, or save money to finance a business. A point has arrived where we can afford to reap the first harvest. Because we have not permanently forsworn the warmth and richness of animal consciousness. We have set out to develop ways in which we can have the enrichment without its disadvantages: laziness, incompetence, lack of purpose. We chose purpose, and accepted the sudden drop in the pressure of consciousness that went with it. The east always found it easier to achieve ecstasy than the west, because the eastern temperament tends to be less purposive (this may not continue to be true, though), and so far, that has been the equation that governs human existence: purpose and the tightening of the belt, *or* happiness and drifting. But expressed in this way, we can see that it does not have to be so. We left purpose to the robot, because consciousness had to be economised: we had to use it for immediate problems. And now a time has come when it is not only true that we can afford to relax—and take the horse out of its harness—but when it has become a matter of urgency that we do so. The new complexity of our civilisation *demands* a more leisurely, enriched type of consciousness. The old obsessive energy must be turned into self-knowledge, the attempt to illuminate the realm of the robot, to gain conscious control of its vast resources of power.

For I must repeat the assertion with which I began: we possess such immense resources of power that pessimism is a laughable absurdity. Yeats's old Chinamen are gay because they *know*.

They have broken through. They no longer suspect—as Faust
does—that knowledge may be the death of us, by revealing new
vistas of futility, and the ultimate impossibility of knowing
anything at all. They have pushed knowledge further still: and
what they now know fills them with a tremendous, quiet satisfaction. That is why 'their ancient, glittering eyes are gay'.

Why do I believe that *this* is the crucial point in human evolution?
Why not in the year 2000 or 25000?

There are two reasons, and I have already discussed the first:
that we can *choose* when we shall turn the questing intellect that
has built the cyclotron and the moon rocket to the scientific
exploration of man's inner being. And now is a good time to
choose—now that there is more leisure available to more people
than at any time in history.

But I also believe that the inner forces of history are pushing us
towards the moment of choice. Man has been having 'mystical'
experiences for as far back as written records extend; but they
were restricted to a few rare souls. In the 19th century, we suddenly discover what can only be called a mass hunger for mystical
experience—that is, for rejection of the imperatives of everyday
existence and for an intenser form of inner-experience. Romanticism is the expression of a deep instinctive desire for the life of
the mind, and we are still in the midst of the romantic period.
The stomach of the romantic rejects everyday existence as Bombard's stomach rejected the squashed fish; but he has no clear
idea of an alternative to it. Like Wagner, he believes that the world
of the mind is based upon 'wahn', illusion, and that to reject
'life' is the same thing as choosing death. What he is failing to
grasp is that human beings are the only terrestrial creatures for
whom the word 'life' has two distinct meanings. For an animal,
'life' is what it sees when it opens its eyes in the morning; that is
all. But even a fairly unintellegent human being—let us say, a
provincial lad on his way to see the Cup Final in London—can
say 'Eh, lad, this is life!', and mean that he suddenly perceives that
'life' means something bigger than his individual life. Human
beings are the only creatures with some ability to grasp 'life'
in this bigger sense. And *this* is the aim of our evolution, the
purpose for which we rejected animal 'oneness' with nature.
We are capable—in theory—of living 'life' in the broader sense.

The trouble is that our habits are against it. Imagine a soldier from Napoleon's army, returning from the Russian campaign to his small village where nothing ever happens. He sees clearly that these people are wasting their lives by living so narrowly; he knows 'life' is bigger. But if he stays in the village for six months or so, he too will forget this broader life, and allow his senses to shrink to the confines of village gossip. The problem is to stretch the mind 'beyond immediacy', and our chief defect is that it takes crisis or misery to make us do it. And yet we possess a power possessed by no other animal—this power called imagination—and its purpose is not—as I have already remarked—to allow people to live in 'a world of imagination', but to enable them to point the mind towards the broadest possible meaning of 'life'. In the 19th century, the impulse became so powerful in the higher types of human being that it outstripped their interest in the narrower sense of 'life'. In the 20th century, this disgusted rejection of 'life' has become stronger. Wagner and Tennyson represent a rich autumn; Kafka and Beckett a bleak, grey winter. It is impossible for rejection to go further; the turning point has to come.

Kafka and Beckett represent an extreme of exhaustion and life-rejection. Elsewhere, a more positive form of romanticism has developed. In *The Rock*, Eliot repeats the phrase: 'Make perfect your will'. And both Proust and Hermann Hesse are aware that the main problem is the low pressure of everyday consciousness, which rises only occasionally to moments of intense self-awareness. Proust's attempt to re-possess his own past can be construed as an attempt to convince his consciousness that it has *got* to stop drifting and 'perceiving', that intensity is given to the present moment by that vision of purpose and meaning that is grasped in the lightning-flash of the orgasm experience. Axel says negatively: 'Live? Our servants can do that for us.' Eliot is more positive when he asks: 'Where is the life we have lost in living?' for an accurately-expressed question is already halfway towards the answer. Proust's *Recherche* and Hesse's *Steppenwolf* are asking the same question, and perceiving vaguely that the answer would lie in successfully carrying the meaning-content of the 'orgasm' into everyday consciousness. Everyday consciousness is flat because the will collapses when it lacks an objective, a long-range purpose. But a purpose is something that can be expressed in terms of

G

knowledge. The answer, therefore, is to direct all one's conscious discipline to carrying the insight of intensity-consciousness into everyday consciousness—which would mean, in effect, that everyday consciousness could become attuned to purpose, and transcend its own limitations.

Part two

Introductory

A healthy consciousness needs to be fed by streams of 'newness', to be constantly reminded of the complex richness of the external world: hence the importance of holidays. Man has discovered that this inner-newness can be produced by other means; by art, music and poetry. Poetry is an attempt to mould and direct the 'intentions'. Its purpose is to irrigate consciousness, and it could be compared to a farmer's construction of ditches to carry water to the fields where it is most needed. Fundamentally, it is man's attempt to control his inner-life instead of leaving it to the mercy of external stimuli.

In the second chapter of Part One, I spoke of some of the mechanisms that poetry employs in this 'moulding of intentions'. But this leaves a larger question untouched. Why does a particular poet wish to mould the intentions to a certain end?

A non-musician, listening to a symphony, may feel that a composer is a kind of Prospero who commands spirits of the air to produce harmonies. In fact the musician and the poet are living creatures, enmeshed, like the rest of us, in the 'triviality of everydayness'. The first step in the direction of art is the deliberate creation of a self-image, accompanied by an act of dedication, not unlike the vows taken by a monk. It now becomes the artist's problem to somehow reconcile the self-image with his everyday personality. Joyce and Brecht stand at opposite extremes in this matter, Joyce choosing the way of the monk—silence, exile and cunning—while Brecht insists upon the identity of the poet and the ordinary man.

Clearly, the nature of the poetry will depend upon the way the poet deals with this problem. If the fundamental nature of the poetic experience is always the same, then the difference between poets will be largely dependent on the solution he chooses, upon his decision about the relation between his self-image and the world of contingency.

The poets dealt with in the next four chapters have been chosen to illustrate different approaches to this problem of the self-image.

1

Rupert Brooke

It would not be accurate to say that Rupert Brooke is currently unfashionable, for he has never been fashionable in the literary sense. Even at the height of his reputation—shortly before his death in 1915—no one took him very seriously. His position could be compared to that of John Betjeman in the sixties. It is significant that, although his collected poems have never been out of print since 1918 (and had gone through thirty impressions by 1947), no biography of him appeared until nearly forty years after his death.

When Christopher Hassall's biography finally appeared in 1964, a weekend reviewer, Philip Toynbee, took the opportunity to write a final dismissal of Brooke, which included the assertion: 'There is not a single line of real poetry in all Brooke's work.'

It seems to me that this remark betrays a curiously literal and naïve view of what constitutes poetry. Poetry does not come in lines as chocolate comes in squares. It happens to be written in lines as music is written in bars or a novel in sentences. But one can no more judge a poet by how many good lines he has written than a composer by the number of whistlable tunes in his work. A poet is like a philosopher in one fundamental sense; what counts is not how well he expresses himself, but *how much he has to express*. I have tried to argue that a poet is a certain type of person: one who is subject to unpredictable states of 'promotion', a sense of 'enlargement' that is oddly impersonal. When Eugene Marchbanks walks out of Candida's house at the end of Shaw's play, Shaw comments in the stage instructions: 'But they do not know the secret in the poet's heart.' The secret is his ability to transcend his disappointment in love, to transcend his present immature personality in a sudden flash of 'promotion'. In a letter (to James Huneker) explaining the play, Shaw speaks of the poet walking out into 'Tristan's holy night' and realising that the little domestic fool's paradise of Candida and her husband is not for him.

If this ability to experience 'promotion' is the mark of a poet, then it is impossible to deny that Brooke was a poet. The early poems are full of descriptions of such moments: for example, *Seaside*, written when he was twenty:

> Swiftly out from the friendly lilt of the band
> The crowd's good laughter, the loved eyes of men,
> I am drawn nightward; I must turn again
> Where, down below the low untrodden strand,
> There curves and glimmers outward to the unknown
> The old unquiet ocean. All the shade
> Is rife with magic and movement, I stray alone
> Here on the edge of silence, half afraid.
>
> Waiting a sign. In the deep heart of me
> The sullen waters swell towards the moon,
> And all my tides set seaward.
>   From inland
> Leaps a gay fragment of some mocking tune,
> That tinkles and laughs and fades along the sand
> And dies between the seawall and the sea.

The idiom here is romantic—as in the music of Bax and Delius with which it is contemporary. Ears that are accustomed to the drier idiom of Eliot and Auden will object to the clichés, 'rife with magic', 'the friendly lilt of the band'. But that need hardly be of serious concern. Fashions come and go. Nowadays we are able to listen to Delius without worrying that he was apparently unaware of the existence of Schoenberg and Stravinsky. We have even learned to enjoy the merits of Victorian academic painting without a guilty conscience. It is not Brooke's fault if 'in the deep heart of me' evokes a memory of Cole Porter's 'O such a hungry yearning burning inside of me'. Put all this aside, and the poem is seen to be the honest expression of a personal emotion, and the record of a certain kind of promotion experience.

Like all poets, he also experiences the converse state: of boredom, sterility.

> I said I splendidly loved you; it's not true.
> Such long swift tides stir not a land locked sea.

Observe that here again, Brooke compares himself to the sea; but the sense of expansion, of limitlessness, is gone.

The tendency to be dismissive about Brooke is due less to the feeling that he is a minor poet than to what an advertising man would call a 'bad public image'. Even his name sounds as if it had been invented by W. S. Gilbert as a companion to Reginald Bunthorne. But what was Brooke really like as a human being?

Brooke was the son of a housemaster at Rugby. He was never underprivileged, and he took a certain pleasure in not being underprivileged. He was not oppressively or snobbishly 'upper class'; but, like many young people, he derived a mildly theatrical pleasure from contemplating the advantages of being 'public-school' and upper middle-class.

It is impossible to read much of Brooke without being aware of this slightly theatrical attitude. Physically, he was extremely attractive. There is a story that Henry James enquired whether Brooke was a good poet; on being answered in the negative, James remarked: 'Thank goodness. If he looked like that and was a good poet too, it would be too unfair.' Brooke was aware that he was good looking, that he looked well in tennis flannels, that he belonged to England's privileged minority of 'golden youth'. He was also aware that he had a good brain and that he *was* a good poet—in spite of his good looks and privileged status.

What is impressive about Brooke is that he transcended all these 'advantages'. There is a touch of original John Betjeman about many of the poems—middle-class comfort contemplating itself with absorbed delight (which is not necessarily a bad thing) —but his intensely active and curious mind is always turning away from this narcissistic self-absorption and mocking itself.

All this helps to express the peculiar charm and potency of the Brooke legend. As one reads the Edward Marsh *Memoir* or Christopher Hassall's *Life*, it seems that Brooke is one of the most fortunate poets who was ever born. From the beginning, everything went well with him. As the son of a housemaster, he was in a uniquely fortunate position, with all the advantages of a public school education, and none of the disadvantages of being away from home and family. He was popular, intelligent, and a good athlete, playing both soccer and rugby football for the school. A contemporary wrote: 'Gradually, most of us in the House came under his spell.' And Brooke wrote, in a typical letter from school: 'I'm enjoying everything immensely at present. To be among 500 people, all young and laughing, is intensely delightful and interesting. . . . Wonderful things are happening all around me. Some day when all the characters are dead—they are sure to die young—I shall put it all in a book. . . . The rest are only actors; I am actor and spectator as well. . . .' The last sentence catches the essence of Brooke: actor and spectator. It also, perhaps, explains his somewhat incongruous admiration for Henry James.

What is ultimately bad about Brooke—or at least annoying—comes from the actor element. He was a little too conscious of being golden, privileged youth, and it can become a little tiresome over the 550 pages of Hassall's biography.

And yet, in another sense, Brooke's permanent importance derives from this element of narcissism. With the exception of Belloc, the poets he admired were despairing romantics. After Brooke's death, the tradition of despair and defeat became a kind of absolute premise for modern literature. Two years before Brooke's death, the archetypal modern hero had already appeared in *Swann's Way*: the poet who admits that he is an oversensitive neurotic, but who insists that weakness and neurosis are inseparable from talent. Joyce's self-pitying Stephen Dedalus appeared three years later. Brooke was lucky; he had no chip on his shoulder, no cause for neurosis, no sense of underprivilege, no reason to feel that life was 'against him'. He lived and wrote his poetry on the premise that the gods meant well by him. Apart from a few older contemporaries like Shaw, Wells and Chesterton, he is the only writer of the 20th century who has taken that unfashionable view. Brooke's poetry has certain affinities with Chesterton's. But Chesterton allowed his sense of physical well-being to lull him into artistic complacency and intellectual dishonesty. (Shaw's sketch of him in *The Domesticity of Franklin Barnabas* makes one wonder how anyone ever put up with him.) Brooke never drowned in his own optimism; it simply forms the basis of his *weltanschauung*. Apart from his optimism, his mind has the same kind of tough honesty that is found in Yeats.

One of the reasons for the post-1918 decline in Brooke's reputation is that he was thought of as a 'Georgian poet'—that is,
one of a group of more-or-less tweedy and healthy poets, all in
revolt against the aesthetic despair of the nineties. In fact, Brooke
has almost nothing in common with Bridges or Masefield or
Binyon. He would have been the kind of poet he was in any
age.

The interesting thing about Brooke's work is the conflict of
romanticism—much of it due to immaturity—with tough-
mindedness. One would expect a poem called *Wagner* to be a tribute to the 'old magician'; instead, it is a description of a fat
sensualist who likes love music that is cheap and who sits quiver-
ing with ecstasy as the waves of *Tristan and Isolde* break over him.
Even at twenty-one, Brooke was too self-critical to be swept
away by the Wagnerian magic.

Brooke was dead by the time he was twenty-eight. His up-
bringing had been so pleasant and free of conflict that he was late
in maturing. This means that most of his poetry must be classi-
fied as juvenilia. (It must be remembered that if Yeats had died
at this age, we should know him only as the poet of *Innisfree*
and *When you are old and grey and full of sleep*. The earliest characteristic poems of Yeats's maturity were wrtitten when he was in
his forties.) This means that there are very few of Brooke's
poems that could stand in anthologies. This is also because it is
intensely personal poetry. Brooke plays the part of the young
poet as consistently as the early Yeats, although his poetic personality is totally unlike Yeats'. So one reads his poems rather as
if they belonged to a single sequence, like Newman's *Dream of
Gerontius* or Shakespeare's sonnets. And like *A Shropshire Lad,*
each one is best enjoyed when considered as part of the whole.
Brooke's hundred or so poems form a kind of poetic journal.
They reveal a complex, interesting, romantic, self-critical,
humorous and intensely alive personality. One enjoys them because one comes to like and respect Brooke. And once one is in
this receptive frame of mind, even the over-anthologised sonnets
of the 1914 sequence become intensely moving.

It may well be that poetry that is so much a part of the poet's
personality cannot be regarded as poetry of the highest order.
But this hardly seems to matter when one is absorbed in Brooke's
world. It is real poetry springing out of the genuine poetic

impulse; there is nothing 'phoney' about it. How one judges it
in relation to other poetry hardly seems important.

The poems fall into a number of groups or types. The influence
of Dowson is strong among the early ones. *Evening*, written
when he was eighteen, begins:

> Lo, now, the splendour of the sun setting!
> And the little fields are dim with mist.
> Dewy and merciful through the shadows,
> Robed in purple amethyst,
> Comes the hour of forgetting.

There are half a dozen or so of these 'soulful' Dowson-type
poems: *Sorrow* begins:

> I whispered to my sorrow, 'Come! Let us go hence
> Far through the dusk, we two, to some dim shadowy place . . .

A few of these 1890-ish poems are extremely successful, *Day
that I have loved* and *The Vision of the Archangels*. Their poignancy
springs from Brooke's perception of the contrast between the
pleasures of human existence and the ultimate fact of death:
classical material, treated here with a certain individuality.

Brooke experienced various types of reaction against his soulful
phase. (One poem begins: 'These are unworthy, these sad whining
moods'.) Another group of poems could be labelled 'fleshly';
these begin with *The Song of the Beasts*, written when he was nine-
teen, which includes the lines:

> Have you not felt the quick fires that creep
> Through the hungry flesh, and the lust of delight,
> And the hot secrets of dreams that the day cannot say . . .
> And the touch and the smell of bare flesh sting. . . .

At a fairly early stage, Brooke is openly writing about the
desires that Yeats refused to acknowledge until the *Last Poems*.
The sonnet *Lust* begins:

> How should I know? The enormous wheels of will
> Drove me cold-eyed on tired and sleepless feet.

Closely connected with these are the 'jealousy' poems, which
obviously spring out of sexual frustration, and have a disquieting
note of cruelty. *Menelaus and Helen* consists of two sonnets. The

first is conventionally romantic and heroic, describing how Menelaus breaks into Troy, intending to murder Helen, and then is overcome by her beauty. The second is pure anti-climax, describing how they grow old together; Menelaus grows fat and garrulous; Helen becomes 'gummy eyed and impotent'. And in the last line, 'Paris slept on by Scamander side'. This is Brooke's central obsession: youth and death. Is it worth growing old if all life is an anticlimax? *Jealousy*, the nastiest of Brooke's poems, describes how the girl he loves and the man she has married will sink into mediocrity and boredom:

> Then you'll be tired, and passion dead and rotten;
> And he'll be dirty, dirty! . . .

And in the last line:

> Oh, when that time comes, you'll be dirty too!

But the soulful and the fleshly are only two aspects of Brooke's poetic personality. There is another Brooke who enjoys being crudely realistic, as in the poem about sea sickness, or the poem called *Dawn* that begins:

> Opposite me two Germans snore and sweat.

Death continues to obsess him, but sometimes with a touch of humour:

> There was a damned successful poet;
> There was a Woman like the Sun.
> And they were dead. They did not know it.
> They did not know their time was done.
> They did not know his hymns
> Were silence; and her limbs
> That had served Love so well,
> Dust, and a filthy smell.

Brooke is slowly casting off the trappings borrowed from Swinburne and Dowson, and creating a personality of his own. Like Yeats or Gide, he seems determined to be honest with himself at all costs, to express only what he felt, to refuse to counterfeit emotions. It is true that there *are* bad poems, poems that seem to be exercises or experiments, such as *Town and Country*, *Mary and Gabriel* and the two *Choriambics*. But there are relatively few, and they only emphasise Brooke's best quality: the feeling of spontaneity and reality, of language that says precisely what it means, as in Donne's: 'For God's sake hold your tongue and let me love'.

> The damned ship lurched and slithered. Quiet and quick
> My cold gorge rose . . .

Much of Brooke's poetry is an obvious by-product of his attempt to grow up, to cast off his feeling of immaturity. One has a feeling of being involved in his personality. If this was all, then Brooke would undoubtedly be a very minor minor poet. But not all Brooke's poetry flows with this muddy personal quality. He *is* fundamentally a poet, which means that he has the capacity to forget himself. One of the early poems, *Pine Trees and the Sky,* is not a particularly good poem, but it is curiously revealing. He describes lying on the grass and watching 'the sorrow of the evening sky' and meditating gloomily on time and death and women, and brooding on whether it would not be a good idea to commit suicide.

> Then from the sad west turning wearily,
> I saw the pines against the white north sky,
> Very beautiful and still, and bending over
> Their sharp black heads against a quiet sky.
> And there was peace in them; and I
> Was happy, and forgot to play the lover,
> And laughed, and did no longer wish to die;
> Being glad of you, O pine trees and the sky!

This is the fundamental poetic experience; being more-or-less self-absorbed and egoistic, and suddenly awakening to the real existence of the external world. The immature and self-dramatising Rupert Brooke vanishes; the senses open. It is the 'negative capability' that Keats regarded as the fundamental quality of the poet, the opposite of what Heidegger called 'forgetfulness of existence'. It was this quality that Brooke continued to develop until his death, and that is found in his best poems. It is the pure poetic experience, the sudden forgetfulness of personality. Personality is a distorting glass that lies between man's inner reality and the reality of the outside world. In the poet, this distorting medium suddenly vanishes; the inner and the outer world face one another directly, with no distorting glass between them.

This ultimately, is Brooke's claim to be a poet—even if not a major one. It is difficult to say whether he might have become a major poet, just as it is difficult to know whether Keats or Shelley had any further development in front of them when they died. By the time of his death, Brooke had outgrown many immaturities, but many still clung to him, including his obsession with youth. He could have been destroyed by it, just as Scott Fitzgerald was destroyed by his romantic obsession with wealth and beauty. He was also, perhaps, a little too handicapped by the security of his childhood and his public school and university education. And yet his development between the ages of eighteen and twenty-eight seems to demonstrate that he had staying power and a ruthless honesty. His later development might well have paralleled that of Yeats, particularly after the disillusioning experience of the war.

As it is, one has to admit that Brooke's death was perfectly timed, and that in retrospect, all his poetry seems a preparation for that final magnificent funeral on Skyros. (Brooke died of blood poisoning.) One can see why he became such a legend. The early poetry mourns the brevity of life. Then there is the middle period poetry glorifying life and laughter—*Grantchester*, *Drawing Room Tea*, *The Great Lover*. This latter in itself read like an elegy, a kind of hymn to life, enumerating all the things he has loved, from 'white cups and plates, clean gleaming', to

> ... the musty reek that lingers
> about dead leaves and last years ferns ...,

followed by the usual lament that:

> Nor all my passion, all my prayers, have power
> To hold them with me through the gate of Death.

Then came the war, and Brooke's first reaction was delight, the feeling that they could now

> ... turn, as swimmers into cleanness leaping
> Glad from a world grown old and cold and weary.

Louis Macniece selected this particular sonnet for attack, constrasting its 'sentimental' attitude to the war with Wilfred

Owen's realism. But this is to entirely miss the point about Brooke. When he wrote the sonnet, the war was merely a symbol of escape from personality; like the pine trees against the white north sky, it had the effect of shocking him out of the Turkish bath of his immaturity and into objectivity. It is doubtful whether a man as honest as Brooke would have remained an ardent patriot if he had lived throughout the war.

Be that as it may, the final poem, *The Soldier*, catches the essence of Brooke. His best poetry is full of his love of England and the English countryside, so that this sonnet strikes one as totally sincere, and not at all deliberately patriotic. In spite of the 1914 sonnets, Brooke was not a patriot. It simply so happened that the war and his personal need to throw off his immaturity, met in fruitful union. The poem *The Chilterns*, written in 1913, shows the same mechanism at work:

> Your hands, my dear adorable,
> Your lips of tenderness
> —Oh, I've loved you faithfully and well,
> Three years, or a bit less.
> It wasn't a success.
>
> Thank God that's done! and I'll take the road,
> Quit of my youth and you,
> The Roman road to Wendover
> By Tring and Lilly Hoo,
> As a free man may do . . .
>
> White mist about the black hedgerows,
> The slumbering Midland plain,
> The silence where the clover grows,
> And the dead leaves in the lane
> Certainly, these remain.

We can see again the rejection of the personal, the 'Rupert Brooke' evoked by an unhappy love affair, and the sudden sense of freedom and objectivity that comes through nature. According to this poem, Brooke had been involved in the love affair for three years. It is not surprising that he welcomed the war as a crisis that would provide him with an escape from emotional servitude. To accuse him of jingoism or militarism on that account is like accusing the children who rush to watch a house on fire of being arsonists.

All this adds to the difficulty of deciding exactly how good a poet Brooke really is. Any critic who has never had a Brooke phase in his teens is likely to make the fatal error of thinking in terms of the Brooke legend—flaming youth* dying for its country. Brooke's life is so fatally novelistic; even the Marsh *Memoir* reads like a novel—the poet who adores life but is obsessed by death. This means that it is easy to form a clear mental image of Brooke. A writer whose life is full of mysteries—like Shakespeare—tempts the reader to keep returning to the work to try to form a clear picture. A writer who has a sharp public image—Shaw is an example—tends to find himself dismissed for the converse reason: it is easy for the reader to feel that he knows 'all about him' without the trouble of making a thorough acquaintance with the work. This is what has happened to Brooke.

But in Brooke's case, it is even less fair than in Shaw's; for Shaw was partly responsible for his own public image; Brooke wasn't. There is another reason, even more to the point. Brooke died young. Therefore the Brooke we know is not the real Brooke, who would have emerged in maturity. He dramatised himself and his affairs, like all young poets. He decided he was a poet at an early age, and lived the part for all he was worth. This is as it should be. 'The great man is the play actor of his own ideals,' said Nietzsche. One *gives oneself* personality by acting out a certain idea of oneself with consistency. A man who is gifted in self-dramatisation may act out a highly convincing ideal of himself, and if he dies at that point, posterity will always identify the ideal with the reality behind it. This has also happened in the case of Shelley and Keats. But there are other examples of writers who outgrew the youthful self-dramatising stage, and we can then see that the 'reality' is something quite different from the 'ideal' self-image of the youth. If Joyce had died in his early thirties, then Joyce would be forever identified with the Stephen Dedalus of *A Portrait of the Artist as a Young Man* (whose title in itself is a flamboyant gesture of self-dramatisation). Luckily, we know the other Joyce—the mild myopic 'artificer' of *Finnegans Wake*, described by Budgen, Léon and the Colums. Otherwise we would be tempted to think of Joyce as the fiery young rebel of Dublin, unfairly ignored by his contemporaries and determined to outdo them all. It is not that this later Joyce is 'truer'

* The title of a novel about Brooke.

H

than the Stephen Dedalus of *Ulysses* and *The Portrait*; simply that
he rounds out the picture, gives it perspective and depth. Most
of the qualities of youth are accidental and temporary. The Joyce
who emerges from *The Holy Office* and *Gas from a Burner* is a kind
Irish Brecht, witty, aggressive and conceited. Most of these qualities seem to have vanished entirely in the Joyce of the last twenty
years whom we encounter in anecdotes of Hemingway, Morey
Callaghan and the rest, and we can see that they were the outcome
of his early sense of neglect.

Yeats is an even more obvious case, for apart from Brooke, he
was one of the most successful self-dramatisers in modern
literature. From the beginning he is determined to impose his
own idea of himself on the world. The Sargent drawing (printed
in the *Collected Plays*) shows Yeats as he wanted to be seen—the
handsome, hawk-like face, the floppy lock of hair over the left
eye, the eyes gazing dreamily into the distance, the slightly
sensual month, the enormous bow tie. (Yeats was in his forties
at the time, the artist has made him look twenty.) It is a triumph
of self-dramatisation, the poet of *The Shadowy Waters* and *The
Land of Heart's Desire*, the man who agreed with Axel that 'as for
living, our servants can do that for us'. If Yeats had died at
thirty, posterity's image of him would have born a close resemblance to that of Brooke.

There is one matter on which Brooke was more honest and
realistic than the early Yeats, that of sex. A number of the love
poems are idealistic and romantic enough; others admit frankly
to his desire to get the girl into bed. A third group are realistic,
and often highly critical of the beloved, or of his own attitudinis-
ing. *The Voice* begins:

> Safe in the magic of my woods
> I lay, and watched the dying light.
> Faint in the pale high solitudes,
> And washed with rain and veiled by night,
>
> Silver and blue and green were showing.
> And the dark woods grew darker still;
> And birds were hushed; and peace was growing;
> And quietness crept up the hill
> And no wind was blowing....

> And I knew
> That this was the hour of knowing,
> And the night and the woods and you
> Were one together, and I should find
> Soon in the silence the hidden key
> Of all that had hurt and puzzled me—
> Why you were you, and the night was kind,
> And the woods were part of the heart of me.

At this point, the revery is broken by:

> The noise of a fool in mock distress,
> Crashing and laughing and blindly going,
> Of ignorant feet and a swishing dress,
> And a voice profaning the solitudes.

> The spell was broken, the key denied me,
> And at length your flat clear voice beside me
> Mouthed cheerful clear flat platitudes.

> You came and quacked beside me in the wood.
> You said, 'The view from here is very good!'
> You said, 'It's nice to be alone a bit' . . .

Once again, the 'peak experience' involves alienation from those he normally loves. But in any case, Brooke is always trying to withdraw from his romanticism to criticise it.

There is always a quality of healthy self-mockery:

> I dreamt I was in love again
> With the One Before the Last,
> And smiled to greet the pleasant pain
> Of that innocent young past.

> But I jumped to feel how sharp had been
> The pain when it did live,
> How the faded dreams of Nineteen-ten
> Were Hell in Nineteen-five.

One feels that the part of Brooke that would have been outgrown was the mystique about people and friendship, Marsh mentions that he often quoted Belloc's lines:

> From quiet homes and first beginning,
> Out to the undiscovered ends,
> There's nothing worth the wear of winning,
> But laughter and the love of friends.

It is an admirable sentiment, but only partly true. Again, Brooke was fortunate. People liked him and took trouble to cultivate his acquaintance. When in America, he wrote a letter to Marsh in which he claims to have written a poem with the chorus:

> Would God I were eating plovers' eggs
> And drinking dry champagne,
> With the Bernard Shaws, Mr and Mrs Masefield, Lady Horner, Neil Primrose, Raleigh, the Right Honourable Augustine Birrell, Eddie, six or seven Asquiths, and Felicity Tree,
> In Downing Street again

The list of his friends may suggest a certain snobbery, but it also demonstrates that a great many people of completely different types found Brooke charming. Henry James knew him only slightly, yet his introduction to Brooke's *Letters from America* (published after Brooke's death and only shortly before James's) shows how powerful had been the impact of Brooke's vital personality. The grief is genuine.

Brooke's most important quality—which hardly appears in the poetry—is the sense of humour. In the letters, it is continual, unforced and delightful—obviously the result of a sheer overflow of vitality not in any way a conscious attempt to be funny. He writes from Cambridge:

'The room I have opens straight on to a stone verandah covered with creepers, and a little old garden full of old fashioned flowers. . . . Every now and then dull spectacled people from Cambridge come out and take tea here. I mock them and pour cream down their necks or roll them in the rose-beds or push them in the river, and they hate me and go away.'

Here one gets the feeling that when he wrote the sentence about dull spectacled people coming to tea, he had no idea of what the next sentence would be; it is an explosion of exuberant nonsense, as in Mozart's letters to his cousin Maria.

On reading the Hassall biography, it is difficult not to feel that Brooke lacked the isolation necessary to produce great work.

In some ways, fate was too kind to him. Yeats suggests in his autobiographies that the fates 'have but one purpose, to bring their chosen man to the greatest possible obstacle he may confront without despair'. Whether or not one accepts the idea of 'fates', one can see what Yeats meant: that great work is usually produced by the challenge-and-response mechanism, by problems to be overcome. Nietzsche and Rupert Brooke may have possessed much the same degree of natural talent, but Nietzsche's hard and lonely life produced great work and great thought. Whether Brooke would have been strong enough to face real challenges can never be known. Towards the end of his life, he was beginning to outgrow the 'young poet' persona; one can sense the shadows of disillusionment in the letters he wrote from the South Seas:

'Oh, it's horribly true, what you wrote, that one only finds in the South Seas what one brings there. Perhaps I could have found Romance if I'd brought it. . . .'

The values of Brooke's youth were too much mixed up with upper-class comfort and admiring friends and pleasant summer days on the river. Inevitably, as he grew older, he found himself in the same position as a woman who attaches too much importance to her beauty. Time gnaws holes in the old values; it is necessary to look around for a replacement. In Brooke's case, the problem was complicated by the fact that he saw himself solely as a poet, and the poetry he wrote up to his death was entirely concerned with these values. Most of his poetry is about the feelings of youth: about girls, and unrequited love, and the open road and the tragedy of death. One might almost say that Brooke specialised in being a poet of youth. The poems have the intimacy of a diary; every one of them is about a feeling connected with growing up. This is also why they are so memorable. One does not have to be young to enjoy them, any more than one needs to be homosexual and obsessed by death to enjoy *A Shropshire Lad*. But this means that Brooke was bound to lose his fundamental subject as he got older. And a poet who loses his subject either has to find another, or cease to be a poet. Yeats almost dried up between the age of thirty-nine (when he published *In the Seven Woods*) and forty-five (when his next volume appeared).

It is difficult to imagine what Brooke would have done if he had survived the war. In the last year of his life, he had spent

much time dining at the Admiralty with Edward Marsh and
Winston Churchill, or being nursed through a cold at 10 Downing
Street. Churchill would have offered him a well paid government
job, as he offered one to T. E. Lawrence after the war. And
Brooke, if he had had any sense, would have refused. But he
was gregarious and would have found it difficult to refuse
invitations to dinner from titled friends. He would have been in
his mid-thirties by this time, in an age dominated by Eliot, Joyce
and Pound, where the 'modernism' of his early poems would
have been regarded as out of date. On the whole, it looks as if he
may have chosen the most sensible course in dying of blood
poisoning. (He was ill an increasing number of times towards the
end of his life.) The poems of 1914—*Tiare Tahiti* and *The Great
Lover*—are still as uncompromisingly elegaic as the music of Delius;
there is no sign of Brooke finding a new subject, until the war
produced a burst of elation at this call to throw off the old
personality and 'all the little emptiness of love'.

It seems to be an ironical commentary that the last lines of
Tiare Tahiti:

> Well this side of Paradise!
> There's little comfort in the wise,

provided Scott Fitzgerald with the title of his first novel, another
glorification of 'flaming youth', and that Fitzgerald found the
problem as insoluble as Brooke, and ended as an alcoholic.

It may be that I have overemphasised the 'golden youth' aspect
of Brooke. This is certainly in accordance with the image he
himself tried to create—as well as of Frances Cornford's epigram
about the 'young Apollo'; but it is a long way from the truth.
Brooke was rather late in coming to sexual maturity, and he seems
to have remained sexually frustrated to the end. The kind of girls
he knew were well brought up young ladies who might discuss
free love around a camp fire, but who then retired to their tents
with two or three other well brought up virgins. Brooke, in spite
of his good looks and charm, had nothing of the seducer about
him. The girl to whom most of the love poems are addressed was
Katherine ('Ka') Cox, who began by treating Brooke with a
motherly sort of affection, without returning his feelings. There
came a point at which she became infatuated with the painter Henry
Lamb, and made it plain to everybody. Brooke was convulsed

with jealousy, and had a nervous breakdown. (The Henry Lamb episode is described in Michael Holroyd's biography of Lytton Strachey.) Later still, she decided that she *was* in love with Brooke, but by that time he had either lost interest, or wanted to revenge himself on her; nothing came of it. It was after the breakdown that his health began to decline. He talked of suicide, and thought he was going mad. The full story has never been told, and may never be told.* All that is certain is that in the last years of his life, Brooke hit an emotional low-water mark, from which he had not fully recovered at the time of his death.

All this explains why Brooke found the war an emotional relief from 'all the little emptiness of love'.

A major part of Brooke's problem, then, was late maturity and the consequent sexual frustration. A few centuries earlier, he would have seduced his first girl at fourteen and written his first sequence of love sonnets at eighteen. Some of the intensity of the poems comes from their turbulence, the attempt to come to terms with his romantic obsession with the Candida figure of Ka Cox. They are poems of immaturity, and the attempt to discipline himself beyond immaturity. It follows that if Brooke's emotional—and physical—experience of women had been different, he would have been a different kind of poet. The importance of early sexual frustration in the life of a sensitive person can hardly be overestimated. It can produce a permanently soured outlook. Early conquests tend to engender a basic self-confidence that is bound to play an important part in one's general outlook. It is perhaps not too far fetched to ascribe Shaw's basic optimism to the fact that sexual conquest always came easily to him. D. H. Lawrence's development certainly owed much to the love affair with Freda at the age of twenty-five. The 'feminine element' is important to all poets, as important as water to a plant. (At least, it is difficult to think of any important poet for whom this

---

* Michael Hastings' pictorial biography of Brooke, *The Handsomest Young Man in England* (1967) originally contained a facsimile of a letter in which Brooke comments bitterly that all Ka Cox needs is someone to fuck her twice a night. This had to be removed from the printed version, at the insistence of Brooke's executors. Hastings told the present writer that the unpublished Brooke documents revealed that he had homosexual leanings, as well as a tendency to anti-semitism. It will obviously be impossible to form a complete, all-round picture of Brooke until a biographer can study the Brooke archives in full.

is untrue.) If Brooke had survived the war, his sexual experience would have been different; like Shaw, he would have found conquest easy. Sooner or later, he would certainly have married and produced children, and entered another range of emotional experience. One is aware of all this in reading his poetry; that it is essentially incomplete, distorted.

Yet although there is some truth in this, it hardly matters. In a sense, if a man is a major writer, he is a major writer from the moment he is born, whether he ever fulfils his promise or not. It is a matter of his natural genius and his attitude towards life. In this sense, Brooke is a major writer. He possessed that degree of vitality and intense curiosity about life that is called genius. When every possible criticism has been made, this remains. Brooke's genius was a natural endowment, like Nijinsky's ability to arch his foot like a bird's. It was a natural way of seeing things. He describes it in a letter to Ben Keeling:

'Do not leap or turn pale at the word Mysticism, I do not mean any religious thing or any form of belief. I still burn and torture Christians daily. . . .

'It consists just in looking at people and things as themselves—neither as useful nor moral nor ugly nor anything else; but just as being. At least, that is a philosophical description of it. What happens is that I suddenly feel the extraordinary value and importance of everybody I meet, and almost everything I see. In *things* I am moved in this way, especially by some things; but in people by almost all people. That is, when the mood is on me. I roam about places—yesterday I did it even in Birmingham!—and I sit in trains and see the essential glory and beauty of all the people I meet. I can watch a dirty middle-aged tradesman in a railway-carriage for hours, and love every dirty greasy sulky wrinkle in his weak chin and every button on his spotted unclean waistcoat. I know their states of mind are bad. But I'm so much occupied with their being there at all, that I don't have time to think of it. I tell you that a Birmingham gouty Tariff Reform fifth rate business-man is splendid and immortal and desirable.

'It's the same about the things of ordinary life. Half an hour's roaming about a street or village or railway-station shows so much beauty that it's impossible to be anything but wild with suppressed exhilaration. And it's not only beauty and beautiful things. In a flicker of sunlight on a blank wall, or a reach of muddy pavement, or smoke from an engine at night, there's a sudden significance and importance and inspiration that makes the breath stop with a gulp of certainty and happiness. It's not that the wall or the smoke seem important for anything or suddenly reveal any general statement, or are suddenly seen to be good or beautiful in themselves—only that *for you* they're perfect and unique. It's like being in love with a person. . . . I suppose my occupation is being in love with the universe.'

This kind of faculty is not acquired. Blake and Wordsworth and Whitman had it, and they were born with it. There may even be a physical explanation for it; according to Aldous Huxley, starvation of sugar to the brain can produce visionary states. Professor Abraham Maslow would say simply that Brooke was subject to 'peak experiences', and that peak experiences come most frequently to people who are naturally healthy and optimistic. Brooke's early life was pleasant and without frustrations, so that his basic outlook was naturally optimistic. The early nature poems are a series of 'peak experiences' modified by a teenager's natural *weltschmerz*. The rather difficult emotional experiences with Ka Cox lowered Brooke's natural vitality, with the result that the last three years of his life were relatively sterile and unproductive (although he wrote, among other things, two plays). Because his vitality was so high, and his basic outlook so unneurotic, there seems to be no reason to doubt that he would have continued to develop—either as a poet or as a playwright—after the war.

Brooke, then, is not a great poet; but he is a real one. That this statement has to be made at all is a sign of the unhealthy influence exercised on English criticism by Eliot, and later by Leavis. Eliot performed the great service of 'Europeanising' English criticism, of making it aware of a 'tradition' that stretches back through Baudelaire, Dante and St Augustine. His criterion was semi-theological, so that any poet without a Christian preoccupation tended to get dismissed. Coleridge and Donne were 'in', Byron, Shelley and Swinburne were hardly worth the trouble of dismissing.

The Eliot attitude was a reaction against a reaction. Romanticism was actually a part of the great scientific reaction against the Church and its narrow authoritarianism; considering the size and strength of its adversary, it was inevitable that it should go too far and dismiss the whole idea of religion as superstition. (Even so, Shelley had outgrown his atheism by the time he died recognising that all poets are basically religious—religion being the feeling that life has a meaning that goes beyond its banalities.) The neo-religious movement—whose figures include Newman and T. E. Hulme—was equally incensed by the pessimistic materialism that it identified with romanticism, as well as by its verbal imprecision and general lack of intellectual discipline. Neither side was fair to the other; in both cases, the violence of the rejection indicated a certain innate sympathy with that which was being rejected. Eliot's attack on Shelley and Swinburne tells us something about Eliot, but nothing about Shelley or Swinburne. We know that Shelley was subject to self-deception, particularly in matters of sex; we know that Swinburne was as immature at sixty as he was at sixteen, and that he cared more for sound than sense. We know that the militant atheists of the 19th century swallowed both poets lock, stock and barrel, and tended to regard them as saint and martyrs of free-thought. All this leaves the central question untouched: did Shelley and Swinburne really possess genius? To *what extent* were they great poets? Apart from their negative qualities, what had they to contribute that was unique? If you are judging an egg and spoon race, you do not disqualify the winner on the grounds that he is a poor swimmer. But Eliot was always doing something of the sort in judging poets who failed to live up to his religious views.

Eliot was by no means entirely wrong. It *does* matter, in judging Swinburne's poetry, that he remained a permanent adolescent who referred to De Sade as 'the Master'. Nor is it irrelevant in judging Shelley's poetry that he treated his first wife with unconscious sadism. What is wrong with Eliot's attitude is that he allows his moral judgements to blind his critical faculty. The kind of intensity and passion that Shelley and Swinburne brought to poetry is too rare to be dismissed on moral grounds; it occurs only half a dozen times in a century. It is the basic quality of a poet, the rarest and most desirable quality.

The poet is a man who naturally and instinctively rejects the banality of everyday existence. In the early stages of his development, he probably has no more idea of what is happening to him than a caterpillar has when it changes into a butterfly. He may rationalise this inner conflict in a number of ways. The Manichees rationalised it by believing that matter was created by the devil, and 'spirit' by God. Rousseau—a stage more subtle—blamed all evil on society. Shelley was inclined to accept this view. Swinburne was more or less a Manichee, who believed that God—if he existed—was evil (a view he borrowed from Sade). Whitman and D. H. Lawrence were anti-Manichees, glorifying the world of matter and suspicious of the human ego and its tendency to rationalise.

Brooke, on the whole, followed Whitman. Life had treated him too well for him to distrust matter. But, like anyone who lays great stress on the natural 'gifts' of the world, he was haunted by a sense of its impermanence. Followed out to its natural conclusion, his attitude would have resulted in Buddhism. The other alternative is a kind of mystical humanism, a sense of the brotherhood of men and 'the eternal reciprocity of tears' that one finds in Wilfred Owen's later poetry. (This seems a more likely possibility when one considers that Owen's early poetry has much in common with Brooke's, with the same tendency to pantheism and Keatsian sensuality.) The only thing that is certain is that there *would* have been a development. Brooke had too much vitality to stagnate or capitulate to mediocrity.

In the first *Duino Elegy*, Rilke suggests that lovers who died young are a symbol of that 'other world' of insight and intensity. The Hero symbol, he says, is a symbol of conquest of this world. But a symbol that continues loses some of its intensity; and lovers who died young are in some ways a more effective symbol of intensity, of the revolt against banality, because their existence is curtailed. One might add that the young poet has the same kind of self-completeness as a symbol. In this sense, Brooke *is* a symbol —not of patriotic youth dying for its country, but of everything that is meant by the word 'poet'. The incompleteness of his work is not important; the symbol is complete in what we possess. In the same way, the symbol is complete in the early poetry of Hofmannsthal or Rimbaud, who both ceased to write poetry at a relatively early stage and developed in other directions. It is no objection to their poetry to say that it is immature. Neither is it any objection to Brooke's poetry to point out that it is less technically accomplished than that of Hofmannsthal or Rimbaud. Brooke is an Englishman, and the English have never cared particularly for style.

The point I am ultimately trying to make is that we are limiting our minds if we dismiss Brooke as Eliot dismissed Shelley. It is permissible to dismiss a writer whom one has outgrown in every sense, as a schoolboy outgrows Billy Bunter or Henty. But when Eliot dismissed Shelley, he was dismissing a man who possessed certain important qualities that Eliot himself did not possess, and, worse still, did not even recognise that he lacked. Shelley should only be dismissed by someone who possesses the same degree of vitality, idealism and vision—and such a person would not dismiss him. The qualities that make a poet are rare, and ultimately 'undismissable'. Even if one outgrows the poetry—that is, one ceases to read it for pleasure—the poet himself remains a symbol of the most important thing about human existence, an evolutionary aspiration. In this battle there are only two sides, and unless you are suicidal or hopelessly confused, you do not shoot your own men in the back.

2
W. B. Yeats

There is an interesting book about Wordsworth called *Words-worth's Anti-climax*** that attempts to analyse the reasons for his poetic decline. I have often thought that it would be an interesting idea to devote a series of studies of writers to the same theme: *Swinburne's Anticlimax, Browning's Anticlimax, Hemingway's Anti-climax, Aldous Huxley's Anticlimax*. It is true that in the case of prose writers, the decline may be less obvious—at least, less jarring—than in the case of a poet. It could be argued that Joyce's *Finnegans Wake*, Mann's Joseph novels, the historical extrava-ganzas of John Cowper Powys (to take three writers who seem to me of comparable stature) are creative aberrations that would never have been accepted from writers without an established reputation; but prose can afford to spread its effects thin, because it can have so many purposes: from political speeches to Church ritual, from guide-books to works of philosophy. Poetry, like music, is a special medium, an artificial medium, and we judge it by a more rigid standard of rules.

The problem of creative decline is interesting because it implies its opposite: the notion that an artist, like a great scientist or mathematician, might continue to produce original and valuable work to the end of his life, might perhaps even reserve his greatest contributions for the last. It is easy enough to understand Rupert Brooke's obsession with youth when one contemplates Words-worth or Swinburne. In retrospect we can see that Browning was being over-optimistic when he said: 'Grow old along with me/ The best is yet to be'. One might even go so far as to say that if the work of most 19th-century poets was divided into two halves, and the second half thrown away, the loss to literature would be slight.

* By Willard L. Sperry, Russell and Russell, New York, 1966.

The cases of creative longevity become an absorbing study, because there are so few of them. Mention Goethe, Beethoven, perhaps Hugo and Ibsen, and the list for the 19th century is almost complete. And in the 20th century, it is even more rare. Among musicians, it is difficult to decide, because atonal techniques may disguise a fundamental lack of development. Among poets, only Rilke and Yeats qualify unmistakably. Everyone who has written about Yeats has pointed out this ability to continue developing. What interests me far more is the curious, erratic manner of the development, and the contradictions that remain at the core of even the most mature work.

The first book about Yeats I ever read was by Louis Macniece, and I was struck by his insistence that the early poems are relatively worthless, and that only the later ones entitle him to be regarded as a great poet. At sixteen, it seemed self-evident to me that the early poems have a unity of poetic mood, and establish as distinct a poetic personality as any of the *fin de siècle* period, while the later poems reveal the evaporation of the poetic 'mood'.

The view is worth considering, I think, as a counterbalance to the usual one. We must return to the fundamental question: What is poetry? It is a *contradiction* of the everyday life-world: that is its nature. I am born into an environment that moulds me and that tells me who I am and what is expected of me. I may be lucky, like Rupert Brooke, or Victor Hugo, or Wolf's favourite poet Mörike, and find myself in a sympathetic environment. But it is statistically more probable that I shall find myself in the provinces, or the suburbs of London or Glasgow or Swansea. In the long run, it does not make all that much difference; I face the same problem: of developing a personality and set of ideals, and then setting them up in opposition to my environment. I do not say 'imposing them on my environment', because this may not happen. My environment may remain unaware of my existence. But I project an image of myself which is more consonant with the fulfilment of my needs than the 'I' who responds when a parent or schoolteacher calls me by my name. Yeats admitted (in a B.B.C. talk): 'Some people say I have an affected manner, and if that is true, as it may well be, it is because my father took me, when I was ten or eleven, to Irving's famous "Hamlet". Years afterwards I walked the Dublin streets when nobody was looking, or nobody that I knew, with that strut Gordon Craig has compared to a movement in a dance, and made the characters I created speak with his brooding broken wildness.' Yeats is a typical poet of the industrial age; he has to impose his imaginative self-image on sordid streets and down-to-earth people. 'Another day, a woman asked me to direct her on her way and while I was hesitating, being so suddenly called out of my thought, a woman from some neighbouring house came by. She said I was a poet, and my questioner turned away contemptuously. On the other hand, the policeman and tramway conductor thought my absence of mind sufficiently explained when our servant told them I was a poet. "Oh well," said the policeman, who had been asking why I went indifferently through clean and muddy places, "if it is only the poetry that is working in his head!"' Sometimes the act convinced; sometimes it didn't. Wordsworth could climb the hills and look down on the Lakes, or borrow a boat to take a moonlight row—as he describes in the *Prelude*. Shelley was adored by female cousins, to whom he told stories of enchanters; and before he was out of his teens, had eloped with a girl with a peaches-and-cream complexion, whom he subsequently deserted. Yeats also fell in love with a pretty girl, but she only made him the confident of her quarrels with her lover; and if he lost sleep, it was not because of daydreams about how nice it would be to have her in his bed, but 'through anger with her betrothed'. The later love affair with Maud Gonne was equally abortive, and he is too tactful to say whether his affair with Florence Farr—who had been Shaw's mistress—ever reached physical consummation. What was there to do, then, but to project a self-image with 'cloud-pale eyelids, dream-dimmed eyes', the noble young poet walking through the mortar-and-brick wilderness of London, dreaming of some John the Baptist who might cry out and empty these houses of their down-to-earth inhabitants? (It was the same image that drove T. E. Lawrence among the Arabs.)

The poet, I have argued, is the man who is subject to sudden 'peak experiences' when 'everything we look upon is blessed'; and I have cited Yeats's own experience in the 'crowded London shop'. In these moments, the sheer 'interestingness' of the world, its magic, its richness, becomes self-evident. But because the young poet is sensitive and unsure of himself, he is inclined to 'identify' with other people; his fan turns in sympathy to theirs. How, then, does he reconcile these two moods, these states of mind? When he is tired and depressed, he looks at the world through the eyes of a tram conductor and asks: 'Is it magic? Of course not. It's the Old Brompton Road. . . .' How does one reconcile the peak experience with everyday awareness, without betraying the experience and writing it off as some kind of illusion, a flash of mere physical well being? William Blake, faced with the same problem, asserted that there are two worlds: this world of everyday reality, of trams and butchers' shops, and the ideal or symbolic world hinted at in all myths and romances. And in a paradoxical sense, the symbolic world is more real than the everyday world. No, not even in a paradoxical sense; for we know that trams and butchers' shops pass away, and forests and stars remain. The forests and stars are therefore more real than the Old Brompton Road, even if our lying senses refuse to agree.

What is the truth about the contradiction of the 'two worlds'? Obviously, there are not two. What I am speaking of are two modes of apprehension of the real world, two states of consciousness. If I am ill—let us say, in a slight fever—my consciousness is hardly more than a mirror reflecting my environment, seeing things blankly, without attaching meanings to them. I confuse illusion and reality; dreams seem real, and reality seems a dream. What does this mean? It means that my consciousness and my 'awareness' are two different things. I am conscious of this room. If I am reading a great novel, I am *aware* of its characters and events, not conscious of them in the sense that I am of this room. But normally, these two modes of consciousness work in double harness. I look at that tree with the rain dripping from its branches, and it seems to evoke a poetic mood. Why? Because my actual physical perception of the tree—which would be *merely* a tree in a fevered state—blends naturally with poetic images of trees, of dim Sunday afternoons as a child with rain beating on the windows. . . . My *inner* awareness is supplying the meanings, the 'relations'; my perception only supplies me with a photograph of the tree. And the more deeply this inner world is stirred, the more my will relaxes its practical drive and allows me to sink towards the bosom of my subconscious, the more richly meaningful and magical will this perceived world be. *There*, then, are Blake's two worlds. This is why certain drugs can enrich perception: they arrest my will and disturb the habitual relation between perceptual consciousness and 'awareness'. When I say 'That tree in the rain is beautiful', what do I mean? I mean not only that the rain stirs memories of childhood and makes me aware that I am in a comfortable, dry room. There is far more. I *reach out* for it eagerly, expectantly, happily, as a child reaches out for its pillowcase full of toys on Christmas morning. If it were not raining, I might glance at the tree, and there would be a half-formed thought: 'That is merely a tree'. That act of reaching out, as impulsive as a child flinging its arms around an uncle's neck or a girl running to her lover, is as much an 'act' as jumping to my feet when I sit on a pin. When I sit on a pin, I am not aware of saying: 'This is painful—I must get up quickly'. Perception and activity are associated so closely that I am unaware of the gap. If I am in a fevered state of delirium, it may take me a second or so to notice: 'I experience a pain—I ought to get up'.

In short, the difference between 'poetic perception' and 'ordinary perception' is a difference of chosen impulse, so to speak. I reach out for the tree as I might reach out for a sandwich when I am hungry. The act is as intentional—purposeful—as a boxer hitting a punching bag. And just as a boxer strengthens his arm by hitting the punching bag often enough, so I may strengthen the muscle of intentionality by making it punch out at the tree when I have no particular reason to do so. If I now merely narrow my eyes and concentrate hard on the tree, it becomes for a second *more real*, and a spark of delight shoots up inside me.

Young people tend to be passive; they hope for something interesting to turn up. On a dull day, they yawn, and the eyes grow dull: another way of saying that the muscle of intentionality is not being used. Inevitably, it gets weaker.

A Martian would find it very odd that human beings are not aware of the simple mechanisms of perception, that they think of consciousness as a mirror reflecting reality. However, once he had this key to human behaviour, he would understand Blake and Yeats. If one fails to recognise the simple intentionality of perception, then how does one reconcile the two states of mind— boredom and intensity? *By blaming the world:*

> I wander through each dirty street
> Near where the dirty Thames does flow

> And see on every face I meet
> Marks of weakness, marks of woe.

And Yeats tells how a friend of his father's quoted Ruskin as
saying: 'As I go to my work at the British Museum, I see the
faces of the people become daily more corrupt.' Yeats quickly
convinced himself that it was true.

One begins by finding scapegoats:

> The world is too much with us; late and soon,
> Getting and spending, we lay waste our powers.

Or:

> The wrong of unshapely things is a wrong too great to be told;
>
> I hunger to build them anew, and sit on a green knoll apart.

Why? Because:

> All things uncomely and broken, all things worn out and
> old, ...
> Are wronging your image that blossoms a rose in the deeps of
> my heart.

What is being created is an alter-ego in opposition to 'the
world'—in defiance of the world. Yeats was later frank, in poetry
and in the autobiographical writings, about early humiliations,
about gaucheness and inadequacy. 'I began to make blunders
when I paid calls or visits, and a woman I had known and liked as
a child told me I had changed for the worse'; and he speaks in a
poem of 'the unfinished man and his pain/Brought face to face
with his own clumsiness'. He seethes with ideas and convictions;
and, as often as not, they lead him to make a fool of himself. In
retrospect, most of these incidents sounds funny, since they
reveal a Quixote-ish failure to make contact with reality. Left
alone for a moment with the historian Bury, Yeats declares
without preamble: 'I know you will defend the ordinary system
of education by saying that it strengthens the will, but I am
convinced that it only seems to do so because it weakens the
impulses.' Bury 'smiled and looked embarrassed, but said nothing'. On another occasion, 'I had said to the photographer when
he was arranging his piece of iron shaped like a horse-shoe to
keep my head in position: "Because you have only white and black

paper instead of light and shadow you cannot represent Nature. An artist can, because he employs a kind of symbolism." To my surprise, instead of showing indignation at my attack upon his trade, he replied: "A photograph is mechanical."' 'At seventeen years old I was already an old-fashioned brass cannon full of shot, and nothing kept me from going off but a doubt as to my capacity to shoot straight.' 'Once when I was in Dowden's drawing-room a servant announced my late headmaster. I must have gone pale or red, for Dowden with some ironical, friendly remark brought me into another room and there I stayed until the visitor was gone. A few months later, when I met the headmaster again, I had more courage. We chanced upon one another in the street and he said, "I want you to use your influence with So-and-so, for he is giving all his time to some sort of mysticism and he will fail in his exam- ination." I was in great alarm, but I managed to say something about the children of this world being wiser than the children of light. He went off with a brusque "Good morning".' And Yeats, no doubt, brooded on the incident for days afterwards and thought of the things he should have said.

All sensitive people experience these embarrassments. The important question is how they deal with them. Shaw waited until his mid-forties—when they were safely behind him—and then made the idealist's failure to communicate the subject of his best comedy, *Man and Superman*. Aldous Huxley was perhaps the first English writer to make satirical comedy of these youthful agonies of shyness and effrontery. But this method also involves a form of self-betrayal, since the self that is mocked is also dis- owned. (The English public school system of character training, based upon the notion that self-assertion is 'bad form', tends to favour the development of the satirical method.)

Detachment is one way of escaping the immature self. Equally effective is the method of involvement. Man is most aware of his shortcomings when he is surrounded by the trivial, and least aware when he is totally involved in a physical or emotional situation, Shaw chose the method of involvement when he be- came a socialist and spoke on street corners. Straightforward conviction involves the possibility of straightforward action. Emotional involvement is a more complex matter. Only the contemplation of tragedy or crisis can produce the same simple unity of emotion that is created by violent action. 'We begin to

live when we have conceived life as tragedy,' writes Yeats in
Four Years. If all human beings are involved in the same tragic
situation, then the difference between a self-conscious youth of
seventeen and a self-possessed man of seventy is unimportant. If
anything, the youth of seventeen is better off because he is further
from death.

Now intellectually speaking, pessimism is as valid as optimism.
And emotionally speaking, the 'tragic sense of life' pays richer
dividends than its opposite simply because its opposite is *not*
optimism or the sense of purpose, but mere casual acceptance of
the 'triviality of everydayness'. When life is well organised and
well protected, tragedy becomes synonymous with seriousness
and the sense of purpose.

Yeats, like Shaw, tried socialism—William Morris's idealistic
brand—but his temperament was less suited to it than Shaw's.
'I was unlike others of my generation in one thing. I am very
religious, and deprived by Huxley and Tyndal, whom I detested,
of the simple-minded religion of my childhood, I had made a new
religion, almost an infallible church of poetic tradition. . . .'
At William Morris's, Yeats used to engage in arguments with a
young workman whose ideas on religion were 'pure Karl Marx'.
'Then gradually the attitude towards religion of almost everybody but Morris, who avoided the subject altogether, got upon
my nerves, for I broke out after some lecture or other with all the
arrogance of raging youth. They attacked religion, I said, or some
such words, and yet there must be a change of heart, and only
religion could make it. . . .' This was the beginning of Yeat's
break with socialism. The way of social involvement was closed
to him for the time being. The creation of the poetic alter-ego
became his chief concern. It had to be tragic, this poetic *weltanschauung*, permeated with a sense of the brevity of life, the frail-
ness of beauty, the inevitability of frustration and defeat. The
beginning of the poem that opens his first published volume of
poems states the problem:

> The woods of Arcady are dead,
> And over is their antique joy;
> Of old the world on dreaming fed;
> Grey truth is now her painted toy.

One's first inclination is to criticise both the manner and the

matter. The woods of Arcady never existed except in the imagination of the pre-Raphaelites. There was never a time when the
world fed on dreaming—certainly not the Middle Ages. One
wonders how truth can be 'grey' and 'painted' at the same time.
Still, these are quibbles. The meaning is clear enough:

> But O, sick children of the world,
> Of all the many changing things
> In dreary dancing past us whirled,
> To the cracked tune that Chronos sings,
> Words alone are certain good.

That is to say, words that conjure up the Arcady of the pre-
Raphaelites, that hang an embroidered curtain over the bare,
unsightly walls of reality. And having announced his poetic
principle, Yeats proceeds to practice it in the rest of the volume.
The aim is to evoke an autumnal mood of beauty mingled with
fatigue, sadness, desolation. One of his favourite words is 'sorrow'.

> There was a man whom Sorrow named his friend,
> And he of his high comrade Sorrow dreaming,
> Went walking with slow steps along the gleaming
> And humming sands; where windy surges wend

Or:

> 'What do you make so fair and bright?'
> 'I make the cloak of Sorrow:
> O lovely to see in all men's sight
> Shall be the cloak of Sorrow,
> In all men's sight'

The verbal imprecision irritates: 'where windy surges *wend*'?
Yeats is not really concerned with words but with music, with
incantation. This 'sorrow' is not the real emotion, felt by human
beings who have lost someone they love, but a vague, rather pleasant mood associated with falling leaves and the sound of the sea.
It is akin to that of Delius's music, except that certain images take
the place of chords: flickering stars, slumbering trout, whispering
leaves, murmuring waves. One of the favourite themes is of
practical men turning away from action to become dreamers.
Love is always tragic—or at least, 'sorrowful'; either the lover
has been deserted, or his beloved has died, or the lovers simply

fall out of love. In the latter case, there are no recriminations; they wander through the autumn leaves and talk about the brevity of passion.

The interesting thing about Yeats's first three volumes is that, like the music of Delius, the poetry is completely successful *within its own terms*. In order to criticise it, one must stand outside it and say 'This is shallow', 'This is unrealistic'. In speaking of this period, Yeats talks about 'my immense self-confidence'* and, in fact, the foundation of the poetry is a clear self-image. He is not, like Morris, the 'idle singer of an empty day'. He takes his role far more seriously, and sees himself as something closer to Coleridge's visionary of *Kubla Khan*:

> Weave a circle round him thrice
> And close your eyes with holy dread. . . .

The poet is a privileged being, magician, who has the power to confer a kind of immortality on his beloved. In these poems, he never for a moment admits that the beloved might reject him. If a 'beautiful friend' goes weeping away, it is because:

> She looked in my heart one day
> And saw your image was there. . . .

He is immune from the ordinary disappointments of love because, like Childe Harold, he is steeped in the wisdom of sorrow and of experience. Yet there is also a cult of youth—as in Brooke:

> And the young lie long and dream in their bed
> Of the matching of ribbons for bosom and head . . .
> While I must work because I am old,
> And the seed of the fire gets feeble and cold.

The old belong to the world of ugliness: 'all things uncomely and broken, all things worn out and old'. He seems to feel they are to blame for being old as the stupid are to blame for being stupid.

But it is easy to place too much emphasis on this negative aspect of the early Yeats. It is more constructive to try to grasp the logic of his position. He takes it absolutely for granted that all sensitive persons must agree that the world is a detestable place. It seems

* B.B.C. talk, *I Became an Author* (1938). Included in *Selected Prose*.

so obvious that he cannot imagine how anyone could disagree unless he is one of 'them', the stupid and insensitive (hence his failure to appreciate Shaw). He seems to see the world divided into two warring factions, like Milton's heaven and hell, except that 'the children of light' are outnumbered. When he walks from his home to the British Museum, he is passing through enemy territory. He is in a world of cracked pavements and potential violence. A night watchman hawks phlegm into his throat and spits it into the gutter; a cockney woman argues shrilly with the next door neighbour. But this world is not even Hogarthian: Hogarth is an *artist* of the sordid, and this world is in no way artistic; it is too full of irrelevant detail. It is a world of chance and contingency that is unaware of the poet's existence. He feels beleaguered, outnumbered. The circumstances demand an extreme attitude; 'if you are not with me, you are against me'. (He later idealises his Sligo relatives, merchants and sailors; but in the early days he probably included them among the enemy.) He admires the poets of that 'tragic generation' who preferred to drink themselves to death—Lionel Johnson, James Thomson, Ernest Dowson, even Oscar Wilde—because their choice seems so logical. How can a sensitive man bear this nauseating world? He sympathises with Poe's Dupin who spends all day indoors with the curtains drawn and walks out only at night, and Huysmans Des Esseintes, who is rich enough to create a small island in the chaos and live entirely for a world of imagination and sensations. Yeats himself creates a character called Michael Robartes who lives in a room hung with black velvet. Yeats is too poor to do this; but he sets out to create his own mental world of anti-matter, a 'land of heart's desire' where the 'little people' play tricks on farmers and steal children.

The audience who laughed at *The Land of Heart's Desire* when it was first performed at the Avenue Theatre, Charing Cross, saw it as a piece of whimsical fantasy without even the charm of humour. The modern reader may feel the same. For Yeats, such an attitude would represent the worst kind of stupidity. The land of the fairies may not, strictly speaking, exist, but it is the symbol of something absolutely *real*. The world of the poets—particularly the romantic poets—is an attempt to symbolise a reality that has its own self-sustaining existence. As soon as the poet turns away from the everyday world to the work of the great poets, he can *see* this other world of beauty, meaning, 'luxe, calme et volupté' as clearly as if it were a mountain ten miles away.

So when Yeats creates his world of fairies and autumn sunsets and dripping trees, he does not feel that he is trying to escape 'reality'. He is like an I.R.A. man *mounting an attack* on the reality he detests. He and his fellow poets are human beings living in a world of the mostly sub-human. The sub-humans seem contented with their mental and physical slums. Poets can conceive a world less offensive to the sensibilities. Since the actual power seems to be in the hands of politicians who are as coarse and unimaginative as the mob, all the poet can do is to create a blueprint of his ideal world, as Keats and Shelley created theirs. His aim is to build a kind of *mental shelter* in which other sensitive souls can take refuge. It has to be a self-complete world, a complete alternative to the real world, such as might be found on some imaginary planet. Dowson and Johnson failed in this respect; they glimpse the ideal world from afar, and the mood of the poetry is of sadness and resignation. Yeats did not fail; he built determinedly, using fragments of Irish myth, occult lore, eastern religions, to create his own landscape of the mind. The result is a landscape that is genuinely a total creation, like the landscape David Lindsay was to create a quarter of a century later in *A Voyage to Arcturus*.

To the young poet, it seems that as man gets older, he sells out to the world of sub-humanity and dirt, and that perhaps the only way to avoid compromise is to die. It never strikes him that part of his problem is that he has 'one skin too few', and that as he gets older, his vital mechanisms will supply the deficiency until the actual world ceases to jar his sensibilities every time he goes outdoors. The idealism may remain as strong as ever. The perception that most people are sub-human is seen to be accurate enough; but they no longer excite rage or disgust. It is seen to be a problem of evolution—social and biological. In short, the poet ceases to live in a sharply dualistic universe, and has to learn to pursue his ideals with less sound and fury and more precision. This is eventually what happened to Yeats.

But at twenty-five, Yeats had enclosed himself in a self-image like a suit of armour. Instead of playing Hamlet as he walks through the streets, he can play at being Shelley. He feels that this identity he has created for himself corresponds more closely to his inner reality than the gawky poet who is known to his friends as Willy. He is encased in this idea of himself as a madman might be encased in the notion that he is Julius Caesar.

I have pointed out elsewhere* that Shaw did much the same thing: built up a persona with which to confront the world and cover up his shyness, a puppet known as G.B.S. who was always right, always more brilliant and far sighted than any of his adversaries. But Shaw created G.B.S. when he was in his late thirties, and the suit of armour ended by rusting on him until it became his prison. Yeats started earlier. The self-image was already functioning efficiently when he published *Crossways* in 1889 (when he was twenty-four). It continued to serve for the next ten years, in *The Rose* (1893), and *The Wind Among the Reeds* (1899). But by 1904, when *In the Seven Woods* came out, he was approaching forty, and no longer experienced the same need for a curtain of words—or music—to protect him from the everyday world. There is a clumsiness in the verse that must have convinced old admirers that he was losing his touch:

> I thought of your beauty, and this arrow,
> Made out of a wild thought, is in my marrow.
> There's no man may look upon her, no man,
> As when newly grown to be a woman . . .

What has happened, in effect, is that misty-eyed poet of the Celtic twilight has vanished. Yeats has stopped pretending to be the dreamy magician, murmuring soulfully about the hosts of the Sidhe and pearl-pale high born maidens. No doubt people who were not entirely sympathetic to him—like Chesterton and Belloc —felt glad that he had stopped 'putting it on'. The volume contains the well-known *Folly of Being Comforted*, and it sets the tone: advancing age, disillusionment, 'new commonness . . . crying about the streets'. There is an attempt to cling to the old mood in poems like *The Withering of the Boughs* and *Red Hanrahan's Song about Ireland*, and in such lines as:

> I am contented, for I know that Quiet
> Wanders laughing and eating her wild heart
> Among pigeons and bees . . .

* *Bernard Shaw: A Reassessment* (1969).

but it is little more than a gesture. And the disillusion of the love
poems also sounds a new note:

> Never give all the heart, for love
> Will hardly seem worth thinking of
> To passionate women ...

Poetically speaking, Yeats was approaching his 'change of
life'. It is a sign of his remarkable power to sustain a self-image
that it had taken so long. Shelley and Rupert Brooke were
approaching it before they were out of their twenties. Even
Keats said, just before his death, that he felt as though he was
living a 'posthumous existence', expressing this same sense of
having come to the end of a dream that has sustained him. But
then, Shelley, Keats and Brooke had nothing to fall back on.
Each had been concerned, like Yeats, with the creation of an
'alternative world' of ideal beauty. Brooke catches it in his *Song
of the Pilgrims* when he speaks of a voice:

> ... that fills
> The soul with longing for dim hills
> And faint horizons ...

Then the daylight hardens; the visionary gleam has apparently
fled. And the poet, like Goldsmith's betrayed maiden, feels
there is nothing for it but to die. The only alternative seems to be
a lifetime of anticlimax, the 'long littleness of life' for which
Brooke was so 'magnificently unprepared'.

Fortunately, Yeats was of a practical turn of mind. The descendant of generations of tough, enterprising Anglo-Irishmen,
he could never bring himself to accept that this ideal world he was
trying to create was no more than a delightful illusion. The poet
in *The Shadowy Waters* cries:

> It's not a dream,
> But the reality that makes our passion
> As a lamp shadow—no—no lamp, the sun.
> What the world's million lips are thirsting for
> Must be substantial somewhere.

And in the *Autobiographies*, he quotes the long passage from
Shelley's *Hellas* about the Wandering Jew who lives 'in a sea
cavern 'mid the Demonesi', and who can be contacted by anyone

who is bold enough to seek him out, and adds that he was attracted to the followers of Madame Blavatsky because 'they had affirmed the real existence of the Jew, or of his like' (i.e. the 'Tibetan Masters' who were supposed to have dictated Madame Blavatsky's books). Yeats joined the theosophists and the magical 'Order of the Golden Dawn' hoping to discover that there are secret Powers hidden behind the surface of reality. For Shaw, there is such a power behind the world: the force of godhead or evolution. This was too vague and abstract for Yeats, who wanted signs and wonders. At a seance, he convinced himself that there were spirits present; at a magical conjuration, that certain symbols have a universal power over all minds because they represent that unseen reality. He travelled around the west of Ireland collecting folk tales and legends, and, by some intellectual sleight of hand, convinced himself of the reality of fairies.

Perhaps it was the Irish background that made the crucial difference to survival. Brooke and Shelley and Keats were Englishmen with the typical 'no-nonsense' English background; so when they discovered that the wider world is no more magical or ideal than Piccadilly, it seemed that the search had come to an end. Yeats was born in the west of Ireland among hills and lakes, and a peasantry that accepted ghosts, fairies and goblins as they accepted the Holy Trinity. When Yeats was nine, the family moved to London, then later to Dublin, then back to London again. If he had spent all his childhood and youth in Sligo, it would have become a symbol of the things he hated: dreariness and small mindedness and superstition. London and Dublin transformed it into a symbol of beauty and simplicity, the equivalent of Wordsworth's lakes. He revisited it often enough to keep the enchantment alive. He had been unable to take a permanent interest in socialism because it contradicted his feelings about magic and religion; but this did not apply to the cause of Irish liberty. He yoked his poetic talent to the Young Ireland literary movement, and later, with Lady Augusta Gregory, founded the Irish Theatre. The idealism could, to some extent, find practical expression. And Yeats's mind sought constantly for new symbols to embody his sense of a reality opposed to the 'common daylight'. When he met Lady Gregory, he became aware of the other aspect of Anglo-Irish life: the great houses, family portraits, 'hard riding country gentlemen', the 'lords and ladies gay/That were

beaten into the clay/Through seven heroic centuries'. These
became a psychological antidote to the 'new commonness in the
streets'. It was also at about this time—of his poetic 'change of
life'—that he met J. M. Synge, who was fundamentally as romantic
as Yeats, and yet curiously hard-headed. Synge came to find in
the Irish peasantry his own symbol of opposition to the world of
the 20th century. But his attitude differed from that of Yeats
in certain fundamental respects. Synge was a Rabelaisian in the
original sense of that term; the earthy side of physical life in no
way detracted from his enjoyment of it. Although the comedic
impulse behind his work places him in the tradition of Lever and
Carleton—or even Samuel Lover—Synge is primarily a nature
mystic. Like Yeats, he was a religious man who had rejected the
religion of his childhood; he replaced it with a religion of nature:

> Still south I went and west and south again,
> Through Wicklow from the morning to the night,
> And far from cities, and the sites of men,
> Lived with the sunshine and the moon's delight.
>
> I knew the stars, the flowers, and the birds,
> The grey and wintry sides of many glens,
> And did but half remember human words,
> In converse with the mountains, moors and fens

The Irish peasantry of Wicklow and the Aran Isles, instead of
disturbing this mood of mystical contemplation, somehow
deepened it. *The Playboy of the Western World* was attacked because
it seemed to present the peasantry in the worst possible light;
yet in another sense, it idealised them. He contemplates them
from his detached height—this expatriate Irishman who has
travelled in Italy and Germany, and studied French classical
literature in Paris—and sees them as embodying ancient, earthy
simplicities. When he went to the Aran Isles, he was like a time
traveller going back into the past to study a simpler age.

When Synge died in 1909—aged thirty-eight—Yeats had
learned the important lesson from him: that it is possible to be
a mystic, and yet be thoroughly at home in the world. In 1910, the
year after Synge's death, the new Yeats emerges definitely in
The Green Helmet. The poem *At Galway Races* would be unthink-
able without the influence of Synge:

> There where the course is,
> Delight makes all of one mind,
> The riders upon the galloping horses,
> The crowd that closes in behind:
> We, too, had good attendance once,
> Hearers and hearteners of the work;
> Aye, horsemen for companions,
> Before the merchant and the clerk
> Breathed on the world with timid breath . . .

One is inclined to suspect that Yeats had also been reading Nietzsche, with his opposition of the heroic virtues and the timidity of the bourgeoisie. It should be added that from this point on, the horse becomes in Yeats's work the symbol of the powerful and the irrational:

> Violence upon the road, violence of horses . . .

The *Galway Races* poem is evidence that Yeats had successfully completed the delicate Caesarian operation of releasing himself from the old self-image, and thereby opening up a new range of possibilities. (Shaw never succeeded; he left it too late.) The new self-image began to emerge clearly in his fifties:

> But I grow old among dreams,
> A weather-worn, marble triton
> Among the streams.

The title of the poem in which these lines appear is—significantly—*Men Improve with the Years*. This was published in 1919. There was an intermediate period, after *In the Seven Woods,* when he tries on various images. There is a romantic gloom that is too ironic to be called despair:

> Sweetheart, do not love too long:
> I loved long and long,
> And grew to be out of fashion
> Like an old song.

(He is referring to the long, frustrating involvement with Maud Gonne.) He speaks of having grown: 'As weary hearted as that hollow moon'. *The Green Helmet* opens with a poem that describes a dream in which Yeats is the oarsman in a 'ship of death'. And a

poem called *Words*, restates the dilemma of the early poems with
a new emphasis:

> I had this thought a while ago,
> 'My darling cannot understand
> What I have done, or what would do
> In this blind bitter land.'
>
> And I grew weary of the sun
> Until my thoughts cleared up again,
> Remembering that the best I have done
> Was done to make it plain;
>
> That every year I have cried, 'At length
> My darling understands it all,
> Because I have come into my strength,
> And words obey my call';
>
> That had she done so who can say
> What would have shaken from the sieve?
> I might have thrown poor words away
> And been content to live.

This is the dilemma Ibsen stated in *When We Dead Awaken*:
that the dedicated artist must turn his back upon life. In the earlier
poems 'words alone are certain good', and 'as for living, our
servants can do that for us'. Now he feels that life is something to
be lived and enjoyed, and keeps wishing that he had his 'burning
youth'.

Many of these intermediate poems are satirical or savage.
To a poet, who would have me praise certain bad imitators of his and mine:

> You say, as I have often given tongue
> In praise of what another's said or sung,
> 'Twere politic to do the like by these;
> But was there ever dog that praised his fleas?

Some of the best poems written in his late forties have this
bitter flavour, because indignation sometimes inspires him to
noble rhetoric, as in the lines *To a Shade*:

> ... Go, unquiet wanderer,
> And gather the Glasnevin coverlet
> About your head till the dust stops your ear,
> The time for you to taste of that salt breath
> And listen at the corners has not come:

> You had enough of sorrow before death—
> Away, away! You are safer in the tomb.

He has even learned to smile at himself:

> ... When I was young,
> I had not given a penny for a song
> Did not the poet sing it with such airs
> That one believed he had a sword upstairs;

It must be admitted that many of the poems written between *In the Seven Woods* (1904) and *Responsibilities* (1914) are unmemorable. They spring out of negative emotions, and good poetry cannot permit itself to be purely negative. The outlines of despair have to be softened until they become sadness, or hardened into a rage that expresses itself like Lear or Othello. Satire must bite epigrammatically. Defeat must be somehow universalised. In short, all negative emotions must be charged with vitality until they become somehow positive. Between his fortieth and his fiftieth years, Yeat's creativity hit a rock-bottom. Even the opening poem of *Responsibilities*—praised by Eliot for its honesty:

> Pardon that for a barren passion's sake,
> Although I have come close on forty-nine,
> I have no child, I have nothing but a book ...

—is fundamentally negative and self-pitying.

But the barren period was almost over. Yeats was finding a new image of beauty: cold, savage and impersonal:

> Suddenly I saw the cold and rook-delighting heaven
> That seemed as though ice burned and was but the
>   more ice. . . .

and in two of the poems, this has become a magnificent gaiety, reminiscent of Synge:

> Three old hermits took the air
> By a cold and desolate sea,
> First was muttering a prayer,
> Second rummaged for a flea:
> On a windy stone, the third
> Giddy with his hundredth year,
> Sang unnoticed like a bird:
> 'Though the Door of Death is near
> And what waits behind the door,

> Three times in a single day
> I, though upright on the shore,
> Fall asleep when I should pray.'
> So the first, but now the second:
> 'We're but given what we have earned
> When all thoughts and deeds are reckoned,
> So it's plain to be discerned
> That the shades of holy men
> Who have failed, being weak of will,
> Pass the Door of Birth again,
> And are plagued by crowds, until
> They've the passion to escape.'
> Moaned the other, 'They are thrown
> Into some most fearful shape.'
> But the second mocked his moan:
> 'They are not changed to anything,
> Having loved God once, but maybe
> To a poet or a king
> Or a witty lovely lady.'
> While he'd rummaged rags and hair,
> Caught and cracked his flea, the third,
> Giddy with his hundredth year,
> Sang unnoticed like a bird.

For Yeats, this is a completely new tone. He has caught the insane, Rabelaisian gaiety of Synge, and infused it with the religious seriousness that is peculiarly his own. The poem surges with a kind of laughter. The laughter is implicit in the ideas of the poem, which derive from the *Bhagavad Gita*. The end of man is 'salvation', union with the divine, and he is reborn endlessly until he achieves it. There is no point in mourning for lost youth: there is no way back. But there *is* a way forward. The misfortunes and miseries of the poet should not provoke self-pity, as in most of the 'tragic generation'. The 'woes that flesh is heir to' are not tragic; life pokes us with a pointed stick to create the will to throw off the 'triviality of everydayness'. (Shaw took a similar view; he makes Hesione tell Ellie Dunn in *Heartbreak House* 'It's only life educating you, pettikins'.)

This view of destiny was not adopted for this particular poem. Yeats had been a disciple of esoteric Buddhism in his Dublin days and had sat at the feet of the guru Mohini Chatterjee. In *Hodos Chameliontos* he writes of destinies whose purpose is 'to bring their chosen man to the greatest obstacle he may confront without despair. They contrived Dante's banishment, and snatched away his Beatrice and thrust Villon into the arms of harlots, and sent him to gather cronies at the foot of the gallows.' It was a view that developed steadily throughout his lifetime.

The second poem of *Responsibilities* that achieves this gaiety sounds even more like Synge; this is *Running to Paradise*

> As I came over Windy Gap
> They threw a halfpenny into my cap,
> For I am running to Paradise;
> And all I have to do is to wish
> And somebody puts his hand in the dish
> To throw me a bit of salted fish:
> *And there the king is but as the beggar.*
>
> My brother Mourteen is worn out
> With skelping his big brawling lout,
> And I am running to Paradise;
> A poor life, do what he can,
> And though he keep a dog and a gun,
> A serving-maid and a serving-man:
> *And there the king is but as the beggar.*

How does one reconcile the philosophy of this poem—and of *The Three Hermits*—with the title of the volume, *Responsibilities*? It cannot be reconciled. Yeats was like a butterfly emerging from it's chrysalis; the old self could hardly understand the new. Most of the poems in *Responsibilities* belong to the negative mid-period. One of them, *The Dolls*, sounds a note of cruelty that is rare in Yeats.

Yeats was never to resolve the conflict, except on an intuitive level. A part of him continues to mourn lost youth:

> O who could have foretold
> That the heart grows old?

Or:

> The holy centaurs of the hills are vanished;
> I have nothing but the embittered sun;

> Banished heroic mother moon and vanished
> And now that I have come to fifty years
> I must endure the timid sun.

But elsewhere he can write of his ambition to write a 'poem maybe as cold/And passionate as the dawn', and of himself:

> I would be—for no knowledge is worth a straw—
> Ignorant and wanton as the dawn.

The image of a cold, impersonal delight keeps intruding on the poet complaining about lost youth. His conscious philosophy remains pessimistic:

> What portion in the world can the artist have
> Who has awakened from the common dream
> But dissipation and despair?

He clings to the early philosophy: words create a world of illusion to protect the artist from the unbearable crudeness and futility of real life. The strength he derives from his Irish background now becomes clear in poem after poem, where he writes of the Pollexfens and Middletons and Yeatses of Sligo. He writes in *Under Saturn* of 'a child's vow sworn in vain/Never to leave that valley his fathers called their home', apparently unaware that he can look back on it with this rich melancholy only because he left it. The man approaching sixty replaces the supernatural daydreams of his youth with a nostalgic past that is almost equally imaginary;

> You heard that labouring man who had served my
>   people. He said
> Upon the open road, near to the Sligo quay—
> No, no, not said, but cried it out—'You have come
>   again.
> And surely after twenty years it was time to come.'

Fortunately, Yeats also possessed an instinct for multiplicity that was able to combat this tendency to gloom and subjectivity. It had saved him in his twenties from the consequences of his intense romanticism—which might have ended by making him suicidal. It was his interest in ideas, in theories and systems. A man without ideas has nothing to do but contemplate himself and the stock of mental images drawn from his experiences. It is difficult for 'newness' to enter his universe, and recharge his vitality. Yeats had always been a thinker; unsystematic and intuitive; yet capable of pursuing an intuition and crystallising it in words. The *Autobiographies* are remarkable because of the pressure of ideas. (I can think of no other autobiography—with the possible exception of Goethe's—that is so stimulating in this way.)

In 1917, an accident gave a new impetus to this passion for ideas. His wife attempted automatic writing, and Yeats became convinced that certain 'powers'—the 'destinies' that banished Dante, perhaps—were trying to communicate with him, in order to explain the varieties of temperament in human beings. The design that came into Yeats head—or was put their by the 'powers' —was closely related to the designs upon which Arnold Toynbee and Oswald Spengler were working at the time. It was an attempt to see a unifying pattern in history. The evolution of the human soul—and of history—is made to correspond to the twenty-eight phases of the moon. (The system is conveniently if obscurely summarised in the poem of that title.) And it is typical of Yeats that although he claims a kind of supernatural authority for his system, he ends the preface to *A Vision* (the work in which it is expounded) by admitting that he regards the phases as 'stylistic arrangements of experience comparable to the cubes in the drawing of Wyndham Lewis'.

The system is an interesting attempt to arrange men according to their degree of subjectivity and objectivity—that is to say, between the temperaments of the mystic and the hero. The 'system' has never caught on—understandably, for much of it seems wilfully eccentric. But the studies that produced *A Vision*— including a great deal of history and philosophy—had the effect of recharging Yeat's mind, making him forget his lost youth and the bitterness of Dublin politics. Fed by this objectivity, the poetry takes on a new toughness. The Yeats of the early poems had been essentially passive and feminine; their mood is close to that of Keats's *Ode to the Nightingale* or Shelley's *Lines Written in Dejection near Naples*. In the mid-period, the mood has become weary and bitter. *A Vision* seems to have been a real turning point. The poet's self-image has again solidified. Instead of the good-looking poet with the dreamy stare, he becomes a stern-faced old man with bushy eyebrows and a strong jaw. The language takes on a sinuous, athletic quality:

> Although the summer sunlight gild
> Cloudy leafage of the sky,
> Or wintry moonlight sink the field
> In storm-scattered intricacy,
> I cannot look thereon,
> Responsibility so weighs me down.

The best known example of this harsh, resounding use of words is the much anthologised *Byzantium*, whose language seems to have been chosen to imitate the clash of cymbals:

> ... Or, by the moon embittered, scorn aloud
> In glory of changeless metal
> Common bird or petal
> And all complexities of mire and blood.

The interesting question raised by *Byzantium*, and by some of the other poems that use the same linguistic devices—*News for the Delphic Oracle, The Delphic Oracle Upon Plotinus*—is whether they have any 'meaning' in the sense of a continuous argument, or whether they are not exercises in sound and imagery, like *Kubla Khan*. In these poems, Yeats seems to have reverted to his doctrine that 'words alone are certain good'.

On the other hand, the poetry of anger and the poetry of ideas takes on a self-sufficient, satisfying quality that it had not possessed earlier. *The Leaders of the Crowd* is effective because the scorn is counterbalanced by positive values:

> They must to keep their certainty accuse
> All that are different of a base intent;
> Pull down established honour; hawk for news
> Whatever their loose fantasy invent
> And murmur it with bated breath, as though
> The abounding gutter had been Helicon
> Or calumny a song. How can they know
> Truth flourishes where the scholar's lamp has shone
> And there alone, that have no solitude?
> So the crowd come, they care not what may come.
> They have loud music, hope every day renewed
> And heartier loves; that lamp is from the tomb.

At the same time, one observes the Thomas Mann-like opposition of 'life' and 'intellect'. For Bernard Shaw, intellect was always a positive value, so that he could write of 'my peculiar doctrine that a point will be reached in human mental development when the pleasure taken in brain work by St Thomas Aquinas and the Webbs (and saints and philosophers generally) will intensify to a chronic ecstasy surpassing that now momentarily induced by the sexual orgasm'. Yeats was never quite so certain; he continued to feel guilt towards his seafaring ancestors, the feeling that the life of the mind was a poor second best:

> The intellect of man is forced to choose
> Perfection of the life or of the work,
> And if it take the second must refuse
> A heavenly mansion, raging in the dark.
> When all that story's finished, what's the news?
> In luck or out the toil has left its mark:
> That old perplexity an empty purse,
> Or the day's vanity, the night's remorse.

And in the passage from *Hodos Chameliontos* already quoted, he writes: 'We have dreamed a foolish dream these many centuries in thinking that they [the 'destinies'] value a life of contemplation, for they scorn it more than any possible life, unless it be but a name for the worst crisis of all'.

The poetry of ideas, which in the past had tended to be clumsy, now becomes limpid and clear:

> I thought: 'There is a waterfall
> Upon Ben Bulben side
> That all my childhood counted dear;
> Were I to travel far and wide
> I could not find a thing so dear.'
> My memories had magnified
> So many times childish delight.
>
> I would have touched it like a child
> But knew my finger could but have touched
> Cold stone and water. I grew wild,
> Even accusing heaven because
> It had set down among its laws:
> Nothing that we love over-much
> Is ponderable to our touch.

Or, in the second of *Two Songs from a Play*

> Everything that man esteems
> Endures a moment or a day.
> Love's pleasure drives his love away,
> The painter's brush consumes his dreams;
> The herald's cry, the soldier's tread
> Exhaust his glory and his might:
> Whatever flames upon the night
> Man's own resinous heart has fed.

Here the clarity of the expression enables one to see clearly Yeat's tendency to 'reductionism' that seems to have replaced the idealism of his youth:

> What the world's million lips are thirsting for
> Must be substantial somewhere.

According to this view, great art or great philosophy is an attempt to express a reality which man is capable of grasping, or at least, of glimpsing. There are values beyond the narrow limits of human consciousness, and in mystical flashes, we may become aware of these. In his reductionist mood, Yeats is inclined to the illusion theory of value. I make love because of some impulse that has accumulated in me, just as I might go for a walk to 'walk off' energy. The lover embracing his mistress imagines that his passion is conjured up in him by a perception of her beauty, as anger might be conjured up in a placid person at the sight of cruelty. In reality, says Yeats, I *endow* her with meaning, with beauty, because the love energy in me tingles to express itself; post-coital sadness is the recognition that it was all an illusion. It is the old Berkeleyan argument. If I am hungry, the smell of food strikes me as delicious; if I feel sick, it strikes me as nauseating. Which is it really? The question is meaningless. If I was simply not hungry, the smell would not strike me as anything in particular.

It is obviously a fundamental question for mysticism. Forgael's view of the hidden reality that 'the world's million lips are thirsting for' is that there is a deeper reality behind the 'triviality of everydayness', and that the poet's 'longing for dim hills' is the result of an *apprehension* of this. The 'reductionist' view is that some obscure hunger of frustration creates the sense of this 'superior reality'. The idealist view would be that the apprehension of the reality—or the glimpse of it—creates a craving, just as the smell of a good meal could arouse the appetite, while an unappetising smell would only arouse nausea.

In the same way, a philosopher or an artist striving to express an idea feels as if he is trying to paint the portrait of someone he only glimpses occasionally by flashes of lightning. No matter how subjective and distorted the expression, it is an attempt to express something objective. It follows that if, in place of the flashes of lightning, he had a good, continuous light, he would be able to paint the portrait with far more accuracy and detail. That is to say, the work of art—or philosophy—does not depend upon how much energy he has to put into it; he can call upon more if necessary. It depends upon the 'sitter', the object. The painter's brush does *not* 'consume his dreams', for what he paints is not a dream. Yeats's early tendency to make his poetry out of wishful thinking has deeply influenced his view of the nature of all art and thought.

This pessimistic tendency remained the conscious philosophy of Yeats's poetry until the end. He seems to take a dark pleasure in Buddhistic life-denial:

> Civilisation is hooped together, brought
> Under a rule, under the semblance of peace
> By manifold illusion; but man's life is thought,
> And he, despite his terror, cannot cease
> Ravening through century after century,
> Ravening, raging and uprooting that he may come
> Into the desolation of reality . . .

What Then? questions the value of everything he has done:

> His chosen comrades thought at school
> He must grow a famous man;
> He thought the same and lived by rule,
> All his twenties crammed with toil;
> '*What then?*' sang *Platos's ghost*, '*What then?*'

This is the view one would expect from someone who feels that all art and literature are no more than the striking of coloured matches, the burning of man's 'resinous heart'.

Inevitably, he contradicts this view sometimes:

> Grant me an old man's frenzy,
> Myself must I remake
> Till I am Timon and Lear
> Or that William Blake
> Who beat upon a wall
> Till Truth obeyed his call;
>
> A mind Michael Angelo knew
> That can pierce the clouds,
> Or inspired by frenzy
> Shake the dead in their shrouds;
> Forgotten else by mankind,
> An old man's eagle mind.

Was it 'truth' that obeyed William Blake, or were the prophetic books only the spluttering flashes of his own 'resinous heart'?

Towards the end of his life, Yeats lost the interest in ideas, and returned to earlier topics: love and Ireland. A 'monkey gland' operation had increased his sexual energy, so that the love of these later poems is healthily sensual:

> From pleasure of the bed,
> Dull as a worm,
> His rod and its butting head
> Limp as a worm,
> His spirit that has fled
> Blind as a worm.

The Crazy Jane poems are Rabelaisian, and Synge's presence can be felt in all of them. Some of the most spontaneous, purely rhythmic poetry occurs in the later songs:

> Come gather round me Parnellites,
> And sing our chosen man;
> Stand upright on your legs awhile,
> Stand upright while you can,
> For soon we lay where he is laid,
> And he is underground;
> Come fill up all those glasses
> And pass the bottle round. . . .

> And here's a final reason,
> He was of such a kind
> Every man that sings a song
> Keeps Parnell in his mind.
> For Parnell was a proud man,
> No prouder trod the ground,
> And a proud man's lovely man,
> So pass the bottle round.

In some of these later songs, he uses a kind of chorus, which is intended to add another dimension to the drinking-song atmosphere, but as often as not, only makes one wish it wasn't there.

> Could Crazy Jane put off old age
> And ranting time renew,
> Could that old god rise up again
> We'd drink a can or two,
> And out and lay our leadership
> On country and on town.
> Throw likely couples into bed
> And knock the others down.
> *From mountain to mountain ride the fierce horsemen.*

The *Last Poems* (1936–39) are full of this kind of glorification of physical recklessness and violence, which brings to mind the *Odyssey* of Kazantzakis. And this obsession with the physical underlines the 'reductionism', the disillusionment with his old idealism. The attitude to politics has become savagely cynical:

> Parnell came down the road, he said to a cheering man:
> 'Ireland shall gain her freedom and you still break stone'

His attitude towards his own talent has also grown cynical:

> You think it horrible that lust and rage
> Should dance attention upon my old age;
> They were not such a plague when I was young;
> What else have I to spur me into song?

The Apparitions seems to be an admission that the supernatural machinery of *A Vision* was a hoax:

> Because there is safety in derision
> I talked about an apparition,

> I took no trouble to convince,
> Or seem plausible to a man of sense,
> Distrustful of that popular eye
> Whether it be bold or sly.
> *Fifteen apparitions have I seen;*
> *The worst a coat upon a coat-hanger.*

On the other hand, it may refer to all Yeats's lifelong super-naturalism.

He finds reasons for this disillusion in his own past:

> A girl that knew all Dante once
> Live to bear children to a dunce;
> A Helen of social welfare dream.
> Climb on a wagonette to scream.
> Some think it a matter of course that chance
> Should starve good men and bad advance,
> That if their neighbours figured plain
> As though upon a lighted screen,
> No single story would they find
> Of an unbroken happy mind,
> A finish worthy of the start. . . .

And *The Circus Animal's Desertion* seems to hit a kind of rock-bottom of 'reductionism', when he speaks of the myths that formed the subject of so much of his poetry:

> Those masterful images because complete
> Grew in pure mind, but out of what began?
> A mound of refuse or the sweepings of a street,
> Old kettles, old bottles, and a broken can,
> Old iron, old bones, old rags, that raving slut
> Who keeps the till. Now that my ladder's gone,
> I must lie down where all the ladders start,
> In the foul rag and bone shop of the heart.

Here again, his life work as a poet is dismissed as a patchwork of illusion. The most extreme Marxist or positivist could not frame a more contemptuous indictment: a poet who has always run away from life, who has lacked the courage to believe that it can be changed, who has smoked dreams like opium—and who now has to admit to his moral bankruptcy, to the barrenness of his inner life. What has happened to the poet who believed what the world's million lips are thirsting for must be substantial somewhere?

It would seem that he has succeeded in prolonging his life beyond that of most romantic world-rejecters, but has never truly succeeded in 'remaking' himself. The anticlimax may not have been as obvious as in the case of Wordsworth or Swinburne, but it is just as certain. When the early Yeats died, no phoenix rose from his ashes: only a tired man who refuses to die and lacks the courage to live.

In a sense, this is true. Yeats does not belong with Goethe and Beethoven, among the small number of men of genius whose creative flight became more powerful and assured with middle age. When one has made full allowances for his creative endurance, he remains a man who somehow missed his road.

But there is another aspect of Yeats that refuses to fit into this pattern of failure: that inclines one, in fact, to feel that the poems of cynicism, nostalgia, 'reductionism', were only the expression of a mood of a greater man, that the reductionism is only a kind of game. He writes in *Hodos Chameliontos*:

'I know now that revelation is from the self, but from that age-long memoried self, that shapes the elaborate shell of the mollusc and the child in the womb, that teaches the birds to make their nest; and that genius is a crisis that joins that buried self for certain moments to our trivial daily mind. There are, indeed, personifying spirits that we had best call but Gates and Gate-keepers, because through their dramatic power they bring our souls to crisis. . . .'

There follows the passage about how 'they' contrived Dante's banishment and Villon's imprisonment.

Yeats had always been preoccupied by such problems as why birds can build nests without training from the mother bird. He was aware that the 'self' that looked back nostalgically to the past, or raged about Irish politics, was the 'trivial daily mind'.

> Eternity is passion, girl or boy
> Cry at the onset of their sexual joy
> 'For ever and for ever'; then awake
> Ignorant what Dramatis Personae spake;
> A passion-driven exultant man sings out
> Sentences that he has never thought. . . .

The most important statement of this view appears in the poem that he chose to place last of all in *Last Poems*, *Under Ben Bulben*:

> You that Mitchel's prayer have heard,
> 'Send war in our time, O Lord!'
> Know that when all words are said
> And a man is fighting mad,
> Something drops from eyes long blind,
> He completes his partial mind,
> For an instant stands at ease,
> Laughs aloud, his heart at peace.
> Even the wisest man grows tense
> With some sort of violence
> Before he can accomplish fate,
> Know his work or choose his mate.

These are the visionary, mystical moments, when man 'completes his partial mind'. His everyday, conscious self is only a small part of the mind, like the final crescent of the moon. In moments of crisis, the full moon suddenly appears. Petty miseries and oppressions vanish. And essentially, *all* human miseries are petty, as Kirilov realises. A superb gaiety bubbles out of the soul, the gaiety of the old Chinamen of *Lapis Lazuli*.

Yeats understood this—at least, part of the time. And so, in a real and profound sense, he had finally cast off the chrysalis of the early romantic self-image, and achieved a new greatness. This remains the paradox of Yeats: that so much of his verse should be pessimistic, so much self-pitying and defeated, so much cynical and 'reductionist', and yet a small percentage of his greatest work should place him securely among the mystics who have transcended the everyday self and its sufferings.

The later Yeats had become an evolutionist. His view of the purpose of life differed in no essential from that expressed by Shaw in *Man and Superman* or *Back to Methuselah*. In one of the last poems, *The Man and the Echo,* the two Yeats's fight it out. First speaks the guilt-tormented man:

> All that I have said and done,
> Now that I am old and ill,
> Turns into a question till
> I lie awake night after night
> And never get the answer right.

> Did that play of mine send out
> Certain men the English shot?
> Did words of mine put too great strain
> On that woman's reeling brain?

When he feels that the answer is to 'lie down and die', the echo supports him. He replies:

> . . . That were to shirk
> The spiritual intellect's great work,
> And shirk it in vain. There is no release
> In a bodkin or disease,
> Nor can there be work so great,
> As that which cleans man's dirty slate . . .

Like Shaw, he finds the myth of original sin useful to express the reality of the human condition, and he sees that the job of the artist is to struggle to raise man to godlike heights. This is stated explicitly in *Under Ben Bulben*:

> Poet and sculptor do the work,
> Nor let the modish painter shirk
> What his great forefathers did,
> Bring the soul of man to God,
> Make him fill the cradle right.

This last line makes clear that he is thinking in terms of evolution, not of some other-worldly mysticism.

> Michael Angelo left a proof
> On the Sistine Chapel roof,
> Where but half-awakened Adam
> Can disturb globe-trotting Madam
> Till her bowels are in a heat
> Proof that there's a purpose set
> Before the secret working mind:
> Profane perfection of mankind.

This 'secret working mind' that drives the artist is the great unconscious drive of evolution.

It is interesting to note that this verse hardly rises above doggerel:

> Where but half-awakened Adam
> Can disturb globe-trotting Madam
> Till her bowels are in a heat.

One of the most curious things about Yeats is that so much of his major work is *not* good poetry in any sense at all:

> [He] who understood
> Whatever had been sighed, sung,
> Howled, miau-ed, barked, brayed, belled,
>   yelled, cried, crowed,
> Thereon replied. . . .

This can be explained in terms of his desire to give his poetry the earthiness of folk-rhymes. But in much of the later work, he is simply concerned to cast ideas into verse form, ideas that strike him as worth expression in the gnomic medium of verse rather than in prose. It is an amusing observation that one of the 'great' poets of the 20th century should be such a bad poet in the sense in which the word is generally understood. It argues that poetry is not so much a matter of words or style as of actual thought-content.

Even at the end, Yeats remains paradoxical, self-contradictory. The passage I have just quoted on the fundamentally evolutionary role of great art, is followed by a typical expression of Yeats's other aspect:

> 'Irish poets, learn your trade,
> Sing whatever is well made,
> Scorn the sort now growing up
> All out of shape from toe to top,
> Their unremembering hearts and heads
> Base-born products of base beds.
> Sing the peasantry, and then
> Hard-riding country gentlemen,
> The holiness of monks, and after
> Porter-drinkers' randy laughter;
> Sing the lords and ladies gay
> That were beaten into the clay
> Through seven heroic centuries;
> Cast your mind on other days
> That we in coming days may be
> Still the indomitable Irishry.

Here one has all the aspects of Yeats that seem to have been wilfully chosen to create a patchwork self-image: the snobbery, the later obsession with sex and booze, horseplay and heroism, Irish patriotism. The significant idea that emerges here is the injunction: 'Cast your mind on other days'. The base-born are condemned because of their 'unremembering hearts and heads', the tendency to live in the present. The answer, Yeats implies, is a sense of tradition. But not the 'tradition' of T. S. Eliot or T. E. Hulme, the tradition of spiritual effort symbolised in the Christian church—although the 'holiness of monks' is a passing glance at it—but the tradition of hard-riding and hard-drinking gentry, of roystering and copulating and gaming. In short, it is the bookish poet looking back nostalgically on what he thinks he has missed. And then, as a final contradiction, Yeats ends the poem with his epitaph:

> Cast a cold eye
> On life, on death.
> Horseman, pass by!

where the Buddhistic withdrawal is opposed to the Shavian evolutionism and the simple life-affirmation of the following section. To complete the confusion, one might add that *Under Ben Bulben* starts with a section that seems to imply that Yeats still accepts the notion of reincarnation:

> A brief parting from those dear
> Is the worst man has to fear.
> Though grave diggers' toil is long,
> Sharp their spades, their muscles strong,
> They but thrust their buried men
> Back in the human mind again.

This brings to mind the 'credo' section of *The Tower*, which must rank among Yeats's finest rhetoric:

> And I declare my faith:
> I mock Plotinus' thought
> And cry in Plato's teeth,
> Death and life were not
> Till man made up the whole,
> Made lock, stock and barrel,

Out of his bitter soul,
Aye, sun and moon and star, all,
And further add to that
That, being dead, we rise,
Dream and so create
Translunar Paradise.
I have prepared my peace
With learned Italian things
And the proud stones of Greece,
Poet's imaginings
And memories of love,
Memories of the words of women,
And all those things whereof
Man makes a superhuman
Mirror-resembling dream.

But here, there is no implication that the superhuman dream
serves any purpose but to save man from the 'rag and bone shop
of the heart'. In *Under Ben Bulben,* he takes the final step, and thereby contradicts the idea he had first embraced at eighteen, and
wrestled with for more than half a century.

3

A. L. Rowse

In his second volume of autobiography, *A Cornishman at Oxford*, A. L. Rowse remarks: 'For thirty years the new idiom of Eliot and Pound has been poetic orthodoxy—all my working life in fact—and my poetry has been out of it, disconsidered, myself discouraged.' This is true; Rowse belongs to the school of direct personal utterance, the same tradition as Hardy and Housman. In America, the tradition was kept alive by the dominating influence of Robert Frost, which acted as a counterweight to the intellectualism of Eliot and Pound: in recent years, 'personal utterance' has seen a revival in the work of Robert Lowell and W. D. Snodgrass. In England, it may be said to have gone out of fashion with the death of Rupert Brooke (who was, after all, a friend of Robert Frost). Rowse's poetry is 'naïve' in Schiller's sense of the word; he expresses personal feelings directly, without embarrassment, and without any attempt to 'disinfect' them with the use of abstract language or intellectual cross-references.

> In the late afternoon of my life I lie and doze
> In the residents' lounge of the hotel at Lytham
>   St Anne's,
> The candid sun full on my February face
> White and drawn with long winter's overwork.
> Behind me the silvery chime of a Victorian clock
> Tinkles the afternoon tea-time away.
> No one about: no one walks on the sands:
> The sea-side resort is deserted, the turreted stands
> Of the pier silent and empty as a cathedral.

These lines—the opening of *St Anne's-on-the-Sea*—chosen almost at random, immediately catch Rowse's peculiar quality, the ability to conjure up silence and loneliness. All Rowse's best poetry has this still, contemplative quality, like something over-heard in the silence. There is often a quality of sadness that is reminiscent of Ernest Dowson, except that it is curiously free of self-pity:

> The moon, the snow, the light of winter afternoon,
>   as if one were seeing life go by
>   from under the sea:
>   the leafless twigs that sway, O so gently,
>   in the wind and the light,
>   the fronds and ferns that wave under the sea:
>   life seen through the refraction of water. . . .

One notes here that the poet is not afraid to use the phrase 'O so gently', that could so easily sound sentimental. His mind is so absorbed in its object, the cold, still light of the winter afternoon, that he is totally preoccupied with describing what he sees as honestly and accurately as he can. The result is that the phrase does *not* jar; it assists the work of invocation.

This is the root of Rowse's success as a poet. The utterance is so direct that it produces an effect of shock. It produces the feeling of a man standing by a window in an empty room, talking to himself, unafraid of being overheard because he is so convinced that no one is interested anyway. The poem on All Souls—the college of which Rowse is a Fellow—has this quality:

> Evening. Silence, and the questioning of birds.
> A bugle blows its erotic note over the city;
> The light creeps round to the north face of the tower
> The grey, stone chimneys are very still and void of
> Life, silently saying, There is no love, no love,
> Here there is neither marrying nor giving in marriage,
> No heart to hold, no loved limbs to cherish.
> The happy birds go winging upon their business,—
> The soldiers in the streets on theirs—
> Beyond the walls, the roofs, the eaves.
> Than walls of stone or bars of iron more subtle
>   and binding
> These intellectual integuments,
> Because self-willed.

As one reads the autobiographies—*A Cornish Childhood* (1942) and *A Cornishman at Oxford*—it becomes clear that one of the reasons for Rowse's honesty is his low opinion of most of his fellow human beings. ' . . . these perpetual irritations from stupid people became no laughing matter. They built up a resentment which I have no desire to overcome, and they fortified me in my conviction—which everything that has happened since in world affairs confirms—that in political matters, as in all matters involving general thought, human beings are idiots.' (Yeats felt much the same, but his expressions of scorn for the 'mob' are restricted to his poetry, where it is given force by his rhetoric. Rowse is not that kind of poet: the explosions occur mainly in the autobiographies.) Rowse obviously has the feeling that his poetry is directed at a very small number of people, and that with these, he can reveal himself openly.

Such an attitude means inevitably that Rowse is something of a dual personality—at least, on the surface. There is no discontinuity between the Yeats of the autobiographies and the Yeats of the poetry; even the titles, *Reveries over Childhood and Youth, The Trembling of the Veil,* indicate that he is still wearing the poet's personality, so to speak. The style often seems artificial; it is obviously not *intended* to be colloquial. Yeats never appears *en pantoufles.* Rowse's autobiographies often sound as if they have been transcribed direct from his speech:

'I fear I was very simple and direct, with no return upon myself; I cannot think how people put up with me as they did, for I had masses of friends. (As I still have, in spite of the deliberate qualification I have imposed as the result of unfortunate experiences at the hands of some. Very easy to get yourself demoted from the rank of friend to that of acquaintance, if you misbehave.)'

It is hard to see any connection between this Rowse, and the poet who writes:

> Silently, softly,
> With unhurried, moth-white wings
> The visiting owl voyages over the cornfield
> At the oncoming of night:
> The great wings but skim the blades of wheat,
> Making no noise. So Death comes
> To the small creatures that wait.

In the mirror I catch sight as I pass
Of the white owl-like face
Of the sick man, with great dark eyes
Looking out of the glass.

This is the nocturnal hour
When predatory fears
Put forth their power.

The poet here is a man on his own, a solitary. One is reminded of
the Journals of Amiel, of W. N. P. Barbellion, of Rilke's autobiographical *Notebooks of Malte Laurids Brigge*. It seems strange to
hear him talking about 'masses of friends' and of 'demoting'
friends who misbehave themselves.

To some extent, the paradox is resolved by a study of the autobiographies.

Alfred Leslie Rowse was born in St Austell, Cornwall, in 1903.
His father was a clay worker, and for many years his mother
ran a rather unprosperous village shop at Tregonissey.

' . . . the village had a not unattractive appearance in my early
years, with its cob-walled cottages washed yellow and cream,
the colour of the clotted cream on top of the pans in the dairy
at the farm. A few were a deeper shade, saffron. A little group of
thatched cottages in the middle of the village had an orchard
attached; and I remember well the peculiar purity of the blue
sky seen through the white clusters of apple blossom in spring. I
remember being moonstruck looking at it one morning early on
my way to school. It meant something for me; what, I couldn't
say. It gave me an unease at heart, some reaching out towards
perfection such as impels men into religion, some sense of the
transcendence of things, of the fragility of our hold upon life,
mixed up with a schoolboy's dream of an earlier world (I was then
reading Q's *The Splendid Spur*), of England in the time of the
Civil War, the gallant bands of young horsemen careering out in
the morning, Spring, the pure sunlight falling over the hills in
waves under the cloudless blue. It was always morning, early
morning, in that daydream. . . .'

And in the following paragraph, he says:

'Later on, though still a schoolboy . . . when I read Wordsworth's *Tintern Abbey* and *Intimations of Immortality*, I realised
that that was the experience he was writing about. In time it

became my creed—if that word can be used of a religion which has no dogma, no need of dogma; for with this ultimate aesthetic experience, this apprehension of the world and life as having value essentially in the moment of being apprehended *qua* beauty, I had no need of religion.'

'It seemed to me . . . that what was characteristic of the experience was that in the moment of undergoing it, in contemplating the light come and go upon the façade of a building, the moon setting behind St Mary's spire outside my window . . . in listening to Beethoven or Byrd or seeing the blue sky through the apple-blossom of my childhood, in that very moment it seemed that time stood still, that for a moment time was held up and one saw experience as through a rift across the flow of it, a shaft into the universe. But what gave such poignancy to the experience was that, in the very same moment as one felt time standing still, one knew at the back of the mind, or with another part of it, that it was moving inexorably on, carrying oneself and life with it.'

Throughout *A Cornish Childhood,* one is aware of this intense, Proustian sensitivity, the sense of passing time, the poignancy of physical beauty. Rowse, unlike Proust and Yeats, was not a member of the well-to-do middle classes. In *A Cornishman at Oxford,* speaking of the reasons for his happiness at Oxford, Rowse comments: 'D. H. Lawrence was quite right: the mental life of the working class is too restricted and cramping for an intelligent boy to endure it. One would perish of inanition; they never understand anything, haven't read anything, or heard or seen anything, could never answer the questions my mind was full of, from childhood on.' But, like Yeats, Rowse was at least lucky in the scenery of his childhood; it is hard to imagine how he would have survived in the slums of a large town. The Cornish scenery compensated, to some extent, for the narrow, dull world of his childhood.

His escape was slow and painful. Fortunately, the headmaster noticed his intelligence and decided that he should try for a scholarship to a university. Overwork produced an ulcer, and a diseased appendix was not diagnosed in time to prevent peritonitis. First attempts to obtain scholarships were unsuccessful—three were required to make up the minimum of £200 a year that was needed. The attempts dragged on for two years, with periodic breakdowns in health. During this time he kept a diary, and had also begun to write poetry. Poetry became 'my secret religion, the activity which I hugged to myself, the tower into which I could always retreat for consolation for my troubles, my angers, my disappointments . . .'. Eventually, the scholarship was obtained; two months before his nineteenth birthday, Rowse went up to Christ Church, Oxford.

One might assume that, at this point, the struggles were over. In fact, they were beginning again. There followed three years of lunching on bread and marmalade, nights made sleepless by acute stomach pains, impecunious holidays spent at home with nothing to do but study and take long walks. The family fortunes were going downhill; his elder brother and sister had now left home, and both parents were in failing health. If Rowse developed a certain tendency to pessimism, this is surely understandable. Death and misfortune continued to strike around him in the family, and he was almost a permanent invalid. But in his twenty-second year came the major breakthrough, Fellowship of All Souls, Oxford. Now at least there could be no slipping back into the life he was trying to escape. By this time, he had taken another major decision: to be a historian rather than a literary man. His original aim in going to Oxford had been to study literature, with the eventual aim of becoming a critic or novelist. History meant, to some extent, turning aside from his obsession with poetry and literature. In terms of its end product, the choice has been justified; as a historian of Tudor England—particularly Cornwall—and the biographer of Shakespeare and Marlowe, Rowse has achieved a secure place. In accepting the security of All Souls, Rowse provided himself with the basic conditions he needed to work. It also meant that he could provide support for his parents in their later years. But the question that rises in the mind of any reader of *A Cornish Childhood* is whether a temperament like Rowse's could ever be satisfied with academic distinction. It is the temperament of the poet, the artist, even of the mystic. How far could Proust or Lawrence have flourished in an academic environment?

One becomes aware of the problem in turning from *A Cornish Childhood* to *A Cornishman at Oxford*. After the struggles described in *A Cornish Childhood*, the reader thinks of Oxford as a haven, a new life. Rowse ends the book with the lights of Oxford mirrored in the water as the train draws in. The knowledge that he achieved a Fellowship of All Souls at twenty-one confirms the feeling of a final breakthrough: All Souls is a college without undergraduates where life is serene, civilised, even contemplative. *A Cornishman at Oxford* quickly dissipates this 'happily-ever-after' atmosphere. There is hard work and illness and socialist meetings and friends—and also enemies. Even after his election to All Souls, there are further disappointments and breakdowns in health (a serious one came close to killing him in the late thirties).

It becomes possible to understand why the poetry has this quality of honesty. It is still the 'secret religion', the expression of a part of Rowse that has not found its haven at Oxford. It is also possible to understand the ambivalence of his attitude towards people, the bursts of impatience and resentment. One remembers Yeats's lines about hermits—and presumably poets:

> [They] are plagued by crowds until
> They've the passion to escape.

All poetry is, by its nature, a turning-away from 'the triviality of everydayness'. Human life is a series of responses to the world, and the responses are on many different levels, from the pleasure of playing dominoes and gossiping in a pub to the inner cataclysms of the religious convert. Each human situation evokes a different level of response, a different level of the personality. The self awareness of a mother feeding her baby has so little in common with her self-awareness when quarrelling with the next door neighbour that she is virtually two different people. The poet is one who has experienced his profoundest responses—and therefore his profoundest moments of self-awareness—when alone. He may have many other levels of response: to people, to travel, to politics. But the core of his vitality, the root of his 'secret life', lies in that intimate aesthetic response which evokes his profoundest sense of identity. And when self-expression emerges from this 'secret life', the 'personality' vanishes, or at least becomes no more than a thin layer of water that diffracts the light. All poets therefore have a dual nature: one that is evoked by the 'everyday', one that responds only to the aesthetic vibration. Yeats, as I have pointed out, attempted to build a bridge between his two halves, by dramatising the everyday self until it no longer seemed a grotesque travesty of his poetic self-image. (It is significant that younger poets who met him in the later years felt that there was an element of charlatanism about him.)* Rowse's more introverted, Proustian nature has never felt this need for a heightened self-image to unite his two aspects. The consequence is that in turning from *A Cornishman at Oxford*—or even his historical works—to the poetry, one becomes sharply aware of the dual personality, the poet and the 'man of the world'. The man of the world is a brilliant Celt 'with one skin too few' who has become a successful historian and a member of the 'establishment'. This 'public Rowse' has many facets to his personality. The historian impresses not only by his ability to re-create the life of the past, but by a most un-Celtish delight in facts, the prosy economic details of life in the past. There is an openly avowed aestheticism, a religion of beauty, and, as in Jacob Burckhardt— one of Rowse's favourite historical writers—this is accompanied by a feeling of pessimism about the modern era. Rowse is here at one with Nietzsche and with Yeats; the reign of creeping mediocrity, the 'base born products of base beds', the 'new commonness in the streets', gradually displaces the 'beautiful noble things' that are the glory of western culture. In all this, Rowse is very close to Yeats, as well as to the Eliot of *The Waste Land*. (Eliot encouraged Rowse to write poetry in the thirties.) Rowse has certainly followed Yeats's invocation to 'cast your mind on other days'.

But in spite of the similarity of aesthetic, Rowse differs from Yeats and Eliot in a fundamental respect. Their response to the slow destruction of old values was to look for alternatives: in the case of Eliot, to religious mysticism, and of Yeats, to his own strange mythology. Rowse confesses to a 'temperamental affinity for Swift'; his pessimism is savage and absolute. It is this Swiftian veneer that produces some of the crashes of discord in the autobiographies: 'When, years later, I read Pareto I recognised a kindred spirit—someone with a very acute nose for human interestedness, hypocrisy and humbug, who recognised the constant habit humans have of dressing up their own interests or prejudices as objective generalisations, when they are really mere rationalisations of their own interests. Who is taken in by it? Certainly not Pareto, nor, I may say, A. L. R.' In most of the pronouncements of human idiocy, there is this touch of shrillness and egoism. But real egoism is incapable of the self-forgetfulness required for poetry. The reader who approaches Rowse through the poetry

* See Stephen Spender's remarks in *World Within World*.

soon becomes aware that these outbursts are not really Swiftian in spirit. They spring out of a kind of humorous malice, and perhaps a Shavian desire to give his audience what it expects. If Rowse is sincere in his belief that most human beings are idiots—and he undoubtedly is—the spectacle no longer excites fury, but an indulgent contempt. And even this finds no echo in the deeper levels from which his poetry springs. For the most remarkable thing about the poetry is its objectivity, the sense of the ability to be as totally absorbed by an object as water is by a sponge.

> The whole bay brimming with the silent sea,
> The call of a curlew, the creaking of a plough,
> A black and satin plane slides suddenly over
> Wheeling to the coast,
> The smell of November in the air,
> The mould, the dead brambles, the year over. . . .

And when he chooses to write with anger, he carries the same conviction as Yeats: as in *Homecoming to Cornwall, December 1942*:

> In the moment of breathing in my native land
> I remember to hate: the thousand indignities,
> The little humiliations, the small insults
> From small people, the hidden enmities,
> The slights that hurt the sensibilities
> Of a child that, longing for affection, learned
> To reward envy with contempt, to speak
> The biting word that freezes sympathy,
> The instinctive expectation of a blow
> To pride or self-respect or decency;
> And as a man to mark the averted gaze
> Of petty shopkeepers on their dunghill pavements;
> The meanness of the moneyed middle-class,
> The slow passivity of the workers that know
> Not their own interest or their enemies.
> But, most of all, the vast misunderstanding
> That divides me from my people I lament,
> The self-willed folly that condemned me long
> To opening the eyes of fools, the task
> Of a Tregeagle* or a Sysyphus. . . .

* Tregeagle was a bailiff in Cornish legend who was condemned to empty Dozmare pool with a sea-shell with a hole in the bottom.

In reading this passage—which may refer to Rowse's period as
a Labour candidate in the 1930s—one becomes aware of the
basic Rowse problem. It is pointless to ask whether he would be a
better poet if he could transcend these feelings—the over-sensitive
child's response to hostility—and take a more Olympian view.
It is like asking whether Proust would have been a better
novelist if his parents had not indulged his nervous sensibilities
as a child. It is conceivable that he might have been a more balanc-
ed and happy human being; it is also conceivable that he might
never have become a novelist. The 'one skin too few' that produces the temperamental excesses of the *Recherche* also produces
the minute observation that is its essence. Yeats comments
perceptively: 'I have sometimes wondered if I do not write
poetry to find a cure for my own ailment, as constipated cats do
when they eat valerian.' The objectivity of Rowse's poetry is to
some extent the soothing of a burn by pressing it against something cold.

> The window open to the grove:
> The leafless trees are very still,
> The sky is clear with February light,
> The stream runs swiftly from the mill;
>
> Along the paths the people walk,
> Fresh from church they sniff the air,
> Considering the crocuses,
> Frilled aconites and snowdrops there.

The verse also runs like a clear stream, interposing no obstacle
of language between the reader and the object. One is inclined to
believe that Rowse is simply fortunate in possessing a Celtic gift of
language, of saying things with grace and precision. But the
early poems—quoted in the autobiographies—disprove this. The
language is anything but unobtrusive:

> All is at peace now in the moon-splashed glade:
> Nothing moves, save a little rippling wind. . .

Rowse comments on his first poem—a Keatsian sonnet called
Star-Jewels: 'It was very rich and literary, not a good poem.' And
although he continued to write poems throughout the under-
graduate period and subsequent years, the earliest poems included

in his first volume of verse—*Poems of a Decade*—were written in 1931, when he was twenty-eight. There can be no doubt that, in spite of the apparent clarity and ease of the style, Rowse is an obsessive craftsman. The interesting result is that the quality of the poetry continues to improve steadily throughout the five volumes: *Poems of a Decade* (1941), *Poems Chiefly Cornish* (1944), *Poems of Deliverance* (1946), *Poems Partly American* (1954), and *Poems of Cornwall and America* (1967). Two of his finest poems, *The Road to Roche* and *Passion Sunday in Charlestown Church* occur at the end of the fifth volume. But in another sense, the sense of theme and preoccupation, there is very little change between 1931 and 1967. From the beginning, Rowse is the poet of solitude:

> Into a quiet, lonely place I come,
> To a coign of cliff and a lane that drops to the sea:
> The shrill voices of the winds have here
> No place, nor the winds' fingers in my hair.
> All that was before is strangely far,
> And I have entered on a secret stillness:
> A frightened hush falls on the throat that sang,
> On the stream that babbled dreamily in the sun,
> On whispering osiers and ivied stones.
> There are a thousand timid eyes that watch
> In the startled silence; only the monotone
> Of gathered waves that break upon the shore
> Below, lulls suspense with regular beat.

There are certain influences present in these early poems: Hardy, Yeats, Housman—even Hopkins can be detected in the irregular metre of the last line quoted. But from the beginning, Rowse is also fully himself, for the central theses are already here: childhood, the sense of the past, the sense of the brevity of human existence, loneliness, the ascetic renunciation involved in the choice he has made for himself. An Oxford garden symbolises it all:

> This is my life, to watch the seasons pass
> Over the garden's clear enchanted glass.
> There goes by the procession of the hours,
> The days, the years, nor stirs the ordered flowers.
> And there as on a magic plane I see
> The ceaseless flow of time away from me:

Not in my heart, but in the external world
This evidence of my weak mortal hold.

The arctic moon becomes a symbol of his renunciation:

The fingers of the moon upon the frozen world
Have caught the aloof heart in a net,
Caught and enmeshed there is no longer hold
Within this arctic region where life is not:

The fine and subtle fingers of the night
Seek out the lunar shadows that we are,
Sifting in the crevices the white
Dust fallen of the crumbling sphere:

The wind of death at the corners of the house
Is furtive behind the barren leaves;
Though we, but shadows moving in the caves,
For screen from the approaching death have these:

The frozen eagle poised still in vain for flight,
The patterned poplars and the momentary light.

But this mood of sadness is not the dominant note in these
early poems:

How usual is the world of Spring:
The floods are out across the plain;
The punctual birds are on the wing,
Scattering the dew like grain.

Over the meadows and the fields
There blows a wind of daffodils;
Each passing year no difference yields
Upon the seasonable hills.

Yet still I think sometime to meet
A tiger, amber in the rain;
And turning down the narrow street,
The Holy Ghost in Magpie Lane.

But when he writes of people, the misanthropy flares up:

Nature I hate and what's unnatural choose
For rule of life, rather than hourly lose

The sense of separateness from the common world,
Admit a likeness that I never willed

To all that's human, similar and mean:
Rather the animal than the inane.

The poet's fundamental dilemma becomes clear. Faced with the 'common herd', he experiences revulsion; everyday life produces a powerful impulse of asceticism. But the asceticism in turn is unsatisfactory. When he is alone, the poet finds it too easy to think about the brevity of human life. The asceticism is not really a satisfactory response to the revulsion. In the second of two misogynic poems on marriage, he admits this:

So let me speak that have no children: I
That know not how to live nor how to die.

Rowse's honesty is as total as Yeats's. The anti-marriage poems certainly have the Swiftian ring:

The thought of marriage is enough to make men mad:
To think that in the end a man is had

Neck in the noose, foot in the trap caught fast,
Winged and brought down, snared and secured at last

By nature's forces, malign, inscrutable,
Himself no more an independent will

But only a straw, a conduit through which the power
Of human need to multiply may pour,

This parody of purpose, begetting more
Men so that all may proceed as it was before . . .

But there are times when the sense of separation sounds a note familiar to readers of T. E. Lawrence:

At the point at night,
    where the copulating cars draw up,
    the lustful lovers sit huddled inside,
    dark above the soft explosion of the sea;
    or here where the beam of St Anthony's light
    lays a dark track across the harbour mouth
    to Pendennis and envious me:

> I envy their abstraction from the world,
> their absorption in each other,
> their self-sufficiency:
> the primal couple as of ape or dog
> making a fruitful unity.

This tone is typical of Rowse in the late thirties—a time of bitterness and frustration; but little of this can be found in subsequent volumes. It was at this period—the end of the thirties—that Rowse had his most severe breakdown of health. And recovery brought with it a new sense of affirmation, as in *Cueillir des Roses: July 1941*:

> Never have I known till now
> Such sense of joy in life,
> Such pleasure in the moment,
> The days that pass not idly by
> But full of purposeful activity
> And happy contentment like a bee
> That visits in the summer garden,
> The drunk and sleepy flowers weighs down,
> Passing from one to the other all the day
> In the hot sun. The violated flowers,
> Fluttered by the butterflies,
> Raped by the bees, now sway
> This way and that under their thrust,
> Hang their heads in ecstasy
> At the embrace; then, the moment over,
> Recover their primal chastity. . . .

The sexual image certainly conveys this new gratitude for being alive. The sense of the beauty of nature returns again:

> The mingled oats and barley in the field,
> The feathery grasses at my feet,
> The varied movement of wind in corn,
> The night-wind blowing in the trees,
> The melancholy ashes that speak of rain
> The church clock of my childhood
> Speaks yet again over the hillside,
> Knocks at my unrepentant heart. . . .

Poem after poem has this sense of joy in nature:

It is the hour of twilight, when the day's work is over:
I stand at the dip in the road, a flittering bat overhead,
A diminutive frog crosses rapidly at my feet,
In my ears the drowsy night cries of the gulls,
The particular sound of the sea splaying up over the beach.
There is the crushed tobacco scent of new-mown hay.
Now I enter the region of honeysuckle,
The smell of the wood, the corn, and things growing.

In fact, this volume is so full of this sense of acceptance—and
of heroism and danger involved in the war—that it is strange to
turn to its final pages and find a poem that dates from the illness-
period called *Les Horreurs* which lists the things he has come to
dislike: a woman wheeling a pram, providing 'cannon-fodder for
the future', girls 'that express their common souls upon the
pavement':

I am tired of being carried like a corpse around the country,
of carrying myself, a woman pregnant with pain,
my disease, my mind;
of writing poems in a book where nobody understands;

Give me rather the steeled and strong hands of the engineer,
the warmth of body of the furnace man
in the colliery's interior glow,
the loneliness of the aviator,
the skill of the driver taking
                a difficult curve,
the presence and the sense of danger,
        external to the self.

The more positive note comes here as a relief. In a sense, the
negative is an alien intruder in Rowse's poems, for his fundamental aesthetic is positive. He speaks of it in discussing Joyce
in *A Cornishman at Oxford*; of the argument about aesthetics in
The Portrait of the Artist, in which Stephen Dedalus 'works out that
the apprehension of the world and experience as beauty is their
final redemption, the only lasting value that transcends time, environment and circumstance'. For many writers, this would be merely
an empty credo; but it is the essence of Rowse as a poet; almost
his justification as a human being. Rowse may be a pessimist

in many respects, but in this matter he is completely positive. The feeling for beauty is fierce, obsessive, the dominating passion of his life. No Mohammedan could be more fanatical about his prophet than Rowse is about his creed of beauty. One has the feeling that if all his pessimism and personal sufferings were placed on one side of a scale, and his sense of beauty on the other, the sense of beauty would be the heavier. In many respects, the Rowse who emerges through the poems is a self-divided man; but in this fundamental sense, he is unified, and is able to confer unity on his work.

In the autobiography, Rowse comments that he could never be a novelist, because he lacks the necessary interest in the ordinary doings of people—except after they are dead. This is a misleading statement. To begin with, Rowse has written a number of fine short stories. But, more important, the poetry itself is full of the stuff of novels. Rowse's best and most typical poems are not the short lyrics, but long poems like *The Old Cemetery at St Austell, Invocation for a Cornish House: Summer 1941* (both to be found in *Poems Chiefly Cornish*) and *The Road to Roche*. In these Rowse emerges as a kind of English Proust, writing of his country and his past. *The Old Cemetery* has certain points of resemblance to Gray's *Elegy*. This in itself is significant, for the mood of Gray's *Elegy*—the melancholy serenity and detachment—is the mood of many of Rowse's poems. It is also the mood of *Swann's Way*. But in *The Old Cemetery,* the historian complements the poet, and the result is a tougher texture than in Proust.

> There in the distance are the dark woods of Penrice,
> Mysterious, aloof, funereal;
> Lost in their depths lies the house of the Admiral,
> The last Sir Charles: whose family did well
> In the time of the Commonwealth and showed a nice
> Sense of the moment, laid out their money with skill,
>
> Adding acre to acre and field to field.
> The squawk of pheasants now for generations
> Has announced the vicinity of the squire. Yet still
> Their tribute to mortality they yield,
> Having come to an end with a young heir killed
> In Nineteen Fourteen, in the last war of nations.

For him the white gate on the road to Trenarren
Stands open in vain, in vain the long curve of the drive
Leads across deer park and ploughland in the wavering
Moonlight, to the wide portico welcoming
The returned, the family portraits in the hall:
He has become a tablet on a wall.

Rowse speaks here of his love of music—a love so strong, as he
explains elsewhere, that he has often been afraid to indulge it:

The little chantry chapel in the church
Is filled with their memorials. Here as a boy
I used to sit in the darkling evening
Deep-ensconced in a pew, listening
To the organ's music, rapt with such extreme
Joy, my mind enchanted moved in a dream,

In which were mingled melodies and urns,
A woman weeping over a bier, coloured
Armorial bearings, glints of crimson and gold,
White marble stained with the late westering sun's
Last gleams. . . .

Such a passage makes the reader aware of another affinity—with a
writer rather less fashionable than Proust: Walter Pater. The atmosphere here brings to mind *Marius the Epicurean* and the unfinished
Gaston de Latour. And one is reminded of Yeats's comments on
Pater: 'Three or four years ago I re-read *Marius the Epicurean*,
expecting to find I cared for it no longer, but it still seemed to me,
as I think it seemed to us all, the only great prose in modern
English, and yet I began to wonder if it, or the attitude of mind
of which it was the noblest expression, had not caused the disaster
of my friends'—that is, of the 'tragic generation'. It would
hardly be inaccurate to call Rowse 'the last Aesthetic'. His
attitude to life is as detached as that of De Lisle Adam's Axel, and
he accepts death as the inevitable termination of beauty:

Amid so much human mutability
This pleasant garden is a place of rest and peace:
Death loses its horrid aspect, is seen to be
A natural term of life's unquietness:
Here all conflict is stilled, quarrels, cease
Here is neither friend nor enemy.

M

To become aware of this is to recognise that Rowse's choice of
the academic life may have been a deep instinct of self-preservation: not simply from the insecurity of the literary life, but from
his own tendency to world-rejection. The creed of the beauty and
impermanence of life killed Lionel Johnson and Ernest Dowson,
and destroyed Wilde. If Pater, Housman and Delius survived, it
was because they could contemplate it from a position of relative
security. Rowse's Fellowship provided the security, and his
involvement with the facts of history the counterbalance to his
dangerously subjective temperament. It is the sense of history
that provided the backbone for *Invocation for a Cornish House,* with
its lovely coda:

> So now tonight, when the bearded barley drinks
> The moon, and the corn is stippled with night-gold,
> The bent blades swaying, are praying now to Venus
> And Mercury to avert the blows of Mars
> And spare their seedlings the ravages of wars:
> So, too, I pray, preserve this house that I
> May gather the fruits of so many years dreaming,
> Researches into memory's observant eye,
> Achieve some signal thing before darkness falls
> On these loved walls and shuttered windows, on the sea,
> The distant headland, the ripened corn and me.

A reader who had followed Rowse through the first three
volumes of poetry might well have found himself wondering
how he could continue to develop, or whether, given his temperament, his material and his outlook, whether it would be possible
to develop at all. The answer appears in *Poems Partly American*
of 1959. One might have predicted that travel in America would
destroy Rowse's poetic impulse rather than nourish it. But
this is to reckon without the curious eye of the historian, and the
passion of a Cornishman visiting a land that became a home to so
many Cornish miners. There are flashes of aversion:

> Read your Daily *Illini*! You guys got
> Your *Illini*, Keep up with your campus news!

But for the most part, the land seems to awaken a new poetic
zest:

> Gulls, skyscrapers, funnels, masts,
> The wind whipping a rope in the sun
> Or fluttering in the black veil of a nun,
> Light breaks over New York and among
> The cliffs and canyons of the middle town. . . .

Rowse's sense of place is never stronger:

> The leaves are falling in Columbus, Nebraska,
> Raked together by men with the tired faces
> Of professors, full of disappointed hopes:
> No longer keen as the cruel winds that blow
> Across the prairie's winter emptiness. . . .

Or:

> The saddle-back hills and cattle millionaires
> Of Omaha are a November night away:
> I awake to find the country white with frost,
> Snow fences already up along the track.

He obviously takes an immense delight in the changing scenery and changing seasons. It seems strange that Europeanised Americans like Henry James, T. S. Eliot, Henry Miller, should find America so repellent, while an 'aesthetic' Englishman like Rowse seems to feel perfectly at home there:

> Mild south-westerly blows across the field
> Awaking reminiscential oceans in the trees,
> Wind flutters in loose trousers of young men
> In cherry-coloured sweaters, orange, red and green.
> The figures weave, unweave, converse,
> The trees hold up their spreading crowns
> Beneath the mild forgiving sky
> In this autumnal pause before winter comes. . . .

Possibly this increasing mellowness is the result of age. Certainly, it can be found in the English poems in this book. In *Blackpool out of Season, November in Blenheim Park, Buckinghamshire,* and in the fine poem to Kierkegaard, written in Copenhagen, there is the same profound sense of place. The opening poem of the book, *The Choice,* speaks of the old conflict, the view from two windows of his room at All Souls, one of trees in spring blossom, the other of 'the Roman world of stone', 'This learned prison, the walls that shut me in.' But this tone of regret is surprisingly absent from the rest of the book. In poems to Kierkegaard and T. E. Lawrence, one observes Rowse's sense of affinity with these 'outsider' figures, and it seems to symbolise a new view of himself, the equivalent of Yeats's transition from 'the last romantic' to 'an old man's eagle mind'. The poetic character seems to have lost a certain fluidity and acquired a new definition of outline. This can be seen if one compares the American poems—written in the mid-fifties—with an earlier poem, *Approaching Cornwall: Easter 1948:*

> Oh country of my humiliation
> That yet smiles at me in the pools that pass,
> In railway cuttings starred with primroses,
> In alleys where vanished viaducts
> Have left their bones of ivied stones and made
> A desolation in the deepening shade,
> Lit by the shuttling windows of the train
> Approaching Cornwall in the setting sun.
> A presence I already feel like a cloud
> Descends on the mind that yet was free
> A moment before, that now is possessed,
> Moved to unrest with every motion
> Into the obtuse, malevolent West.
> This is Easter time. The Cornish crowd
> Into the compartment, chattering
> As ever with platitudinous vacuity.
> The train moves over the enchanted gulf,
> Trematon mirrored in the evening water,
> Mount Edgcumbe drowned in woods of the sea,
> Sunlit ridges folded with shadow,
> Hills of home where my Passion-tide begins.

The new detachment becomes visible in the poems of the fifties and sixties. Even when he writes of marriage—in *Married Couple*—or of sex—in *The Species*—the observation is ironic, detached; it lacks the old savagery:

> The natural instinct of the male for the female
> Is something universal, hardly comprehensible.
> The fat Jew taximan on the way to Idlewild

Notices the nondescript nurse at the corner of the
block.
'You like them dark?'
'Yeah, I prefer them dark—more aggressive.'
The cab half-slews. 'Want a taxi, miss?'
A smile is exchanged. At the airport
The tall New Englander in navy blue,
Unsmiling Puritan appearance, automatically
Appraises the barely decipherable girl going by.
I have known in an ancient common-room
A young stallion snort at female voices in the quad.
What is it to be shut out from this play of life?
One observes, with Henry James, the human aquarium:
All the fish going round, sad jaws working,
Eyes bulging in ever-unsatisfied stare,
Enclosed within their element, scale on scale, quite unaware
That the female of the species is more deadly than the male.

This, in fact, is social observation, closer to Edgar Lee Masters'
Spoon River Anthology than to any English poet.

This new detachment, the quality of observation, culminates in
The Road to Roche (in *Poems of Cornwall and America*), another poem
describing the Cornwall of his childhood, that achieves a zest
and objectivity that make it one of Rowse's most memorable
poems:

Here is the hard-bitten country of my birth.
In a dank corner between monkey-puzzle and sawpit
Lived drunken Dick Spargo: how he made a living
I've often wondered—occasional cattle-dealing
And his wife's bit of property, I suppose.
Fridays he'd come rolling home from market,
His breeches as tight, and every variety
Of knobbly stick or cane or switch to brandish,
Long moustaches dripping booze at ends.

The poem is too long to quote at length. It makes its effect by
juxtaposing these memories of characters and places:

On an island-site of its own, grim and gaunt
Like a flat-iron, the house of a double murder.
I knew the murderer: a stranger to the village,

> Choirman and St John's ambulance-man,
> Sharp-nosed, evasive, sexy and saturnine. . . .

Then there is Bethesda Chapel:

> . . . . . where Mamie and Frank
> Sang their way into each other's favour
> And further, clinching the matter up Look-out Lane,
> Amid flowering hawthorn and prickly furze,
> Where all the girls got pregnant in the spring.

Again, one has the sense of a development paralleling that of Yeats: the mask of the poetic dreamer abandoned, and a new hardness and vitality.

Still, Rowse is not the kind of poet in whom basic changes occur. The poetry is the expression of a personality and outlook that he has chosen and accepted. This is clear in *Passion Sunday in Charlestown Church*, where, speaking of his father and mother, he says:

> The simple courage, the confidence in life
> Their son has never found, yet had beginning
> In this place. Now come back,
> A public man, scarred with injuries,
> Seared by sad experience, without illusion
> Or any hope, dedicated to despair. . . .

Rowse must be judged, as we judge Housman and Hardy, as the poet of a single mood, an unchanging outlook.

> I do not wish to die—
> There is such contingent beauty in life:
> The open window on summer mornings
> Looking out on gardens and green things growing,
> The shadowy cups of roses flowering to themselves—
> Images of time and eternity—
> Silence in the garden and felt along the walls.
> The room is suddenly filled with sun,
> Like a sacrament one can never be
> Sufficiently thankful for. Door ajar,
> The eye reaches across from one
> Open window to another, eye to eye,
> And then the healing spaces of the sky. . . .

This is the essence of Rowse, this ability to forget the despair, the 'ulcerated heart' in sudden total absorption in beauty.

This poetry is as English as the music of Delius and Elgar, and it has their qualities of beauty, nostalgia, sadness. It has remained unfashionable for the same reason that Delius and Elgar were unfashionable in the era of Walton and Stravinsky: its simplicity, lack of concern with technique as such, seem to relate to it an earlier period. Its colours are perhaps too dark for it ever to achieve the kind of acclaim that came to Betjeman after the publication of his collected poems; but it should at least be known to all who care about English poetry.

Rowse's own explanation of this lack of interest is that people do not expect a historian to be a good poet. He is, after all, the only English historian, apart from Macaulay, who has also been a poet. No doubt he is right. My own feeling is that he is a poet who also happens to be, by some strange chance, a good historian.

4

Nikos Kazantzakis

Although Kazantzakis is known in the west mainly as a novelist, he regarded himself primarily as a poet, and is so regarded by most of his fellow countrymen. In 1960, I wrote a long essay on Kazantzakis, which was published as an appendix to my book *The Strength to Dream*. At this time, there were still many of Kazantzakis's most important books that were not translated: *Report to Greco, St Francis, The Rock Garden, Toda Raba, The Fratricides*. Now it is possible to see Kazantzakis's output as a whole, and to grasp something of the real significance of his masterpiece: *The Odyssey, A Modern Sequel*. I have tried to show in the course of this book that the poet, whether he knows it or not, is the antithesis of the logical positivist or the scientific specialist, since poetry is *by nature* a personal statement that aims at becoming a generalisation about human existence. In the poetic experience, the everyday façade melts; the sense of a world that you know all-too-well gives place to a feeling of wider significances that we are normally too brutish and self-preoccupied to grasp. Whether he likes it or not, the poet cannot take a 'specialist' view of nature, in which one single aspect is chosen for study.

The poet may, of course, decide to stick to the personal, as Rowse does. For Rowse, the realm of general significance is represented by history; and even this he sees in personal terms. Such a poet is at the opposite end of the scale from Kazantzakis, For Kazantzakis, whether he likes it or not, feels a perpetual discomfort in the face of Charles Ives' 'unanswered question', 'Why do I exist?' He turns upon the world around him the raging curiosity that Rowse turns upon history. This is not an attempt at a philosophic synthesis, but at a synthesis in terms of the personal vision. That in the later years of his life this attempt was made mainly through the medium of the novel makes no difference in the present context. The obsessive unity of purpose behind all his work makes it seem irrelevant.

Kazantzakis could be described as an evolutionary romantic. He belongs to the tradition of Goethe, Nietzsche, Bergson, Dostoevsky and Shaw. These writers may seem, on the surface, to have little enough in common; but underlying them all, there is an assumption that might be defined in these terms.

First of all, there is a sense that man has reached a new stage in his evolution, a point at which he is about to become something else. And the ground of this intuitive recognition is the feeling that man possesses far more inner-strength than he ever realises. He thinks of himself as a very ordinary sort of creature, blessed with a capacity to use his brain—Pascal's 'thinking reed'. He is mistaken. He is really a kind of magician, possessed of powers that go far beyond mere reasoning or analysis. In an obscure and yet very real sense, he possesses many of the powers that he used to attribute to the ancient gods—the powers of Zeus, able to hurl thunderbolts or transform himself into a bull or a swan.

This discovery is something comparatively new for the human race; it is barely two hundred years old. First of all, there were the great ages of religion, in which man saw himself as a simple creature of God who was represented on the earth by priests—whether pagan or Christian. Then, with the rise of science, came the great ages of humanism. The cultured men ceased to believe that the Church and the Bible contained all the secrets of the universe. They dismissed the supernatural. Their attitude is summarised in Pope's line, 'The proper study of mankind is man.'

And then after the French revolution came that strange era we call 'the romantic century'. And this was the most important change of all. For the romantic made the important discovery that man is not merely a creature of the physical world, but of the mind. As H. G. Wells once said: the bird is a creature of the air, the fish is a creature of the water; man is a creature of the brain. For most of his life, his attention is occupied by the trivialities of everyday life, and his 'inner life' is comparatively feeble, like a candle in the sunlight. But there are certain moments when this inner-world takes on a strange power of its own. The candle grows brighter and brighter, until it is a blinding glare that rivals the sun. And when this happens, 'romantic man' realises the absurdity of Hume's view that man's mental life is nothing more than a dim carbon-copy of his physical memories and perceptions. No, it is independent in some strange way; it stands alone. It has the power to lift man into a state that can only be described as 'god-like'. Why is man so moved when he looks at a mountain landscape? Is it not because he is reminded of his own inner mountain landscape?

But here is the most important point of all, the key to the whole problem. All animals share one characteristic: lack of challenge makes them grow 'tame', lazy, domesticated. Only challenge brings out the best in them. Yet most animals do not mind becoming tame. They are glad enough to lead a peaceful and easy life.

There is only one kind of animal who loathes the idea of becoming tame. That animal I have called 'the outsider'. He looks around at a society of lazy and more-or-less happy people, and something in him revolts. For he sees clearly that this kind of contentment is the opposite of the god-like. It destroys the will. He clings to that important memory of the moments when the candle began to glow like the sun. He knows that there are enormous inner powers in him, ready to respond to challenges. This is why man has created great music, great poetry, great art: to remind him that mere contentment is a bore, that man is most truly himself when something inside him responds to great challenges, when his inner-spirit exults in the face of storm and tempest, because it has a strength to equal theirs.

There is a strange and absurd paradox about human nature, which is expressed in Fichte's comment: 'To be free is nothing; to become free is very heaven.' In the moment when a human being experiences freedom, inner doors open; he sees over endless plains; his freedom stretches around him like the vast spaces of a cathedral. But within days or hours he has become accustomed to freedom; the mind closes; it yawns and falls asleep. This *sleep* is the greatest enemy of human beings. The cathedral turns into a narrow room with all the windows closed. *Freedom ceases to be freedom*. But how absurd! The freedom is still there, just as a window is still there, even when you have drawn the curtains across it. . . .

This expresses in a nutshell the romantic problem. It is still the central problem for modern man, the problem that blocks his evolution.

A few men recognise this problem clearly, and strive to solve it. In our own century, the number of such men has been pitifully small. A few major writers have recognised it, indeed—Sartre, Camus, Thomas Mann—but have decided it is insoluble. 'It is meaningless that we live and meaningless that we die,' says Sartre, 'Man is a useless passion.'

Kazantzakis is the only contemporary writer who saw the problem, faced it, and spent his life fighting like a demon to solve it. The greatness of his work lies in this demonic quality. It is also heroic; Kazantzakis is the only modern writer of whom one could use the word 'Promethean'.

Before everything else, Kazantzakis is a great artist; this stands out clearly, even in relatively unsuccessful works like *Toda Raba* and *The Rock Garden*. I can think of no major writer except Tolstoy who gives such a sense of physical existence, of intensity of colour and smell and texture, of space and light.

At the centre of all his work lies a revelation which is extremely difficult to grasp. However, I must make the attempt to express it.

It appears, for example, in the twentieth book of the *Odyssey*, in the scene where Ulysses dines with the 'frog-bloated eunuch', the epicurean who believes that man should be cynical and aloof, and sip at all pleasures like a bee at honey. The eunuch is misled by the fact that Ulysses has achieved a god-like detachment into believing that their views of life are similar. And it is almost impossible for Ulysses to explain why this is untrue, for in a profound sense, they have no common language. He can only try to explain his revulsion in symbols:

> One day I met a great striped tiger in a glen
> And my heart leapt with joy, so that I shouted 'Brother!'

This is again the expression of that fierce inner-force that leaps outward to respond to storm and tempest. This is precisely what the epicurean lacks. But it is not enough to say that Ulysses feels a deeper 'love of life'. It is more than that, far more. He is instinctively aware of this paradox of human nature: that when a man relaxes and becomes contented, his cathedral of freedom shrinks into a small dusty room. Ulysses describes landing on an

island where there is a crumbling old windmill, with no wind to
drive its sails:

> I almost choked with wrath, and yelled to my wolf-pack:
> 'Forward my lads, haul up the sails, *give life a shove*.'

I have italicised this last phrase because this is the core of the
problem. All animals are like sailing ships; they need *external
stimuli* to move them; place them in a situation without such
stimuli, and they fall into a state of dullness, like the becalmed
windmill. Most men are animals, and all men, even the greatest,
95 per cent animal, and only 5 per cent of true human potential.
For what distinguishes the truly human is this. It is not a sailing
ship, but a ship with a small engine, that can drive it when there
is no wind. 'Give life a shove.' Man possesses this freedom of the
mind, of the imagination—as Kazantzakis states very clearly in the
great seventeenth book of the *Odyssey* of which I shall speak later.
The world Ulysses understands is a *greater* world than that seen by
the eunuch king. It is a mistake to imagine that their eyes see the
same things. The eyes of a drunken man who has just exhausted
himself with vomiting do not see the same world as the eyes of a
lover who is possessing his mistress for the first time. And yet
this difference must remain forever inexpressible in language,
which reflects the world in dehydrated symbols. In a sense, this is
the central problem of the work of Kazantzakis; it explains why
he agreed with Nietzsche that a sheet of clean paper is in many
ways preferable to a sheet that has been 'defiled' by writing.

Before I go on, let me confess that my own temperament is so
remote from that of Kazantzakis that I am, perhaps, not fully
qualified to write about him. Temperamentally speaking, I am
closer to Shaw—who is always accused by the English of being
'heartless'. Such passion as I possess is intellectual rather than
emotional. I contemplate the life and work of Kazantzakis with a
wonder that is mixed with relief, a feeling of 'rather him than
me'.

I can explain this attitude by referring to one of my favourite
books; *Quest*, the autobiography of Leopold Infeld. Infeld was a
Polish Jew who spent his childhood in the ghetto in Cracow. His
family was heavily religious in the rather literal and unimaginative Jewish way, and he felt himself surrounded by the hatred and

contempt of the *goyim*. One day, in a second-hand bookshop, he saw an enormous work on physics in three volumes, and bought it. From then on, he plunged into the magic world of science; it no longer mattered that he was a Jew living in a ghetto; he was a scientist, a citizen of the world of Mind. There is nothing so exhilarating as reading about men who have made this discovery; that one's personal life does not really matter all that much, for man's true destiny is to lead an impersonal life.

When I read the early chapter of *Report to Greco*, I felt again what I had felt reading *Quest*. Kazantzakis describes his childhood in Megalo Castro in Crete, and his father whose ancestors 'were bloodthirsty pirates on water, warrior chieftains on land', and who had many of the harshest characteristics of his ancestors. As I read the account of his childhood—that clever, over-sensitive boy, surrounded by kindly but basically earthy villagers—I experience again that feeling of stifling, of suffocation, that I experience with *Quest*. I long for the boy Kazantzakis to discover three volumes on physics in a bookshop window and to soar beyond his environment like a bird out of a cage. And, in fact, it *was* science that brought about his mental release. The physics teacher told him that the earth was not the centre of the universe, and that man is not the special creation of God, but of Darwinian evolution. At first, the shock was severe, but he soon recovered from it and embraced the new faith with enthusiasm; he even formed a 'friendly society' with several school friends, whose aim was to preach the new gospel of scientific enlightenment to mankind. At this stage—in his early adolescence—Kazantzakis obviously found it hard to believe that great ideas were not the fire that would burn away all the world's evil and stupidity.

Later, in some of the most moving chapters of the book, he describes how, at the end of his student days, he made a pilgrimage through Greece, and then through Italy, his mind reeling at the revelation of the cultural riches that surrounded him. For most men, this would have been the crowning experience of life, the end of conflict and doubt. It is typical of Kazantzakis that it was only a new beginning. The search began in earnest. Science was not enough, so he turned to history, and to art. These still left him hungry, so he turned to poetry, then to religion, and to the idea of asceticism and spiritual effort. This was succeeded by a phase in which he became obsessed by Nietzsche and D'Annunzio,

and the idea of total moral freedom. Then came a period in which
Christ became his ideal symbol, followed later by Buddha, then
by Lenin. The *Odyssey* derives some of its terrifying vitality from
this vertiginous mixture of ideas. One cannot help feeling astounded by his ability to cope with the mixture, as one is astounded
by a drinker who mixes wine, gin and whisky. But again, I find
myself muttering 'Rather him than me'.

Kazantzakis believed that his major problem was the enormous
strength of the instincts that he derived from his ancestors. He
may well have been right. In a typical passage he says:

> Now and then, sporadically, a sweet voice sounds
> in the very centre of my heart: 'Have no fears,
> I shall make laws and establish order. I am God.
> Have faith.' But all at once comes a heavy growl
> from my loins, and the sweet voice is silenced:
> 'Stop your boasting! I shall undo your laws, ruin
> your order and obliterate you. I am chaos!'

Clearly, he is a self-divided man. He describes how, on a mountain walk, he found himself standing above a small village, and
suddenly felt impelled to scream: 'I shall slaughter you all!' Yet
his books are full of compassion for human suffering. In the sixth
book of the *Odyssey*, in which a sexual orgy is described, there is a
moving account of the death of a slave-woman's child. The
demonic and the saintly wrestle on every page of Kazantzakis.

This element of demonic violence never left Kazantzakis,
Prevelakis tells us that in the last years of Kazantzakis's life, 'an
odour of sanctity issued from him'. And yet at this time, he was
writing his last book *Report to Greco,* with its description of his
pirate ancestors: 'Whooping, the pirates threw their grapnels and
leapt on to the deck, cleavers in hand. Showing no favour either
to Christ or Mohammed, they slaughtered the old men, took the
young ones as slaves, keeled over the women, and burrowed into
Grabuousa again, their moustaches full of blood and female
exhalations.' Clearly, Kazantzakis is still a long way from being a
saint; he is still able to identify too closely with murder. The last
phrase about female exhalations is also typical. He is fascinated by
the odours of the human body, of armpits and loins, as well as
by blood and the idea of violent death. Yet this man could produce superb and profound novels on St Francis of Assisi and Jesus

as well as the portrait of the Christ-like Manolias the shepherd boy in *Christ Recrucified*, who brings to mind Dostoevsky's Prince Myshkin. It is not surprising that, from first to last, his work produced an impression of conflict that can only be resolved by death.

Nevertheless, it would be a mistake to over-emphasise the conflict. What makes Kazantzakis a great writer is the spiritual effort that went into control of his contending forces. It is not surprising that he regarded his *Odyssey* as his great 'work', and all his books as minor works. His books themselves comprise a kind of Odyssey, so that they could almost be read as one single great novel, charting the spiritual and intellectual journey of a lifetime.

Let us briefly consider these 'lesser works' before going on to examine the *Odyssey* itself. They may have appeared to be of minor importance in the eyes of Kazantzakis, but they constitute a body of work that dwarfs that of every other contemporary novelist, and which demands comparison with the *œuvre* of Dostoevsky and Tolstoy.

There is, in the Prologue of his travel book on China and Japan, a passage that goes a long way towards explaining why Kazantzakis is such a good novelist, even when he is not writing at his best:

Neither am I nourished by fleshless, abstract memories. . . . When I close my eyes in order to enjoy a country again, my five senses, the five mouth-filled tentacles of my body, pounce upon it and bring it to me. Colors, fruits, women. The smell of orchards, of filthy narrow alleys, of armpits. Endless snows with blue, glittering reflections. Scorching, wavy deserts of sand shimmering under the hot sun. Tears, cries, songs, distant bells of mules, camels or troikas. The acrid, nauseating stench of some Mongolian cities will never leave my nostrils. And I will eternally hold in my hands—eternally, that is, until my hands rot—the melons of Bukhara, the watermelons of the Volga, the cool, dainty hand of a Japanese girl. . . .

He goes on to tell how, in his youth, 'I struggled to nourish my famished soul by feeding it with abstract concepts', and how Buddha became his god. 'Deny your five senses, empty your guts, love nothing, hate nothing, desire nothing.' Then one day, in a dream, he saw two woman's lips without a face, that asked 'Who is your God?' and when he replied 'Buddha' said: 'No Epaphus' —the god of the senses, of touch.

He follows this up with a magnificently typical story: of how Mohammed went to the tent of a sheik to discuss war; the sheik's wife opened the door, and the wind blew her robe, revealing her breast. Mohammed immediately forgot all other women and cried: 'Thank you, Allah, for making my heart so fickle.'

His first novel, the *Toda Raba* (1929) was written as a direct consequence of the impact of Russia. He was forty-six at the time, a relatively late start for a novelist, although he had admittedly written a verse play on Christ in 1921, a spiritual credo called *The Saviours of God* (a typically Nietzschean title) in 1923, a play about the Buddha and the early cantos of the *Odyssey*, as well as two travel books. (Helen Kazantzakis mentions that he was best known as a travel writer in these early years, and this may explain why it took so long for his creative greatness to be recognised.)

Judged by the standards of his later novels, *Toda Raba* is not a good book. It draws together seven varied characters, including a consumptive Chinese schoolteacher, a Polish-Jewish girl, an Indian monk, an African negro and a Japanese writer, and throws them together in Russia of the post-revolutionary period. It is difficult to say how far Kazantzakis really embraced the ideals of Communism; Kimon Friar has stated (in his preface to *The Saviours of God*) that Kazantzakis fundamentally rejected Marxian materialism, and the smallest acquaintance with Kazantzakis's work would incline one to accept this. What seems almost certain is that all the poet in Kazantzakis responded to the chaos and raw vitality of the new Russia. This is certainly the impression given by this book, which seems to be almost a Dionysian celebration of the chaos, like a poet shouting with delight as he looks at a stormy sea. The book is essential to the understanding of Kazantzakis because it *is* so chaotic; it reveals the forces that he would gradually learn to discipline in the later novels.

In the last analysis, it is difficult not to feel a deep dissatisfaction with *Toda Raba*. It is magnificently alive, but its torrent flows in one direction, carrying all its tremendous force to the same objective. For example, it is hard to feel any deep sympathy for the Jewish Rahel, who always seems to be in a state of nervous excitement bordering on hysteria, and who finally commits suicide under a train when a man she desires rejects her. Obviously Kazantzakis was impressed by her—or rather, by the girl upon whom she is based (apparently a Jewish poetess he met in Berlin). But as he presents her in *Toda Raba*, one has an increasing suspicion that all this conviction and vitality is merely undisciplined frenzy, 'sound and fury, signifying nothing'. Her death is not tragic, or even interesting; she is a hysterical fool.

And the figure of Rahel symbolises for me the dissatisfaction I feel about the book and, to some extent, about Kazantzakis himself. He often seems to invoke Dionysian frenzy for its own sake, like Toda Raba's frenzied dance in front of Lenin's tomb at the end of the novel, when the poet Amita thinks: 'How terrible life is, the way it whirls about and snatches up and scatters all the yellow, white, black leaves of the human race. . . .' In its way, this novel reminds me of another one by a writer not half so great as Kazantzakis: *Mabhattan Transfer* by John Don Passos, with its same incredible thunder of life, the same maelstrom of vitality; even the 'film technique' of cutting quickly from one scene to another is similar. But in Don Passos (as in his disciple Hubert Selby, Jr., the author of *Last Exit to Brooklyn*) there is no purpose, no direction; only this noisy vitality. Kazantzakis is an altogether *deeper* man than Don Passos; ideas mean more to him; yet ultimately, *Toda Raba* is as chaotic as *Manhattan Transfer*.

Yet it is necessary to do Kazantzakis justice. *Toda Raba* was an attempt to embody in fictional form the central ideas of *The Saviours of God*. And he conceived *The Saviours of God* as a post-Marxian credo for human beings. Like Sartre, he seems to have accepted that Marxism is the most typical and basic philosophy of the 20th century. And where Sartre has attempted, in the *Critique of Dialectical Reason,* to broaden and deepen Marxism, Kazantzakis has attempted to create a religion based on the anti-Christian ideas of Nietzsche and Marx. He declares, in effect, that man must cease to regard himself as a slavish creature of God, and recognise that he is God's co-worker. In fact, more than this; without man's creative effort, God dies; through the god-like act of creation, man becomes the Saviour of God. The idea is impressive—and, of course, in total opposition to the self-pitying pessimism that has become so fashionable in the 20th century, from Andreyev to Beckett. But at this point, Kazantzakis the

N

realist steps in, and asks: 'But how about the human beings upon whom this burden falls? Are they strong enough?' *Toda Raba* is his own frank examination of the question. The one thing in common possessed by his eight protagonists—I am including the 'man with the big jaw' who drives Rahel to suicide—is creativity; they do not belong with the sheep of the world. If one sees it in this light, then *Toda Raba* reveals itself as an instance of its author's monumental honesty. He has written the scripture; now he asks how it applies to real life. And since life, unlike the realm of ideas, involves disappointment and compromise, it is not surprising if the novel is not finally satisfying; it accomplishes it purpose, nevertheless.

It seems possible that the creative outburst of *Toda Raba* and the beginning of the *Odyssey* was due to an important circumstance in his life: his divorce from his first wife, and his meeting with Helen, who became his second wife. His first marriage which had lasted fifteen years, had not been happy; and the reason is clear from the self-portrait in *Report to Greco*. Since the age of twenty, he had been a tormented and self-divided man, who began as an aesthete in the D'Annunzio tradition, then discovered Nietzsche, and wrote an Ibsenian drama with a Nietzschean message of power over one's destiny (*The Master Mason*, 1908). He spent ten of their fifteen years of marriage wandering around the world, so it is not surprising that her attitude towards him became ironical and derisive—as reflected in her novel *Men and Supermen*. There is nothing more destructive for a creative genius than to be married to a woman who regards him with a critical and mocking eye. He was divorced in 1926. In 1928, on his second voyage to Russia, he was accompanied by Helen, and by the Greek poet Panait Israti. At the relatively late age of forty-five he had discovered artistic maturity and a deep and durable relationship with a woman. The way was cleared for creativity.

The surprising thing, then, is that it was another five years before he produced his next novel, *The Rock Garden* (1936). The years were not spent in idling; he also wrote two plays (*Lidio-Lidia* and *Othello Returns*, a Pirandellian comedy), four screen-plays and dozens of articles for a Greek encyclopedia; he also translated *The Divine Comedy* and *Faust*, as well as continuing his *Odyssey*.

The Rock Garden is one of his most interesting novels; not a success, and yet of greater value than most 'successful' novels. The chief reason for its lack of success is that, like *Toda Raba*, it is curiously chaotic, combining excerpts from *The Saviours of God* and his travel book *Japan-China* with a love story. Critics have spoken unkindly of the book since its late appearance (more than twenty years after it was written). This is unfair, for it is by no means a minor work. If it combines passages from the two earlier books, this is not due to laziness but to an effort to find the right form in which to express his profoundest ideas. Under the circumstances, it was, perhaps, inevitable that he should use passages from the travel book; but the extracts from *The Saviours of God* are there because he is intent upon making the novel the expression of his whole philosophy. Admittedly, he had already done so, in the *Odyssey*; but this was immensely long, and might easily be rejected or misunderstood (as in fact, proved to be the case when it finally appeared in 1938). *The Rock Garden* contains the essence of Kazantzakis in capsule form. It is not a successful work of art; but it must be recognised as one of his most important works all the same.

The story is simple. The hero is on his way to stay with a friend in Peking—a Chinaman with whom he was at Oxford. In the first part of the book he visits Japan, then Shanghai, and he describes these places with the intense physical intoxication we have come to expect of Kazantzakis. Then he goes to stay with his friend, and falls in love with his sister, the daughter of a mandarin. The girl returns his feeling, but their love is bound to remain unconsummated. China and Japan are at war, and China is also torn with internal struggles that will one day result in Mao Tse-tung's revolution. There are greater issues than whether a man and a woman sleep together. This point is underlined by a kind of sub-plot. The hero's friend has had a love affair with a Japanese girl, Joshiro, and then discarded her; she still loves him. The hero travels to Japan with her and even proposes that they sleep together. (She declines.) At the end of the book, Joshiro is sentenced to death by her ex-lover for debauching Chinese generals, and it is the mandarin's daughter who has to bear the death warrant. As in *Toda Raba*, the contrast is between one's personal little affairs and the great sweep of history. And yet, the author seems to say, how can one turn away from the personal as if it were shameful? What is poetry except this intensely subjective pleasure

offered by the senses? At the beginning of the book, the dilemma
is stated clearly:

'To flirt with Joshiro, to waste time's precious essence in vain
words—how shameful!' But a moment later, he writes: 'Joshiro
had followed me—the sweat beaded like dew on her upper lip;
her marcelled hair was plastered on the back of her neck now. The
odour of her strong, supple body filled me with a degrading
intoxication.' (This curious obsession with the odours and se-
cretions of the human body never seems to leave Kazantzakis.)

This explains why it is necessary to include the passages from
The Saviours of God. This conflict between the personal and historical can only be resolved on a higher plane, by a man who has
become strong enough to transcend both. At the end of the novel,
the hero has been rejected by the girl he loves—and who loves
him—and by her brother, his old friend. The friend says coldly:
'I have other tigers to tame,' and the hero cries: 'I have other
tigers too. I don't need your affection. I don't need anyone. I am
free.' And he adds 'I felt an inhuman cruelty towards myself, a
hideous joy in agony and in mastering agony.' The book ends with
the cold leave-taking of the three, and a brief epilogue in which
the hero walks in a rock garden, symbol of this new-found freedom from mere human emotion.

It can be seen why the book is not a success. Anyone who reads
it is bound to read it as a love story, for the same reason that he
reads *Jane Eyre* or *Madame Bovary*. The book ends with this talk
of self-mastery, which may have expressed the author's deepest
message, but which hardly satisfies the expectations aroused
earlier on. It is not that human beings are incapable of grasping
a message that is so stoically philosophical. There is no reason
why not, if it is presented positively enough. People do not
refuse to see great tragedies because they cannot stomach unhappy endings. But a tragedy is prepared and presented in a
way that disposes the audience to accept it, to be carried beyond
the personal—in fact, to become ashamed of the personal, to
view it as the trivial. This novel never departs far from the author's
personal consciousness; the war is only a dim background noise.
So in the last analysis, the novel fails to 'purge' the reader, to
raise him above the level at which he looked forward to the hero
spending the night in Siu-lan's arms. It might be pointed out that
this development would still have left plenty of room for tragic

development, for her father sees the European as the symbol of the white man who has ruined China, while the hero himself feels a certain ambiguity towards the East, as represented by Siu-lan. The most interesting question is still to come. Is the failure of *The Rock Garden* due to the author's inability to handle his theme? Or is it, in fact, quite deliberate? In my own view, it is deliberate, and reveals something important about Kazantzakis as an artist-philosopher. He never achieves the final aim of the artist-philosopher—to rise above his subject so completely that all conflicts are resolved and some quite new synthesis results. This, I feel, is true even for the *Odyssey*. In this, he resembles D. H. Lawrence, to whom he might be compared. Both in Lawrence and Kazantzakis, there is such a strong element of personal conflict that there can never be the supreme synthesis, the equivalent of Beethoven's Ninth Symphony, or last quartets. In this respect, Kazantzakis also reminds one of Strindberg, of whom Yeats wrote: 'I have always felt sympathy for that tortured, self-torturing man who offered himself to his own soul as Buddha offered himself to the famished tiger.' Yeats means by this the violent rejection of the body and its needs, and his mention of the name of the Buddha makes the comparison doubly apt. In Kazantzakis, the power of the senses and the appetites was immense; so was the power of the soul, the desire to be a Saint Francis and resolve all conflicts in pure absorption in the spirit. (Kazantzakis could not even think of Jesus without wondering whether the total rejection of the flesh was entirely desirable— another point that links him with Lawrence.) This was why he finally decided that his own ideal symbol should be Ulysses, the traveller and seeker. He travelled as a jet aeroplane travels— powered by the explosions of his own dissatisfaction.

The *Odyssey* came in 1938, and is, in a sense, the culmination of his life work. And yet it was to be followed by six more novels, three of them masterpieces, and three of the highest artistic order, as well as by *Report to Greco*.

These six novels in themselves reveal all the conflicting—and still unresolved—aspects of Kanzantzakis. But now, instead of a jangling, discordant conflict, as in *Toda Raba* and *The Rock Garden*, there is something slow and deliberate about their changes of position, like the clapper on some great bell swinging slowly from side to side. *Zorba the Greek*, written during the war and published in 1946, is the lightest and happiest of these books. In a sense, it represents the young Kazantzakis who travelled over Greece as a student, then over Italy, revelling in the physical beauty of the world and disposed to dismiss his mental torments as the result of a sick conscience. Zorba is Rabelaisian man, breezy and delightful. It should also be noticed that the author-hero of Zorba is still involved with his verse drama on the Buddha—i.e. is still in the pre-Russian period of the early twenties. Zorba might be called Kazantzakis's Nietzschean novel, for Zorba stands for the same ideal as Nietzsche's Zarathustra—clear conscience, good digestion, life affirmation, free of the 'troubles and perplexities of intellect'. T. E. Lawrence would have understood the book immediately, with his talk about being the slave of his 'thought riddled nature', and envying a man patting a dog.

There follows a second masterpiece, *The Greek Passion** (1948), the first of that incredible series of works written in the last nine years of Kazantzakis's life. Having embodied his Greek and Nietzschean period in a novel, he now continues with his Christ period. And for the first time, he uses the background of his childhood for creative purposes. (Admittedly, Crete had already appeared in *Zorba*, but as seen through the eyes of an adult man.) This is certainly what makes *The Greek Passion* a masterpiece, for Kazantzakis reveals a wholly unexpected talent for creating human beings who are so real that they seem to walk around in three dimensions. The story is of Manolias, the shepherd boy, who is chosen to play Christ in the village Passion play, and who finds himself becoming steadily more Christ-like. He supports some dispossessed Greeks who live outside the village; but, like Christ, he ends by being hated and misunderstood by all, and is finally murdered by the villagers, who call him a Bolshevik.

Kazantzakis had hit upon a rich spring of creativity; he had discovered his homeland. Now he was in full flood of creation, and novel followed novel in quick succession. *Captain Michaelis†* followed in 1950. It was originally called *My Father*, and, as the opening chapters of *Report to Greco* make clear, the hero is the author's father, a violent, brooding, powerful man, universally respected and feared—the descendant of pirates and murderers. The subject of the book is the unsuccessful rising by the Cretans

---

* Known in England as *Christ Recrucified*.
† Known in England as *Freedom and Death*.

against the Turks in 1889. It is an ideal subject for Kazantzakis, full of the kind of emotions he enjoyed portraying: a tremendous heroism that did not flinch at self-destruction. (One young Greek fighter fired his rifle into an open powder barrel as the Turks burst the doors of a monastery, blowing everyone in it—including six hundred women and children—to atoms.) Captain Michaelis is obsessed by the beautiful Circassian wife of his blood-brother, the Turk Nuri-Bey, and this is also a typical Kazantzakis situation, with opportunities for this usual deeply perceptive portrayal of the explosive violence of physical desire. The description of the small town of Megalocastro is masterly, bursting with real people who almost walk off the page. For English and American readers, it recalls the humour and gaiety of Dylan Thomas's *Under Milk Wood*.

An interesting point about *Captain Michaelis* is the reappearance in it of the 'pen pusher' of *Zorba the Greek*, the intellectual author who is ashamed that he does not possess the strength and inner-unity of his father. And here, I must admit, is the point that is so difficult to understand. In 1950, Kazantzakis was sixty-seven years old, a man who was recognised in his own country as a great writer, and who knew that his own life had reached a level of heroism that went beyond that of the Greek freedom fighters—for it was a lonely, individual heroism, without the support of the crowd. Kazantzakis was also a man of deep religious feelings, who understood profoundly the meaning of the words 'brotherhood of man'. In this respect, as well as in his greatness as a novelist, he reminds us of Tolstoy. How, then, could this Tolstoyan figure write with such deep sympathy of bloodshed? How could he doubt for a moment that the way of the 'pen pusher' was basically more heroic than that of the 'wild beast'/Captain Michaelis, and that, in the last analysis, Captain Michaelis was a fool—hero or no hero?

All this is to say that Kazantzakis has failed to answer the *last* great question. The final impression left by the book is not unlike that left by Hemingway's *For Whom the Bell Tolls*. But Hemingway was not as great as Kazantzakis; he could not see beyond the violence and bloodshed; in fact, he made a cult of them. Hemingway possessed none of the obsessive spiritual force of Kazantzakis. What one expects from Kazantzakis is some spiritual synthesis, like that of *The Brothers Karamazov*. And he never quite

makes it. The opposites are left unresolved: on the one hand, the
spirit, on the other, the flesh and the turbulence of the physical
world.

There are three more novels, each of them powerful and
impressive—but never overwhelming, like *Zorba, The Greek
Passion* and *Captain Michaelis*. The reason for this is not far to
seek. *The Last Temptation* and *Saint Francis* are 'historical' novels,
that leave Kazantzakis's home territory. The last novel, *The
Fratricides*, possesses some of the greatness of *Captain Michaelis*,
but lacks its richness, being written in 1954, when Kazantzakis
was already suffering from the leukemia that was to kill him
three years later.

The Last Temptation (1951) is certainly the most 'Kazantzakian'
of his novels. If *Zorba the Greek* is the most accessible to the ordinary reader, *The Last Temptation* is the least accessible. Kazantzakis has turned his early play of Jesus into a novel. Obviously,
such an undertaking is full of pitfalls. A man who wished to make
it completely convincing would need to possess many qualities.
He would need to be a historian, who could convincingly re-
create the everyday life of Palestine twenty centuries ago, and who
knew the land intimately. He would also need to possess profound psychological and religious insight. No one can deny that
Kazantzakis is abundantly endowed where these latter qualities
are concerned. And when it is a question of re-creating the Crete
he knows and loves, he can certainly breathe life into a specific
time and place. But in *The Last Temptation*, he avoids the problem,
and tries to keep the book on the level of a sort of myth. It has
something in common with the biblical parables of Andreyev—
Judas Iscariot and the rest. And since this is a very long novel—
over five hundred pages—the reader is subjected to considerable
strain. One needs to be very closely in tune with Kazantzakis to
enjoy the book. Its theme is his favourite one of the conflict of
spirit and flesh, and a prologue underlines this point. 'I have
fought to reconcile these two primordial forces which are so
contrary to one another, to make them realise that they are not
enemies, but rather fellow workers. . . .' Anyone who feels that
Kazantzakis exaggerated the conflict—or perhaps deliberately
stoked its fires out of some perverse worship of violence—will
hate *The Last Temptation*. We have all met people who seem to be
perpetually involved in personal crises, until we come to suspect

that they deliberately seek out crisis, because they find tranquillity boring. Even the warmest admirer of Kazantzakis sometimes wonders whether there was not an unconscious desire to prolong the war between body and spirit out of pleasure in the conflict. There is another objection to *The Last Temptation*. Men of powerful imagination are inclined to admire great men whom they imagine to resemble themselves, and they usually end by losing all sense of *objectivity* and turning the admired hero into a reflection of themselves. Frank Harris wrote books on Shakespeare and Jesus in which Shakespeare and Jesus became Frank Harris. Now the one thing that is certain about *The Last Temptation* is that Kazantzakis's Jesus is not an attempt to portray the historical Jesus (which would probably be impossible), but to symbolise Kazantzakis's own conflicts in terms of Jesus. One's feelings about the novel are therefore bound to depend upon how well one can identify with Kazantzakis. In *Zorba the Greek* and *Captain Michaelis* this is not so important, for he is also capable of creating an *objective* world that convinces the reader by its reality; even a reader who was inclined to dismiss Kazantzakis's spiritual conflicts as 'sound and fury' could find himself absorbed in these books. This is not so with *The Last Temptation*.

In such a matter, it is best for the critic to frankly admit personal preference instead of pretending to impartiality. I ask myself whether *The Last Temptation* convinces me, involves me in its flow, and I am forced to answer: No. I am aware that the book is a fantastic *tour de force*. I am also aware that I might have felt very differently if I had read it in 1951, when it was written, and when my own self-conflicts would have led me to sympathise more deeply. But I am now eighteen years older, and I see other solutions to the problem of 'body and spirit'. The mind has curious depths of power that are hardly suspected by consciousness. The real conflict in man is not between 'body and spirit', but between different levels of his mind—what Freud might have called conscious and subconscious. He only knows himself as a consciousness; but everyday consciousness is like the last quarter of the moon, a mere fragment. In certain moments of deep insight, the full moon suddenly appears and man experiences a curious revelation, a knowledge of his true identity. I cannot help feeling that Kazantzakis, in emphasising the conflict of the turbulent body and the ascetic soul, was trapping himself in that 'last quarter' of the mind, making himself too aware of a violent and confused being called 'Nikos Kazantzakis'; *who was not a reality* but only an intermediate stage on an upward road.

This, I think, explains why Kazantzakis's notion of 'spirit' remained so negative, and why the characters who choose spirit rather than flesh are always tormented and unhappy. Kazantzakis uses the words 'spirit' and 'flesh' like two cymbals to clash against one another. But there is a mediator between flesh and spirit; it is called Reason, and it is probably a far greater god than Kazantzakis realised. One gets the feeling that it is always left out of his novels; instead, we get all kinds of violent passions—physical, emotional, sexual, religious—even poetic. There is almost nothing of what Shaw called 'the intellectual passion'.

The climax of the novel occurs when Christ experiences his 'last temptation' on the cross: he faints, and has a long dream in which his guardian angel rescues him from the cross, and assures him that the crucifixion was a dream. He makes love to Mary Magdalene—who is subsequently stoned to death in a scene of characteristic violence—and later becomes the husband of both Martha and Mary, who 'competed to see who could give birth to the most'. He becomes a fat, white-bearded old man, and his former followers and disciples visit him as a crowd of tiny old men, to reproach him for betraying them. He wakes up to find that it has all been a dream, and he is dying on the cross.

Let us agree at once that the conception is powerful, and typically 'Kazantzakian'. At first, one suspects Kazantzakis of indulging his 'fleshly daemon' when he makes Jesus copulate with Mary Magdalene, Martha *and* Mary; but the final awakening on the cross justifies it all, since it is a cry of rejection of the flesh, affirmation of the spirit. If we judged the novel by its last fifty pages, we would have to acknowledge that it achieves greatness. But whether the early part sustains this greatness must remain a matter for the judgement of the individual reader. Most readers will feel either that it is his best novel, or his worst.

Saint Francis (1953) is altogether more successful, perhaps because Kazantzakis knew and loved Italy. And perhaps because its historical epoch is closer in time, it is more convincing than *The Last Temptation*. Besides, the source material on St Francis is so abundant compared to that on Jesus that no doubt it was easier for Kazantzakis to make the period live in his own mind.

The device of putting the narrative into the mouth of the faithful Brother Leo gives the story a depth of conviction. It conveys more convincingly than any of his other novels the genuine depth of his religious obsession. And there are memorable passages that link it with the writings of existentialism; for example, Brother Leo's story of the saint who tells him that there is no road to God:

'What is there then?'
'There is the abyss, Jump!'

The book has the quality of some of the mediaeval lives of the saints and ascetics. It is less 'Kazantzakian' than any of the other major novels. Although Brother Leo confesses at the beginning that St Francis began by loving Clara carnally before he 'reached her soul', there is almost nothing of this physical element in the book.

Aldous Huxley has an interesting essay called *Francis and Grigory* in which he contrasts St Francis unfavourably with Grigory Rasputin, alleging that the piety of St Francis was a form of disguised egoism and exhibitionism, and that Rasputin's healthy attitude towards his sexual appetites is altogether closer to real holiness. I mention this essay, not because I agree with its position (even Huxley decided not to include it in his *Collected Essays*), but because one would have expected Kazantzakis to take a similar view of St Francis. It is interesting that Kazantzakis should have felt drawn to St Francis, who seems in all respects so unlike Kazantzakis. It seems as though, in these later novels, he is deliberately projecting different aspects of himself, in an attempt to create a world that should embody all his conflicts. In a sense, one should read these six novels as a whole—as if they were a single work, like the *Odyssey*. Only then can their achievement be seen in all its complexity.

The Fratricides (1954), the last of Kazantzakis's novels, takes us back to Greece—this time to Epirus. It is less 'weighty' than *The Greek Passion* or *Captain Michaelis* but possesses their same quality of reality. It is as if he has felt misgivings about the violence of Captain Michaelis, and wishes to take a firmer stand. So the hero of this novel is the village priest, Father Yanaros, a saintly man, whose impulse is to reconcile the warring factions. The novel is as violent and bloody as anything Kazantzakis ever

wrote, with scenes in which women are shot and a priest is cruci-
fied. The son of Father Yanaros, Captain Drakos, is cast in the
same mould as Captain Michaelis, a fighter for freedom and the
revolution. One of his soliloquies reveals his essential problem—
and that of his creator:

> Freedom, they say—bah! What freedom? He's the only free
> one—the devil within us—he's free, not us! We're only his
> mule, and he saddles us and goes off. But where is he going?
>   Drakos's past life raced quickly before him. He remembered
> his youth; he had wined and dined; he'd gotten drunk and
> made love to find forgetfulness; but there was no relief. The
> devil would rise within him and cry out: 'Shame on you, shame
> on you, beast!' And in order to escape the voice, he went
> into exile. . . .

Captain Drakos is not intended as a self-portrait by its author,
but there seem to be certain resemblances.

Kazantzakis writes this novel as if he is relieved to have have
done with St Francis and sweetness; here, everything is stormy
and thunderous again, and human beings torment one another and
are carried away by violence or lust. When a woman who has
left her husband to join the communist rebels goes to see Drakos
in the hills, to tell him that another commander has been appointed
in his place, he first of all half chokes her, then rapes her, murmuring 'My love, my love . . .' while she submits with ecstasy;
then, as soon as the love-making is over, they regard one another
with hatred. One is reminded of the emotional confusion in some
of the Russian novels of the early 20th century—in particular, of
Artsybashev. At the end of the novel, when Father Yanaros is
shot, on the orders of his son, the pointless violence seems to have
reached a climax. Obviously, Kazantzakis's intention was to show
the triumph of a saint. But the reader's reaction is to shake his
head and murmur, like Shaw's Caesar: 'Incorrigible! Incorrigible!'
Because this last novel of Kazantzakis has not resolved the conflicts of saint and warrior, any more than *Toda Raba* did. One feels
that, given Kazantzakis's angle of approach, they can never be
resolved. His world remains sundered, divided between God and
devil, flesh and spirit, with no possibility of reconciliation.

Before going on to speak of *The Odyssey*, I should also mention a remarkable play by Kazantzakis, written in 1949, called *Christopher Columbus*,* a powerful study of the 'man of destiny', the man in the grip of the urge to travel. Inevitably, Columbus becomes Kazantzakian, a guilty man who has murdered a Portuguese sailor for a map of the Antilles, but who believes that he has been ordered by God to find America. Its opening act, which takes place in a monastery, immediately exerts its author's obsessive grip; when Kazantzakis writes of religion, he always writes with authority. There is an argument between the piratical seafaring man Alonso, and the saintly abbot; Alonso wants a map of islands where gold is to be found; the abbot believes poverty to be blessed. A traveller arrives at the monastery—Columbus—and he is recognised by Alonso as the murderer of his cousin. Typically, when Alonso asks Columbus if he is afraid to lift up his face, Columbus answers: 'My face and hands are clean, and my heart is a bright clean flame; why should I be afraid?', and he convinces the abbot of his 'mission' by telling about his vision of the Virgin. Yet in the next act, he confesses to the murder of the Portuguese sailor. His supreme conviction persuades the abbot, and even persuades Captain Alonso, who at first intends to avenge his cousin's death on Columbus. Later, the same mystical conviction persuades the queen of Spain, although she is offended by the half-insane way in which Columbus talks of his 'secret marriage' to her. (It is typical of Kazantzakis to introduce a sexual motive; Columbus has dreamed that he will supplant Ferdinand as the king of Spain.) The final act, as might be expected, takes place on board ship, with the sailors on the point of revolt, prepared to murder Columbus if necessary. A nightingale that perches on the rigging saves him, but he now has a vision of angels who warn him that his discovery of the new world will bring him nothing but suffering, and advise him to turn back. He sees a vision of himself as a bull being chased and tormented, and hears the sound of the chains that are being forged for him in Seville. The injustice of it enrages him, but he refuses to turn back. His cry of 'I accept' obviously has a symbolic force that goes beyond this particular play. As the play ends, sailors rush in with branches they have found floating in the sea, and there is a cry of 'Land, ho!' The abbot asks Columbus why he looks so miserable. Columbus,

* I am indebted to Professor Athena G. Dallas for allowing me to read his translation in manuscript.

aware of the suffering that awaits him in Spain, cries 'I *am* happy,' then bursts into tears.

It is hard to judge how effective *Christopher Columbus* might be on stage; skilfully produced, its last act should be overwhelming. Purely as a reading experience, it is not entirely successful. Perhaps it should have been written as a novel, employing the author's panoramic technique; the subject is too rich for brief treatment. Why did Kazantzakis choose to write it as a play? Could he have been aware of Claudel's treatment of the theme, in the play upon which Milhaud based his opera *Christopher Columbus*? If so, one begins to understand his point, for Kazantzakis's Columbus is as different as possible from the Columbus conceived by the devout Catholic. Kazantzakis's Columbus talks about God and the Virgin, but one suspects that the real gods that drive him are some savage deities of nature or life. The religion of the play is not Christianity, but a Nietzschean heroic individualism.

The Odyssey, A Modern Sequel, is the most monumental work of Kazantzakis, and his greatest achievement. In it, he comes closest to presenting a unified world view, transcending the antitheses of flesh and spirit. To some extent, the spirit of the poem emerges in the last two lines of the Prologue, an invocation to the sun:

> Ahoy, cast wretched sorrow out, prick up your ears—
> I sing the sufferings and torments of renowned Odysseus.

There is something Nietzschean in this shout: it says: Rise above your trivial lives and think of something bigger. It promises the heroic, deeds on a larger-than-human scale. But it does not promise anything more; it does not promise some Dantesque vision of the universe, some great Hegelian synthesis in which all the apparent contradictions of the world are reconciled. I make this point because I am inclined to believe that this was the spirit in which Kazantzakis began to write the poem. A restless wanderer himself, he could not imagine Ulysses settling down quietly to old age. This in itself tells us a great deal about Kazantzakis. Most readers who have followed Ulysses through the *Iliad* and *Odyssey* find his return to Ithaca a perfectly satisfactory ending to the story. Not Kazantzakis: his imagination wants to hurl him into fresh adventures. Typically, Penelope feels terrified on recognising her husband and Ulysses feels none of the pleasure, expected in seeing her again. This is a Faustian Ulysses, and Homer would have found him incomprehensible. In a conversation with an old basket weaver, he admits that life is meaningless, yet later in the same book, at a banquet given in his honour, he shocks everyone by proposing a toast to man's dauntless mind instead of pouring a libation to the gods. The basic conflict already begins to emerge.

The *Odyssey* was conceived in a Nietzschean spirit. To the ordinary reader, Ulysses is bound to emerge as wicked and immoral; his creator takes pleasure in revealing his hero's freedom from the usual feelings of decency. Kazantzakis seems intent on creating a savage world, that has more in common with the Chicago of Prohibition than with Homer's Greece. Ulysses quickly gathers a group of boon companions; they begin to build a ship, and spend their evenings raping girls and lonely widows, pretending to be gods. Women whom he has seduced on his travels send his bastards home to him; he gives them labouring jobs in Ithaca. When his daughter by Calypso comes to him, he caresses her with love and lays her on the sand—and then the poet discreetly draws a curtain on the scene with an invocation to 'woman's thick-haired armpits'. Telemachus plots to murder his father, and Ulysses, approving of this sign of manliness, decides to leave Ithaca.

The pattern of the poem is already obvious in these first two books. One gets the feeling that this is the sort of thing that might have been produced by a collaboration between Goethe and the Marquis De Sade. Ulysses is gloriously immoral and revels in it. He lands in the Peloponnese, and sees a girl with a calf. Assuring the girl that he is a god, he makes love to her, then kills the calf, and takes it off to feed his comrades, assuring the girl that she will hear from him in nine months.

The reader's reaction to all this is likely to be very definite. If he is young or sexually frustrated, this idea of a gay seducer will delight him; otherwise, he is likely to feel a kind of impatience with the whole thing, and accuse Kazantzakis of indulging in schoolboy fantasies. There is some justice in this complaint. Nevertheless, the poem still has a long way to go, and it is well to suspend judgement for a while.

Menelaus and Helen are also not as happy as Homer probably

believed when he set them back on Sparta; so Ulysses goes to
Sparta, accepts the hospitality of Menelaus, then steals Helen,
and murders a guard in the course of escaping. In a discussion
with Menelaus, he has poured scorn on the idea of a peaceful old
age, and speaks of a new god of destruction and violence who is
about to arise. In all this, one can hear the voice of Kazantzakis,
shouting to the sleeping village: 'I shall destroy you all!'

Ulysses and Helen sail to Crete, where he is the guest of King
Idomeneus—who at first wishes to kill him. Book Six is a description of an orgy, with a lesbian scene between Helen and the
king's daughter Krino, the death of Krino, gored by a bull, and
universal promiscuity, during which Helen is possessed by a
black slave, and Ulysses copulates with another of the king's
daughters. One of the illustrations in the English edition indicates that the bulls also take part in the orgy. This is the book with
the moving passage about the hard lot of the Cretan peasants,
which awakens Ulysses to sympathy. In Book Eight he leads a
rebellion in which the palace is destroyed, and one of Ulysses'
companions is given the throne. Helen is carried off by a blond
gardener. Ulysses sails for Egypt, taking the king's daughter,
Diktena, but he abandons her when one of his companions
objects that she is of no use to them.

In the Egyptian episode, that occupies the next four books,
Ulysses has become a communist. Like every other kingdom they
have visited, Egypt is decadent. (Kazantzakis seems to take a
certain delight in describing decadence.) Ulysses joins a workers'
rebellion—in which one of the leaders is called Rala-Rahel—and
is thrown into jail. The young Pharaoh lets him go, whereupon
he promptly joins a horde of barbarians who are attacking Egypt.
These are also defeated and he is thrown back into jail. This time,
he earns his freedom by performing a barbaric dance in front of
the Pharaoh, wearing a god-mask he has carved himself. The king
has seen the mask in a dream, and is terrified. (This episode
resembles the one in which St Francis dances in front of the Pope
—who also has had a strange dream.)

His next enterprise is to found the ideal City State, taking with
him all the slaves, criminals and rebels. They ascend to the source
of the Nile, and Ulysses goes to a mountain top to commune with
God—an obvious parallel with Moses.

This fourteenth book is rightly regarded as the most important in the poem. Ulysses ascends the mountain and spends four days there: during this time, Kazantzakis expresses his whole philosophy. In the first day, Ulysses symbolically ascends to a cave above the level of the ghosts and demons—a statement of his pure humanism. On the second day, he praises the hunter, whose jmage he finds on the wall of his cave, and speaks of the eternal ioy of life. He daydreams of his deepest wish, deathlessness, but a worm climbs to his chest to remind him of his mortality. In the succeeding two days, the Nietzschean warrior and the Christian ascetic fight in him, until he identifies with the whole process of evolution, and finally with all nature, animate and inanimate. Kazantzakis once expressed his dislike of mysticism; but there can be little doubt that the vision at the end of Book Fourteen is mystical.

Undoubtedly, this fourteenth book is the great peak of Kazantzakis's achievement; it leaves the reader dazed by the immensity of the author's conception, with all his misgivings stilled. It is no longer possible to dismiss the *Odyssey* as a glorification of total 'freedom'—that is, of immorality—a kind of belated echo of Schiller's *Robbers*. There is something greater at stake here.

This extremely clear statement of the philosophy of Kazantzakis enables me to express my own intuitive rejection of his final position. The Russian philosopher Fedorov said that mankind has one great common aim: the conquest of death. In *Back to Methuselah* Bernard Shaw also recognised that *if* death is an ultimate reality, then it makes nonsense of our idea of evolution. It is death that must be overcome. And perhaps this is possible, since man seems to carry death in his heart, as his most basic form of defeat. In *The Domesticity of Franklin Barnabas*, Shaw makes his biologist hero ask 'Why do people die?' and someone replies: 'Of reasonableness. They do not want to live forever.' Barnabas answers: 'Of laziness, and want of conviction, and failure to make their lives worth living. That is why.'

If one accepts this then all the ideas expressed by Ulysses after the first day—when he sees the worm and accepts the idea of his death—are basically false. They may give an appearance of rising above the problem and solving it, but they are bound to be attempts to solve the insoluble. To me, this is the ultimate criticism of the philosophy of the *Odyssey*.

o

Even so, Kazantzakis has something to add—something of basic importance, which he states in Book Seventeen. After his vision on the mountaintop, the new Moses descends, and they build the ideal City State, with the Ten Commandments on the wall. Ulysses becomes a prophet, and teaches his people about God. Then the volcano above the city erupts and destroys everything, including two of Ulysses' closest companions. Ulysses becomes a kind of saint, and throngs of pilgrims are drawn to him; but he preaches total nihilism: there is neither God nor justice, and goodness is an illusion. He accepts all life's contradictions.

Then comes the interesting seventeenth book. Ulysses becomes life itself; he falls into a deep contemplation, in which his own imagination becomes the creator. He smiles, and three girls are born; he scowls, and war breaks out; he thinks of gold, and a prosperous bazaar appears. He plays a flute, and a long play is enacted in front of him. (One scents the influence of Pirandello here—the creator giving life arbitrarily to his characters.) He ends by addressing the mind as the creator of all things.

This book is the logical climax of the poem. Perhaps it should have ended there. Ulysses has stumbled upon the profoundest of evolutionary truths. The mind is actually a new *dimension* of life, distinct from the physical world and our responses to it. But we are hardly capable of grasping this; we are still 95 per cent animal, machines that respond to external stimuli. We are like two-dimensional creatures who have not yet learned to look upwards and grasp that there is a third dimension. Yet all man's art and literature are a witness to this new dimension of existence. Man possesses an immense freedom, which is grasped in certain moments of ecstasy by mystics and poets. It is a realm that he could enter and make securely his own, if only he became conscious of its existence. His main problem is that he does not know who is he; he continues to think of himself as a creature, an earthbound animal. ('I am nothing and I deserve nothing'.)

In a way, this discovery of Ulysses' negates everything else in the poem. It should bring with it the recognition that *he is not Ulysses*. It should also lead to the recognition that if the mind possesses this freedom, then the immediate problem is to find *methods* for increasing the recognition. Not mystical flashes: they are too brief and unreliable; nor drug-inspired ecstasies of one-ness with the universe. A *scientific* method, an extension of what we at present call science and philosophy.

I feel that it is at this point that Kazantzakis's mind refuses to take the final leap; it falls back. His admirers—although I count myself among them—may dispute this. I can only state my own opinion for what it is worth.

The second half of the *Odyssey* is profounder, more artistically mature, than the first half. Instead of Nietzsche and De Sade, the slave of his own whims and lusts, we now have a Ulysses who has achieved a prophetic status through suffering and thought. His adventures become symbolic, and yet even more interesting. He encounters figures who obviously symbolise Buddha, Don Quixote and Jesus, and rejects all three for different reasons.

The poem has a Wagnerian ending that goes on for three cantos, in which Ulysses sails to the South Pole. It is full of resounding ideas, such as that man sails on the waters of despair, with Death as captain, and that the mind must free itself from its last cage, that of freedom. He relives parts of his life and meets old companions. And finally he dissolves into mist embracing death. It is certainly as impressive as the last scene of *Götter-dämmerung*, a tremendous ending to a work that undoubtedly ranks with the great epics that inspired it: *The Odyssey, Faust* and the *Divine Comedy*. (I also hear echoes of Madach's *Tragedy of Man*, particularly in the last cantos.) But even if the reader rejects the Shavian notion about the conquest of death, it is still open to question whether Kazantzakis has really 'solved' anything. The work leaves upon the mind the same feeling of *final* dissatisfaction that one gets from the novels, as well as from *Report to Greco*.

It is necessary to judge Kazantzakis by the very highest standards: the standard by which we judge Goethe and Tolstoy and Dostoevsky. And it might be objected that, by this standard even Goethe and Tolstoy and Dostoevsky are ultimately unsatisfying. Goethe does not really *solve* the problem he outlines in *Faust*, and the chorus of angels at the end are a confidence trick to disguise this. *Faust* is basically about man's attempt to take possession of this new realm of the mind, to reject the repetitive boredom of animal existence, and his baffled discovery that he is not ready to become a creature of the mind, that a few hours spent entirely in this realm leave the mind exhausted and destroy one's sense of identity and sanity.

The greatest writers of this century have been intuitively aware of this Faustian dilemma, and Kazantzakis is no exception. In a sense, he comes closer to solving it, in the seventeenth book, than Goethe came in Faust. That he did not recognise his solution and build upon it would seem to be a consequence of his tormented restless personality. *Report to Greco* was the work of a man in his seventies, yet it is as turbulent and tormented as *Toda Raba*. The essence of Kazantzakis's work seems to be this 'storm and stress'. He differs from most of the romantics of the 19th century in an essential respect: the 'storm and stress' were a natural expression of his temperament, not a histrionic gesture or a fashionable pose. Of all the great novels of the 19th century, perhaps *Wuthering Heights* comes closest to Kazantazakis in atmosphere—although he might well have disapproved of its feminised romanticism.

In the last analysis, Kazantzakis's importance transcends any question of whether he finally 'solved' the problem with which his work deals. In fact, perhaps it is important that he *failed* to solve them. He becomes thereby a more perfect symbol of the man who refuses to give up the search, who continues to seek the answers until the moment of his death.

5
Postscript

It would be hard to choose four poets more unlike than Brooke, Yeats, Rowse and Kazantzakis. I have done so to emphasise the one thing they have in common: the feeling they convey of the ultimate *frustration of the poet's aim*. Eliot, Yeats and Rowse have all compared themselves to eagles—to eagles prevented from taking flight. In Brooke, this frustration is understandable; it is the direct outcome of the clash between the persona he has chosen for himself, and the actuality of his life as he had to live it. The poet who felt that only the intensities of youth make life worth living, and that most human existence is a steady descent into mediocrity, was bound to find himself at the end of his poetic tether before he was thirty. But then, as I have tried to show, what makes Brooke a poet is not the obsession with youth, early death and so on, but his inborn mysticism. Looking at a Birmingham businessman on a train, he can feel the authentic mystical surge of affirmation, Chesterton's 'absurd good news'. When he meditates alone in a wood at dusk, he has a sense that he might find:

> Soon in the silence the hidden key
> Of all that had hurt and puzzled me.

Silence, as I have pointed out, can be the essence of the mystical experience. Rilke described once how he was leaning in the fork of a tree in the garden when he suddenly experienced a 'silence like the interior of a rose'. Brooke's 'longing for dim hills' is the mystical urge, the need to search for 'what the world's million lips are thirsting for'. But this urge must be rationalised, or at least expressed as a credo, before it can take its place as part of the poetic 'persona'. If Yeats created his credo out of fragments of myth and poetry, Brooke chose simpler ingredients: humour, defiance, the cult of youth, the self-evident goodness of life and nature. It was because he tied his fundamental mystical obsession to this shaky scaffolding that the mysticism collapsed with the scaffolding, and left Brooke with the feeling of having outgrown all the things he valued most.

In the case of Rowse, this act of choice can be seen even more clearly. Here it was dictated to some extent by the way of life he was trying to leave behind. Academic success and the security of All Souls did not bring the 'new life' he might have been justified in expecting. Illness was partly to blame; but so was Rowse's own temperament, the Proustian oversensitivity, the impatience with fools, the tendency to impulsive affection, that could turn into resentment and the nursing of grudges. Rowse chose a credo to fit his character, in which the actual world—about which he felt only cynicism or despair—is opposed to the ideal world of beauty and the meaning that lies in the past. Rowse's poetic temper is akin to Eliot's: the rejection of the idea of 'progress', the sense of tradition, the resignation in contemplating one's own life: ('why should the agéd eagle stretch its wings?'). Unlike Eliot, Rowse has no mystical or religious credo to fall back on: like Delius, he remains aggressively agnostic. Given this set of beliefs, it becomes impossible for the poet to rise above the sense of the tragedy of human existence. One can only turn to the healing power of 'wahn', beauty reflected in art. Rowse is unique because he is perhaps the only poet of the 20th century (I can think of no other) who belongs to the romantic-tragic tradition of Wagner and Delius. As a historian his master is Burckhardt; if he had been a philosopher, it would have been Schopenhauer.

In Yeats, the ultimate failure is obscured by his ability to remain productive until the end. The reason for this creative longevity was *not* that Yeats was an unusually honest man who ruthlessly probed his own illusions. It was that Yeats was far more interested than Brooke or Rowse in creating a credo that should somehow reconcile the poet's 'longing for dim hills' with the actuality of the world we live in. He searched in occultism, mysticism and philosophy for the justification of his sense of 'another reality'. The result is that he is, intellectually speaking, the most interesting poet of the 20th century. His prose works—particularly the autobiographies—could be regarded as a kind of *Summa Theologica* whose aim is to place his own mysticism on a solid intellectual base. The later poetry derives its strength from this broad pedestal. At times, the work achieves a clarity of mystical affirmation: in *The Gyres,* in *Lapis Lazuli,* in *Under Ben Bulben.* But there is also, as in Brooke, a romantic cult of vitality for its own sake and defiance of death:

> Test every work of intellect or faith,
> And everything that your own hands have wrought,
> And call those works extravagance of breath
> That are not suited for such men as come
> Proud, open-eyed and laughing to the tomb.

This is not far from Brooke's:

> Proud, then, clear-eyed and laughing, go to greet
> Death as a friend!

For all his attempt to place his 'mystical' beliefs on a solid footing, Yeats can never resist the temptation to a superficial pessimism:

> Through winter-time we call on spring,
> And through the spring on summer call,
> And when the abounding hedges ring
> Declare that winter's best of all;
> And after that there's nothing good
> Because the spring time has not come—
> Not know that what disturbs our blood
> Is but its longing for the tomb.

And so the mystical affirmation appears only in flashes, and is weighed down by the belief in the ultimate meaninglessness of life. It is worth observing that the above poem—*The Wheel*—expresses the problem of 'the St Neot margin', the human tendency to remain permanently dissatisfied, like the old woman in the vinegar bottle. Yeats might well have reasoned from this that most human beings are little better than children, who are bored with a holiday within a few days, and that only such men as Michelangelo and Blake have the discipline necessary to see beyond the human craving for change. But this would not have made such a neatly rounded poem; the Freudian death-wish makes better poetic material. And so, in the last analysis, Yeats, like Rowse and Brooke, remains trapped in his own metaphysic.

Kazantzakis seems to come closer than anyone to real mystical affirmation, the feeling that man can contact the 'source of power, meaning and purpose' in himself and rise above his apparently tragic predicament. The *Odyssey* represents a greater spiritual effort than Yeats ever made, while the almost Tolstoyan greatness of the late novels indicates that his quest for the 'source of power' came very close to success. But like Yeats, he could never overcome a feeling that 'truth' and 'life' are incompatible. Yeats was afraid that he would lose hs 'theme' if he tried to throw off contradictions and 'seek out reality'. 'What theme had Homer but original sin?' This same ambivalence finally exhausts Kazantzakis; he dies with the object of his quest still out of sight.

I have tried to argue in this book that the poetic and the mystical experience are the *same* experience in every way. Even in a 'pessimistic' poet like Rowse, the poetic experience is a fragmentary mystical experience, the sense of 'absurd affirmation'. If the poet, unlike the mystic or the saint, fails to obtain his vision of pure affirmation, this is not the fault of the vision, but of the poet's clumsy attempt to grasp the essence of his 'flashes of intensity'.

I would suggest that the apparent contradiction between 'intensity consciousness' and the 'triviality of everydayness' can be resolved if one pays less attention to the vision itself, and concentrates instead upon the mechanisms of everyday perception, everyday moods. As soon as one does this, one becomes aware of the basic problem with human beings. We have lost the old animal sense of 'oneness with nature' because we prefer the clarity and power conferred by intellectual consciousness. The consequence is that we find ourselves *trapped in the present*. A few human beings are achieving, little by little, a new kind of 'expanded consciousness'; not the kind that can be induced by psychedelic drugs, but by *stretching* the mind by means of the intellect, the imagination, the emotional sensibilities. Beethoven *wanted* the Ninth Symphony to raise the mind to a kind of mystical perception; it fails to do so, but the failure is of its musical material particularly in the last movement. The idea remains clear enough. Hindemith wrote an opera called *The Harmony of the World* about Kepler, and at its climax, the music is supposed to suggest the whirling of stars and planets. Hindemith's dry, contrapuntal music fails in its purpose. But one could imagine a musician great enough to succeed, to transport the audience into a visionary state with tremendous harmonies that somehow reflect the cosmic order *and* the force of a hurricane.

Neither is art the only mind-stretcher; one could imagine a mathematician finding Newton's *Principia* greater and nobler than any Ninth Symphony. As science probes the universe with its beam of logic, it also carries along the imagination. Every department of human creativity offers the mind new spaces into which to expand.

But it must be admitted that at the moment, even the most highly creative human beings possess this faculty only in embryo, so that as an evolutionary prospect, it may be distant. Fortunately, there is another one closer to hand.

When one turns the attention upon 'the triviality of everydayness', it can be seen that the low level of everyday consciousness can be blamed upon what we might call 'the mind's filing system'. I learn new things every day. These cannot be 'kept' in consciousness; they must somehow be filed away, like books on a library shelf. These shelves, as I have remarked, are not easily available to us. When I sit alone in a room with nothing to do, I ought, in theory, to be able to take down one of the volumes of my own past, or of some subject I have learned, and remain absorbed for hours. In fact, it is only once or twice in a lifetime that we fall into a gentle, reminiscent mood when my past does become, to some extent, accessible to me. The consequence is that no matter how 'well stocked' my mind is, I can quite easily fall into a state of boredom when I have nothing in particular to do and no choices of activity open to me.

Boredom could be defined as having an 'empty consciousness': to be fully awake, yet have nothing to occupy the mind.

Now it is this peculiarity of human beings—our tendency to boredom—that lies at the root of the trouble. To be bored means that one's values are 'in eclipse'. I may have hundreds of things to be grateful for, to feel happy about. But unless some crisis threatens them, making me suddenly aware of how glad I should be to possess them, these do not enter my 'empty consciousness' as definite values. The lover need never be bored; he can sit and think about his mistress for hours, because she is still a dynamic value, not yet taken for granted and consigned to the library shelves. But very few of my reasons for being happy are as accessible as this.

P

Empty consciousness finds it hard to contemplate its positive values. But it has no trouble at all with the negative ones. And inevitably, the mind is full of negative values. Ever since I was a child, I have been learning by trial and error. Christmas cake seems wholly good and delightful, until I have eaten too much of it; then I feel sick. As an adult, sex may seem wholly delightful—until the lover finds himself married with several children. There is a negative side to every delightful thing in the world, if one looks hard enough.

Empty consciousness is inclined to take on a definite negative charge. To begin with, boredom leads to inactivity, and inactivity leads to a feeling of guilt and a running-down of the batteries of the will.

If I study this negativeness closely, I see that the main problem is my *ambiguous* attitude towards most things. If I want something very badly, and it is very hard to get, I may work myself up to a pitch of desire and determination that means that my attitude towards the desired object is wholly positive. I want it wholly and completely, and feel no doubt or ambivalence. But in fact, most of the things I want do not cost me this effort, and so my attitude towards them tends to be vague and ambiguous. My desire may be so enfeebled that I actually cease to desire a thing as soon as I know I can have it, like the narrator of *Wuthering Heights* who admits that he fell in love with a girl, but became cold as soon as she showed signs of returning his feelings.

When I examine this kind of 'ambiguity' intellectually I realise that it is absurd. There is no real and objective reason why I should feel so casual and ambiguous about my dinner; although it is true that if I am overweight, it might be a good idea to do without it. But if I begin to feel indifferent to food, my doctor will tell me that there is something wrong with me, and prescribe a tonic or long walks. He knows that a healthy human being has a very positive attitude towards his dinner.

Yet although I would agree that I may be physically sick if I lose my appetite for food, it never strikes me that I am emotionally sick if I fail to enjoy a Sunday afternoon walk or telling my children a bedtime story.

Because of the limitation of human consciousness, ambiguity has slid into our nerves, and keeps the pressure of consciousness low. I have no *reason* to feel ambiguous about most of the things I have gone to a great deal of trouble to get; it is simply a habit.

If I have been away from home for several months, I shall take a positive delight in telling my children bedtime stories when I get back, because absence—i.e. something *negative*—has destroyed the ambiguity, made me wholly delighted to see them. If there was any kind of threat to my children, I would go to endless trouble to avert it; there can be no question that they represent one of my major values. Why, then, am I capable of looking at them indifferently? Because of this stupid habit of ambiguity that I have allowed to take hold of me as I might take up smoking or biting my nails. Because my life is, on the whole, comfortable and free from major inconvenience, I sink into a trance-like state in which I allow my consciousness to be permanently clouded by a haze of negation.

But I do not need a threat or a crisis to shake my mind awake. Since I possess an intellect and imagination, there is no reason why I should not embark on the task of 'destroying ambiguity' in exactly the same practical spirit that I might set about polishing the tarnish from a brass ornament. As soon as I *know* that my mind is 'tarnished', and that this is not 'normal consciousness', I can take the necessary measures. Up to this point in history, men have deliberately sought out danger and excitement to destroy the ambiguity. But Husserl's discovery of 'intentionality' meant that the danger and hardship are not essential; they only trigger the mechanism. The act of will that snaps us out of our sleep and destroys our indifference is an *intention*—the tightening of a muscle, so to speak. And the point of a muscle is that you can flex it by an action of the will, and can strengthen it by flexing it.

Let us reconsider the question that has emerged periodically throughout this book. What is the meaning-content of the mystical experience, the poetic experience, the peak experience?

We must first understand that the attitude towards life of most people is passive and negative. Imagine a youth who has just left school, and who starts to work in a sheet metal factory. He gets up in the dark, and goes with crowds of other workers to the enormous, cold place that smells of oil and machines. It overwhelms him; it dwarfs him. Looking at the steam hammer he thinks: 'One blow of that would squash me like a fly.' Confronted with this enormous place he feels contingent and insignificant. It seems in every way bigger, more durable than he is. Point out to him that it was built by men, and he would reply: 'Ah yes, big business men . . .', implying: 'Not insignificant people like me . . .'

In the same way, he feels that his body is more powerful than the will that drives it. He only has to feel very hungry to recognise this; he seems to be a mere bundle of cravings, with no thought except food. Again, if he falls in love with a pretty waitress in the works canteen, and she is unaware of him, it only confirms his feeling of being invisible, insignificant.

So far, he only feels passive and unimportant. But if something unpleasant happens to him, the neutrality of his consciousness passes into actual negation. Sitting in a dirty café, drinking tea from a cracked cup, it suddenly seems clear that this is what reality is about—dirt, misery, failure. And if he is merely sitting in his room on a wet Sunday afternoon, his vision remains negative. The spider in the corner of the ceiling becomes somehow another proof that the world is chiefly darkness and dirt.

Now what happens if he goes on a holiday, and experiences that sudden lifting of the heart as the train pulls out of the station? Something he had come to accept as a permanent part of his life is no longer there. He feels that, in a strange sense, he is more real and permanent than the factory he has left behind. *He becomes aware of his long-term self.* The factory is made of dead matter and it might be demolished tomorrow. (Does this not also explain why people love to watch demolition work? As a wall crumples and disintegrates, there is a feeling of triumph, as one's own permanence is illuminated by a flash of lightning.)

Man's relation to his surroundings is fundamentally similar to his relations with other men, in the sense that *dominance* is involved. A bully makes you feel negative, and he may 'get under your skin' until he festers like a splinter in your consciousness. It would produce a feeling of joy and triumph to see his downfall. Is this not the feeling you experience as the train pulls out of the station? The bully, the oppressor of the spirit, has revealed that he can be defeated.

An overweight friend who decided to go on a diet described to me the sense of power and wellbeing it gave him to eat a piece of dry toast instead of his lunch, then to walk two miles back to work. Again, there is a feeling of the power of the will, and also *of its endurance.* It is true that it cannot make the body lose weight instantaneously. But once the will is 'set', like a thermostat, it is invincible.

The feeling of delight in the sexual act has the same cause. Each time Casanova seduces a girl, he experiences the sense of conquest, of power; the usual feeling of 'insignificance' vanishes.

The world is dead matter; man is the most active force on its surface. Passivity and negation are habits we acquire in childhood, but vital human beings slowly throw them off as they get older. Every time we experience a surge of joy, we ceased to be negated by the world of matter. We become aware of the 'long-term self'.

It is not the human *will* that needs to be strengthened; it already possesses all the strength we need. It is the human spirit. *Man must learn to destroy the element of negation in his own consciousness.* When he is bored, he is oppressed by his surroundings. As soon as a crisis arises, and he flings himself into action, his surroundings vanish into anonymity; they take up their proper place as the mere background of his activity.

The danger of the passive and negative attitude of everyday consciousness is that it causes us to waste our lives. Time is the currency of human existence, and every moment wasted in passivity is destroyed as surely as if you burned a pound note.

Sartre is wrong; consciousness is not an emptiness. It has the quality of emptiness, of negation, of existing 'for itself', because of a biological accident. Man has reached a point in his evolution when his strength is precisely counterbalanced by the narrowness and precision he developed in order to make better use of his strength. Narrowness involves loss of insight; involves boredom, passivity. Boredom leads to negation, to self-division, to loss of meaning. In order to reverse the process, it is necessarily merely to understand it: to grasp that the loss of meaning is an illusion. If someone switches off the light when I am reading, I do not assume that the words have vanished. I know that what has vanished is the light by which I saw them. The only reason I believe that 'meaning' has vanished when I have allowed myself to sink into boredom is that I have failed to grasp the intentional nature of consciousness. If I cease to project intentions, it is like switching off a light. To switch on the light again, I have only to arouse consciousness from its passive state by an act of concentration. At first, this may be difficult, because the will-muscle has grown flabby with disuse; but a little effort can soon restore its strength. There is theoretically no reason why its strength should not be increased to a point where man becomes capable of Captain Shotover's 'seventh degree of concentration'.

To summarise:

Phenomenological analysis reveals that the 'peak experience' is intentional in nature. That is to say that the mystical or poetic experience is a perfectly normal potentiality of everyday consciousness, not the explosive ascent to some super-normal plane. It involves simply the destruction of 'ambiguity', the clearing aside of the rubbish that tends to accumulate when we allow consciousness to remain passive for too long.

The romantics were wrong to believe that the 'spirit of beauty' descends upon the poet. The poet descends upon it.

It is this misunderstanding that has produced the pessimistic orientation of western culture during the past hundred and fifty years. The poet set up to be a 'summariser' of human existence: that is, he believes that in moments of inspiration, he has a 'bird's eye view' and can perceive general truths that are hidden from us by the 'triviality of everydayness'. When a scientist has a similar flash of insight into a general law—Newton under the apple tree, Kekulé with his molecular snakes eating their own tails—he takes the trouble to think it through to the end, to subject it to every possible test. But poets are not noted for intellectual integrity; they appear to believe that the service of the muse exempts them from real intellectual effort. And so they serve up a half-baked pessimism as the result of inspired meditation on human destiny.

Let me end, as I began, on a personal note. My own life has, I suppose, been given a certain inner-consistency by the search for the formula of intensity-experience. In childhood, moments of extreme happiness brought an imaginative intuition of a world entirely good, in which misery had vanished and stupidity had become amiable and harmless. My teens were all romantic pessimism, the feeling that the world is so badly and fundamentally out of joint that one can only turn away from it to one's own vision of perfection. (Hence my strong sympathy for Rowse.) But since my temperament is as optimistic as that of Shaw or Wells, I have continued to think about the problem. This matter of temperament is of enormous importance. (Even a thinker as detached and rigorous as Merleau-Ponty ends by allowing innate pessimism to creep into his account of human nature, so that according to him, man's freedom can only be narrowly exercised within a tight 'net of relations' with his environment.) One's temperament determines the nature of one's insights, and one's insights are all one has to work on.

I know Shaw is right when he says 'the brain shall not fail when the will is in earnest'. But the will needs a clear sight of its objectives before it can be in earnest, and this is the task of the brain. Man's evolution has been a struggle to escape the triviality of animal existence. And now he has created civilisation, he is trapped in a new kind of triviality by his formidable ability to focus on minutiae.

The other day, my nine-year-old daughter started to tell me the plot of a story about witches that she was halfway through; then she said: 'I think I'll go and finish it; telling you about it's got me interested again.' She had 'gulped' the story, without making an act of concentration sufficient to 'digest' it, and it produced a kind of nausea. Telling me about it caused it to digest, producing a further appetite.

The first time I clearly noticed this phenomenon was in my teens. I had cycled to Matlock, a matter of some forty-eight miles, and I arrived exhausted. Then I spent an hour being guided around one of the underground caves. When I came out, I realised I was completely refreshed. If I had spent the same hour lying in the shade with a book, *trying* to relax, I would still have been tired at the end of the hour. Why had scrambling around low, dripping passageways refreshed me so completely? Because it had completely absorbed my attention, *allowing my natural powers of recuperation to act.*

Similarly, driving from the Lake District to Blackpool one day, I felt completely exhausted while I still had twenty miles to go. I switched on the car radio and became interested in a parliamentary report. I arrived in Blackpool feeling quite fresh again.

A similar thing happens in my *Adrift in Soho*. The hero is trying hard not to be sick. His attention moves to the rain on the leaves; when it returns to his stomach, he is no longer feeling sick.

In each of these cases, there is a contraction of the attention, which had been *too spread out*. This contraction is not so much a matter of will as of interest. It is what happens to Kierkegaard's bored schoolboy listening to drops of rain on the roof.* For it is surely obvious that if I choose to direct all my attention at any single object or event, I can *endow* it with interest.

The human capacity for the peak experience is greater than we realise. But most of us are suffering from a kind of permanent attention fatigue, not unlike hypnosis; we are misusing ourselves out of ignorance of our capacities.

In the light of all this, it becomes possible to answer the question posed by William James in the epigraph to this book. Why are we 'only half awake' most of the time? What damps our fires and checks our draughts? What is the 'cloud' that weighs on us?

My fires are usually damped because the wind that can set them roaring is an *external* crisis or excitement. Left to myself, I tend to sink into dullness. Man is at his best when facing challenges, and this is because his power of positive action (or thought) is so limited. A great artist in the heat of creation experiences a positive state of mind that comes entirely from within; but even he may get as bored as anybody else on a long train journey. William James elsewhere speaks of a football player who is so carried away by the excitement of the game that he begins to play with a strange perfection; *the game begins to play him.* But the player needs the game if he is to achieve this state of split-second perfection.

In general, it seems that man gets the best out of himself when

---

* In *Either/Or* Kierkegaard writes: 'The gods were bored, and so they created man. Adam was bored because he was alone, and so Eve was created. Thus boredom entered the world, and increased in proportion to the increase in population. Adam was bored alone; then Adam and Eve were bored together; then Adam and Eve and Cain and Abel were bored *en famille*; then the population of the world increased, and the people were bored *en masse*. To divert themselves they conceived the idea of constructing a tower high enough to reach the heavens. This idea is itself as boring as the tower was high, and constitutes a terrible proof of how boredom gained the upper hand. . . .'

As a cure for boredom, he suggests 'the rotation method', the 'principle of limitation': 'The more you limit yourself, the more fertile you become in invention. A prisoner in solitary confinement for life becomes very inventive and a spider may furnish him with much entertainment. One need only hark back to one's schooldays . . . how fertile in invention did one prove to be. How entertaining to catch a fly and hold it imprisoned under a shell . . . How entertaining sometimes to listen to the monotonous drip of water from the roof! How close an observer does not one become under such circumstances. . . .'

circumstances drive him. The process of creation is, as Shaw knew, a matter of driving oneself, of *creating* oneself. But the 'passive fallacy' means that when I think about myself, or look at my face in a mirror, I seem somehow permanent and unchangeable. There seems to be no starting point. The Spanish existentialist thinker Zubiri declares that man can only know himself in action, and the facts of human nature seem to support him.

But consider again James's remark about neurasthenic patients for whom life 'grows into one tissue of impossibilities'. A few paragraphs later, he returns to the subject: 'In those "hyperesthetic" conditions which chronic invalidism so often brings in its train, the dam has changed its normal place. The slightest functional exercise gives a distress which the patient yields to and stops. In such cases of "habit-neuroses" a new range of power often comes in consequence of the "bullying treatment", of efforts which the doctor obliges the patient, much against his will, to make. First comes the extremity of distress, then follows unexpected relief. . . .'

The point that emerges here is that the 'distress' of the neurasthenic patient *is a fake*, a fraud perpetrated by his subconscious, which *can* be cowed by a display of force. In this case, the doctor applied the force, or rather, made the patient apply it. But is there any reason why the patient should not apply it himself? The chief one, obviously, is that he doesn't want to; he is convinced by his 'distress' and fatigue. But the whole point of the kind of analysis I have been conducting in this book is that man should train himself to acquire the kind of detachment necessary for becoming his own doctor. As soon as he *knows* that the fatigue is a fraud, he can take the necessary measures.

In my own case, it was my observation of the power of *crisis* to dissipate the distress or fatigue—and to make one aware of one's reserves of energy—that formed the starting point for my study of mysticism. I called this false fatigue, this 'cloud' of low-spirits or resentment that hangs over the human mind, 'the St Neot margin', and have spoken of it at length elsewhere.

All this points clearly to the most important element in the solution of the problem. When James's footballer began to play superbly, it was because his engine had reached a certain ideal temperature in the excitement of the game, a temperature at which 'reserve energies' became available. Like car engines,

human beings need to 'warm up' before their performance reaches
its optimum. But I can warm up the engine of my car without
taking it out of the garage, by revving its engine. And I can, by a
determined mental effort, hurl off my sloth, and develop a certain
'muscle' of the will, of concentration, that can summon these
same reserve energies.

What has gone wrong with human beings is quite easy to
define. Man's success as an evolutionary experiment is due to these
enormous *reserves* of strength that he can call upon. One does not
have to read much history to be impressed by man's incredible
powers of endurance and recuperation. But reserves have to come
from somewhere. A man who possesses huge financial reserves
has had to build them up by deducting them from his current
income. And this important part of man's vital economy—the
deduction of strength, so to speak—has been taken over by the
robot. As usual, the robot has become *too* efficient. When no
challenge is present and when I have no positive aims to drive me,
he tends to confiscate my spare energies, leaving me only the minimum he thinks I need to get through a quiet day. In doing this,
he reduces me to the level of a cow. If I am not careful, he will
push me into neurasthenia.

Fortunately, he is the servant, I am the master. Once I know
that, I can firmly take back what he had taken away. What is
important is that I should not accept my low condition as normal.
I must recognise that my fires are damped and my draughts are
checked far more than they need be, and refuse to let the robot get
away with this penny-pinching of vital reserves. The first time
one attempts to do this, it may seem quite impossible. First
comes the extremity of distress that James describes in the case
of 'bullying' neurasthenic patients. If one persists, this vanishes,
and the glow of the peak experience beings to appear. Practice
strengthens the 'will-muscle' involved until it no longer causes
acute distress.

But inducing the peak experience is not simply a matter of
sheer force. There is another element involved. If I sit staring out
of a window, thinking of nothing in paricular, or I yawn as I work
at a boring job, my consciousness is being wasted; its energies
flow away as if I had left the hot tap turned on and forgotten to
put the plug in the bath. When, on the other hand, I become
deeply interested in something, I concentrate on it, and cease to

waste energy on the rest of the world. This is what happened in the Matlock cave.

One might say that everyday consciousness is like a leaky bucket. If I am forced to watch someone doing a stupid job, or listen to a boring story, my energies leak away, like Kierkegaard's schoolboy listening to the schoolmaster's voice. But as soon as I focus intently on something, the leak stops; the pressure of my consciousness again begins to rise. My consciousness is normally geared to the outer world; it is hard not to listen to its boring drone.

The 'trick' of mystical consciousness, the mental act that needs to be mastered, is to make consciousness *stand still,* by an act of attention. I do not mean that one has to retreat into one's inner consciousness. I may be looking at a tree, or listening to the sound of running water. What is important is that the normal flow of perceptive consciousness is suddenly arrested. It has to be prevented from grinding on, 'consuming its rag and bone'. This is another habit that can be developed. It is like snapping out of a mood of inattentiveness. The everyday world drags us along, like a slave behind a conqueror's chariot. One must learn to sever the rope, to allow the mind to stand still, to become aware of its affinity with mountains and stones.

To our descendants, it will seem an absurdity that the human beings of the 'scientific age' bumbled and stumbled through life in such a short-sighted way, incapable of grasping the insight of moments of intensity. It will seem obvious that we are little better than imbeciles. They will also smile ironically at Huxley's innocent suggestion that we should take psychedelic drugs to save us from the consequence of our own feeble-mindedness. For it should be obvious even to an imbecile that if our problem is will-lessness and the fragmentary nature of consciousness, then the answer must be to first of all generate an awareness of our possibilities, and then generate the strength of will to bring them into existence.

CITY LIGHTS PUBLICATIONS

Acosta, Juvenal, ed. LIGHT FROM A NEARBY WINDOW: Contemporary
    Mexican Poetry
Alberti, Rafael. CONCERNING THE ANGELS
Allen, Roberta. AMAZON DREAM
Angulo de, Jaime. INDIANS IN OVERALLS
Angulo de, G. & J. JAIME IN TAOS
Artaud, Antonin. ARTAUD ANTHOLOGY
Bataille, Georges. EROTISM: Death and Sensuality
Bataille, Georges. THE IMPOSSIBLE
Bataille, Georges. STORY OF THE EYE
Bataille, Georges. THE TEARS OF EROS
Baudelaire, Charles. INTIMATE JOURNALS
Baudelaire, Charles. TWENTY PROSE POEMS
Bowles, Paul. A HUNDRED CAMELS IN THE COURTYARD
Bramly, Serge. MACUMBA: The Teachings of Maria-José,
    Mother of the Gods
Broughton, James. COMING UNBUTTONED
Broughton, James. MAKING LIGHT OF IT
Brown, Rebecca. ANNIE OAKLEY'S GIRL
Brown, Rebecca. THE TERRIBLE GIRLS
Bukowski, Charles. THE MOST BEAUTIFUL WOMAN IN TOWN
Bukowski, Charles. NOTES OF A DIRTY OLD MAN
Bukowski, Charles. TALES OF ORDINARY MADNESS
Burroughs, William S. THE BURROUGHS FILE
Burroughs, William S. THE YAGE LETTERS
Cassady, Neal. THE FIRST THIRD
Choukri, Mohamed. FOR BREAD ALONE
CITY LIGHTS REVIEW #2: AIDS & the Arts
CITY LIGHTS REVIEW #3: Media and Propaganda
CITY LIGHTS REVIEW #4: Literature / Politics / Ecology
Cocteau, Jean. THE WHITE BOOK (LE LIVRE BLANC)
Cornford, Adam. ANIMATIONS
Corso, Gregory. GASOLINE
Cuadros, Gil. CITY OF GOD
Daumal, René. THE POWERS OF THE WORD
David-Neel, Alexandra. SECRET ORAL TEACHINGS IN TIBETAN BUD-
    DHIST SECTS
Deleuze, Gilles. SPINOZA: Practical Philosophy
Dick, Leslie. KICKING
Dick, Leslie. WITHOUT FALLING
di Prima, Diane. PIECES OF A SONG: Selected Poems
Doolittle, Hilda (H.D.). NOTES ON THOUGHT & VISION
Ducornet, Rikki. ENTERING FIRE
Duras, Marguerite. DURAS BY DURAS
Eberhardt, Isabelle. DEPARTURES: Selected Writings
Eberhardt, Isabelle. THE OBLIVION SEEKERS

N

W CITY LIGHTS PUBLISHERS AND BOOKSELLERS **E**

CITY LIGHTS MAIL ORDER
Order books from our free catalog:

S

all books from CITY LIGHTS PUBLISHERS and more

write to:

CITY LIGHTS MAIL ORDER

261 COLUMBUS AVENUE SAN FRANCISCO, CA 94133

or fax your request to [415] 362-4921